CROSSROADS

Rugby League's Greatest Battle

Billy Roberts

Crossroads: Rugby League's Greatest Battle

Copyright © 2023 Billy Roberts. All rights reserved.

CONTENTS

Preface v
Introduction vii
Part 1 1
Where Are We (Pre-Covid)? 3
    Stage 1 - Hubris Born of Success 5
    Stage 2 - Undisciplined Pursuit of More 7
    Stage 3 - Denial of Risk and Peril 10
    Stage 4 - Grasping for Salvation 13
    Stage 5 - Capitulation to Irrelevance or Death 16
Current Assessment - Quick Overview 20
Rugby League Score Sheet - 2020 23
Part 2 25
Leadership 27
Australian Rugby League Commission 41
Peter V'landys 54
Vision 63
Teams - Workplace Culture 67
Finances 72
Country Rugby League 80
Player Numbers 87
Politics 93
Integrity 100
Rules and Regulations 105
Expansion 112
International 121

World Club Challenge 129
New Zealand...133
Pacific Island Development.......................................139
Media 144

Part 3..**151**
Covid and Rugby League...153

Part 4..**163**
How Does Rugby League Respond?............................165

Part 5..**181**
Solutions 183
Leadership 184
Governance - Australian Rugby League Commission (ARLC)   200
Vision 220
Building a Culture 224
Finance...227
Television...231
Media 241
Country Rugby League and Grassroots 244
Touch Football 260
Grassroots... 262
Middle Management 270
NRL Product 273
NRL Schedule 283
International 289
World Club Challenge 297
Expansion 301
Summary..314
Duty and Honour 318

PREFACE

THIS BOOK WAS written for the people who love rugby league: people who are sick to death with how this great game has been led by current and past NRL management/ARLC and hangers-on involved across the code; people questioning the code's integrity; people annoyed that the media is running corporate agendas that deceive the fans about the truth; people sick to death of how the modern game is played and officiated; people angry that political correctness is interfering with the game they follow; the forgotten folk in the bush who get no support from the game's headquarters, and who are watching the code slowly fade away. This book is for fans watching AFL goal posts pop up all over the nation, with little response, while kids kick a Sherrin on a round oval, rather than play the thirteen-man game. This book is for people wanting to see initiative, passion and urgency from the key leaders. It is for people wanting the game to expand to new regions across Australia and New Zealand, while it continues to be strong in the heartlands. It is for people wanting to see a revitalisation and renaissance of the international game and World Club Challenge concept. The book is written for the people who want the code to prosper and reach the heights we all know it deserves.

INTRODUCTION

All positions in life are temporary.
That is a word of hope for the poor and a word of caution for the rich!
Up, down or sideways, things will change!

AS THE 2023 rugby league season reaches the final phase of the season, the game faces some of the biggest challenges to its popularity and survival in a highly competitive sporting and entertainment market. Since the Super League war in the mid-1990s, the game has lurched from one crisis to another. These have been both on and off the field, with no permanent solutions to the many problems plaguing the game. The independent commission formed in 2012 (Australian Rugby League Commission - ARLC) has not been the saviour that many officials and supporters had hoped for. Instead, the game finds itself still divided, with stern challenges to both its long-term growth and success.

Before the Super League war, which commenced in 1995, the game enjoyed strong leadership from Ken Arthurson and John Quayle. Although things were not perfect, rugby league was booming. There was a clear direction, and strategic plans were implemented to advance the code. In Australia, it was the number one winter sport, certainly in the view of the television networks, who were vying for the media rights. Channel Nine's owner, Kerry Packer, proudly stated that the only sports he wanted on his network were rugby league and cricket, which he regarded as the best winter and summer sports in Australia. Corporate giants were lining up to be involved with the 'product.' State of Origin had grown to be one of the biggest sporting events in Australia, providing an unmatched rivalry and intensity, with Origin games becoming major weeknight events, capturing huge audiences nationwide, with some of the highest television ratings. Powerful and successful marketing campaigns, with Tina Turner as the public face, saw the code cross into new territory in the late 1980s and early 1990s. Rugby league enjoyed mainstream public support and gained a larger female and family audience. Country rugby league was flourishing, with strong regional competitions in New South Wales (NSW) and Queensland (QLD). Premiership games were taken to Adelaide, Melbourne, Darwin and Perth to spread the code nationally. Queensland Rugby League had successfully backed, perhaps reluctantly at first, new teams from Brisbane (the Broncos) and the Gold Coast (the Giants), to enter the then NSWRL competition in 1988. Newcastle Knights entered the competition the same year, further expanding the league beyond Sydney, after Illawarra (Wollongong) and Canberra were accepted in 1982.

The game provided the best television viewing and entertainment product in Australian sport. There was no getting bogged down with wrestling, stop-start play or video referees' interference. Limited structured football led to free-flowing play, and there was the aggression, synonymous with rugby league, which the fans loved. Further expansion was planned and then executed, to give the game an even bigger national footprint, with new teams accepted. In 1995, the Western Reds (Perth), South Queensland Crushers (Brisbane), North Queensland Cowboys (Townsville) and Auckland Warriors (NZ) joined the league. This was coupled with a growing and thriving international scene, with a renewal of the intense rivalry between bitter foes Australia and Great Britain. The 1995 Rugby League World Cup, held in England and Wales, included emerging countries such as Fiji, South Africa, Tonga and Western Samoa, as well as the 'traditional' nations of New Zealand, Australia, France and Papua New

Guinea. Great Britain split into England and Wales. For the first time, a World Cup 'tournament' included nations outside what was regarded as 'The Big Four' – Australia, Great Britain, France and New Zealand. Crowds were good, games exciting and television ratings high. Wales, boosted by rugby union code hoppers, drew strong attention from the UK media. There was a nail-biting semi-final between Australia and New Zealand, and two great contests between Australia and England, including the final at the famous Wembley Stadium in London. There was enormous pressure on Australia, with the selectors ignoring players from Super League aligned clubs. But coached by Bob Fulton, the Kangaroos retained the title they had won 3 years earlier at Wembley.

Super League was born out of Rupert Murdoch (News Corp owner and media billionaire) needing a 'product' or sport to entice people to subscribe to Foxtel, his new pay television service in Australia. A similar service existed in the USA, through major network providers ESPN and FOX Sports, boasting major sports such as NFL, basketball (NBA), NHL, boxing and baseball (MLB). Always abreast of trends in the USA, the rogue and ambitious Brisbane Broncos questioned the direction of the game, leading to in-fighting within the central administration and in club land. The Broncos moved to Super League (News Limited), along with seven other clubs, while the other 12 clubs stayed loyal to the ARL. In 1997, rugby league had split into two rival professional competitions: the ARL (12 teams) and Murdoch (News Corp) led Super League (10 teams), with Super League creating two new clubs: Hunter Mariners and Adelaide Rams. The game was torn apart by a bitter civil war between the old guard – the Australian Rugby League – and the Murdoch-funded Super League. Since the Super League war, rugby league has experienced upheavals that very few sports or organisations could imagine or explain. The fact that rugby league is still standing is testament to the code's unbelievable resilience and popularity. Very few elite sports in the world could have survived the Super League war and come out the other side.

In 1998, the Australian Rugby League and Super League made peace with a return to one competition, the NRL. However, by then there had been massive damage to the game at all levels, with supporters leaving the game in droves, some never to return. There hasn't been a 'happy ending' since the mid-'90s civil war division. Since 1998, the code has struggled to find a path back to greatness, on and off the field. It has failed to find a way to bring new glory days and to provide a foundation and framework for future success, to allow the code to be in safe hands for the generations to come.

Australian Rules Football (AFL) has now become the powerhouse code in Australian sport, and many other sports and entertainment options are fighting hard for their share, in an ultra-competitive sports and entertainment market that now expands beyond our own national borders in the era of global markets.

While rugby league can still produce on-field magic and remind you why you fell in love with the sport, it has been held back for many reasons over the last 25 years. These include having the wrong people in key seats driving the game, weak leadership, huge egos, greedy clubs, forgetting what made the game great in the first place, media partners hellbent on bashing the code, ongoing governance troubles, weak finances, limited assets, inadequate grassroots support, poor operational practices, divided state boards and a lack of middle management capacity.

With the loss of identity of its on-field product, poor off-field behaviour of players, indecision about future design and structure, 'small thinking,' lack of expansion and growth into new markets, abandoning the international game and not having the ability to work together and find solutions, many problems continue to plague the code and its ability to reach the heights it should reach. This list of issues may seem like harsh criticism of rugby league, but when you look at the results over the last 25 years compared with the AFL and other leading sporting organisations, the game has underperformed. It should be in a much stronger position. The endeavours of those in charge have not borne fruit.

This book will explore some of the major issues facing the code, and how we can make it 'The Greatest Game of All' again, and lay the foundations for generations to come.

PART 1

WHERE ARE WE (PRE-COVID)?

"You might as well start with the truth, you are going to end with it," or, as Churchill says more eloquently, "The truth is incontrovertible. Malice may attack it and ignorance may deride it, but in the end, there it is." – William E Bailey and Winston Churchill

Only the paranoid survive – Andrew Grove

FROM THE OUTSIDE looking in, rugby league still holds an extraordinarily strong position in the Australian sporting market, with a record television deal, a profit announcement of $30 million for 2019, strong television ratings on free-to-air and pay television, crowds averaging around 15k per game before Covid, strong media exposure in the northern states and growing awareness of the game in Victoria through the success of the Melbourne Storm, State of Origin being the envy of many other sporting codes, vast media attention during the series and some of Australian television's highest ratings each year, a growing international game and an improved financial position from previous years. But underneath these positives lie some worrying trends that potentially could impact on the future survival of the game and its ability to become once again the nation's strongest sporting code, with the ability to grow internationally.

In business author Jim Collins' book *How the Mighty Fall,* Collins and his team of researchers at Boulder, Colorado (USA) studied numerous organisations and identified how the mighty fall in business, and if there are signs that can be detected to identify the trend of decline. Collins identifies five stages an organisation goes through during the process of decline before it dies or becomes irrelevant. Each stage can last for an extended period. The process is not linear or exponential in speed and it can vary from organisation to organisation.

The Five Stages:

   Stage 1 – Hubris Born of Success

   Stage 2 – Undisciplined Pursuit of More

   Stage 3 – Denial of Risk and Peril

   Stage 4 – Grasping for Salvation

   Stage 5 – Capitulation to Irrelevance or Death

Let us look at Collins' five stages of decline and see where rugby league stands, and if it has entered or passed through some of these stages of decline.

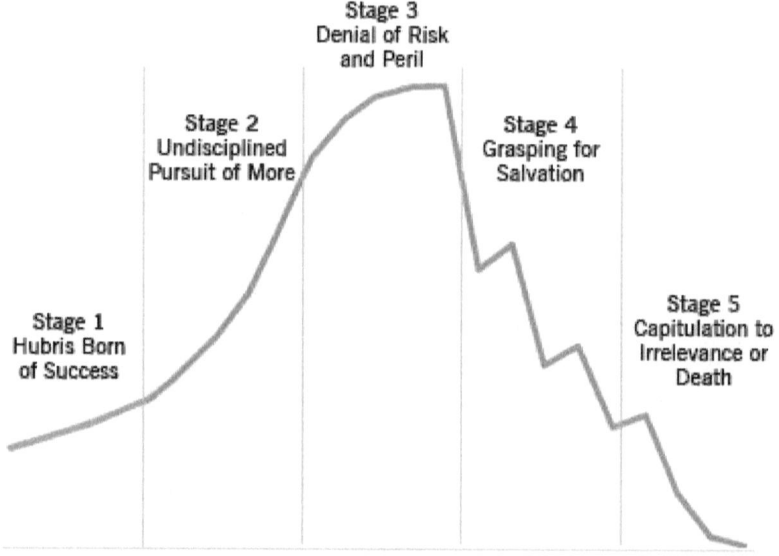

Stage 1 - Hubris Born of Success

Great enterprises can become insulated by success; accumulated momentum can carry an enterprise forward, for a while, even if its leaders make poor decisions or lose discipline. Stage 1 kicks in when people become arrogant, regarding success virtually as an entitlement, and they lose sight of the true underlying factors that created success in the first place. When the rhetoric of success ("We're successful because we do these specific things") replaces penetrating understanding and insight ("We're successful because we understand why we do these specific things and under what conditions they would no longer work"), decline will very likely follow. – Jim Collins

Ego (hubris) is the most destructive emotion for any individual or organisation, and it has been a cancer for rugby league for far too long. Individuals, management, the commission, boards, clubs, players, player unions, media partners, player agents, television networks, newspapers, some individual media representatives, state and country bodies and the International Rugby League have all, at one time or another, been guilty of having put themselves before the greater good, leading to the current position and the many challenges in which the game finds itself in the year 2023. Many people involved with the game over the last 25 years in key positions such as management at board level or senior club roles, or associated with state affiliated organisations, were self-serving and thought success was guaranteed. They have been focusing on power, greed, status, prestige, and their own selfish motives, rather than adding value and laying the seeds for long-term growth and prosperity, in the process, serving the greater good of the game for future generations. The game continues to be unable to achieve unity between stakeholders and to move forward in one direction across the whole sport, with big egos and personalities continually clashing. Rugby league appears to have forgotten what made it successful in the first place, and what can make it successful again.

As you sow so shall you reap – Bible: Galatians 6

CROSSROADS

*For every action, there is an equal
and opposite reaction* – Sir Isaac Newton

Many of the poor decisions of the past are now starting to bite and hurt the code. Country rugby league's demise and decline in certain regions; declining male player numbers across all age groups, including grassroots junior league – especially within the 5-18 years boys' age groups – are indicators that things are not as healthy as proclaimed. When you take out touch football, Oz tag and female participation, the numbers are cause for concern. Another area that indicates the game is in trouble is the lack of expansion into new markets. While AFL executed its national footprint and other sports followed suit, rugby league experienced little crowd growth and flat television ratings (especially in Sydney), with 2020 ratings down, as AFL dominated ratings during the finals. There have been missed sponsorship opportunities with large national and international companies, and rugby league has missed out on greater government funding. The same cannot be said for AFL. Rugby Union's World Cup has become a sporting mega event, even though rugby league was the creator of the World Cup concept, in 1954 in France.

The grassroots game has been forgotten, with the NRL seemingly embarking on a 'strategy' of inactivity and ignorance. There appears to be a belief that we have, and always will, dominate the core fan-base markets in NSW and QLD. This complacency has paved the way for major inroads and growth from the AFL, which is pushing aggressively into grassroots markets nationally, and making great progress.

Many rugby league followers still look back to the glory days of the early '90s, pre Super League. The Tina Turner era has a certain romantic nostalgic feel for many fans, and for good reason. Many wish the game could go back to that era. But the truth is, those days are long gone. The game took for granted that golden period, and many people within the game have been living off those times for too long. Fans, and many involved with the code, are frustrated and angry that greed, division and hubris continue to come before the game itself. Strong statesmen are desperately needed. Men like Quayle and Arthurson, who had their faults and flaws, had the game's best interest in mind during their era. For a generation, leading figures involved in the code have looked out for their own selfish interests, and very few have been serving the game.

Everything has been back to front. Like the old saying: *Give me heat and then I will put the wood on the fire*, you have to sow first to reap a harvest, and you cannot take and take over an extended period without consequences.

Stage 1 general markers and guidelines
- *Success entitlement*
- *Arrogance (ego)*
- *Neglect of discipline*
- *What replaces why*
- *Decline in learning orientation*
- *Discounting the role of luck*

– Jim Collins

Stage 2 - Undisciplined Pursuit of More

> *Hubris from Stage 1 ("We're so great, we can do anything!") leads right into Stage 2, the Undisciplined Pursuit of More—more scale, more growth, more acclaim, more of whatever those in power see as "success." Companies in Stage 2 stray from the disciplined creativity that led them to greatness in the first place, making undisciplined leaps into areas where they cannot be great or growing faster than they can achieve with excellence, or both. When an organization grows beyond its ability to fill its key seats with the right people, it has set itself up for a fall. Although complacency and resistance to change remain dangers to any successful enterprise, overreaching better captures how the mighty fall.* – Jim Collins

The 2016 television deals netted the NRL $1.8 billion from media partners Nine and Foxtel. By February 2018, the game had spent all the money and was looking for a loan from banks, and a $50 million forward payment from media providers, to survive. The NRL was an undisciplined, loosely held-together organisation, with no financial control measures internally, and rapidly leaking cash, which flowed to executives, consultants, clubs, players, community events, employees and all the other areas associated with running the sport. The game had received its biggest cash injection in history, but by February 2018, it didn't have a dime to show for it – no infrastructure, no investments, no real growth, no increase in playing numbers outside female participation and league partners in touch football and Oz tag, no improvement to country rugby league, no expansion in the NRL or genuine growth in the international game. Clubs in the bush, which were on their knees, did not see a cent, and playing numbers continued to decline. The executives of the NRL smoked it all away and were left to start again. In comparison, the AFL, on the back of its own record-breaking television deal with media partners, built a powerful financial base – not squandering cash, but investing in the ownership of Marvel Stadium in Melbourne, Auskick programs were implemented across the country, there was expansion, with new clubs – Greater Western Sydney and Gold Coast Suns – entering the AFL. There was investment, on and off the field, in regional and country leagues, and huge nationwide recruitment of development officers to drive programs and participation growth. Other financial assets were added to the AFL's books. These investments resulted in real growth across the sport and a strong fiscal base to move forward with, that was the envy of other sporting codes.

NZ Rugby, the strongest sport in New Zealand, announced in October 2019 a 5% ownership in Sky TV. In 2021, NZ Rugby sold 5.8% to a US private equity, worth $200m.

The NRL announced a profit of $36 million for the 2018 season and another profit of $30 million for the 2019 season. A $50 million early payment was provided from media companies to the NRL and was still owed. Chairman Peter V'landys has made it clear his number one priority is a better financial nest egg base for the code.

Lack of discipline runs far deeper than just the game's fiscal balance sheet. Country rugby league, especially in NSW, has declined significantly. Once strong regional and group leagues across NSW are much weaker, compared to the pre-Super League era, with many other competitive sports dominating regional markets. Male junior and senior numbers have continued to decline, with new reports glossing over these numbers by including female and touch football/Oz tag participation. There has been no expansion of infrastructure in the non-heartland areas, and there are no new professional teams. Rugby league, which organised the first World Cup in 1954, has been left for dead by rugby union's international calendar. The Wallabies and Socceroos have overtaken the Kangaroos as the nation's most popular winter national teams, in branding and awareness, due to vibrant international scenes and regular matches. The 2019 Rugby Union World Cup in Japan generated around £384m (over $600m Australian) compared to the 2017 Rugby League World Cup hosted in Australia, which made a profit of $5 million. The Rugby World Cup has become a colossus, with many powerful nations taking part and hosting the event, and viewers totaling 500 million around the globe. The 2019 Rugby Union World Cup hosted in Japan is believed to have generated £4.3 billion for the Japanese economy alone.

Discipline and accountability are critical to any individual or organisation's success. In rugby league, the lack of it has caused grassroots and country football to decline, while the image and reputation of the game has been tarnished by repeated poor player behaviour and a failure to expand into new markets, The inactivity of the international game has given other sports the chance to grab a strong share of these markets in the absence of rugby league. The NRL financial base should have been much stronger, with two record television deals in the billions wasted. The NRL, under the former chairmanship of Peter Beattie and current chairman, Peter V'landys, has made a strong financial base a priority, after being caught in a precarious position without cash reserves.

New NRL CEO Andrew Abdo announced in September 2020 a 25% reduction in staff at NRL headquarters and discussions were ongoing with the players union to review players and clubs funding from the NRL. Drastic measures from the NRL were taken after years of ill-discipline and Covid impacting globally on economic activity.

Stage 2 general markers
- *Unsustainable quest for growth, confusing big with great*
- *Undisciplined continuous leaps*
- *Declining proportion of right people in key seats*
- *Easy cash erodes cost discipline*
- *Bureaucracy subverts discipline*
- *Problematic succession of power*
- *Personal interest placed above organisational interests*

– Jim Collins

Stage 3 - Denial of Risk and Peril

As companies move into Stage 3, internal warning signs begin to mount, yet external results remain strong enough to "explain away" disturbing data or to suggest that the difficulties are "temporary" or "cyclic" or "not that bad," and "nothing is fundamentally wrong." In Stage 3, leaders discount negative data, amplify positive data, and put a positive spin on ambiguous data. Those in power start to blame external factors for setbacks rather than accept responsibility. The vigorous, fact-based dialogue that characterizes high-performance teams dwindles or disappears altogether. When those in power begin to imperil the enterprise by taking outsized risks and acting in a way that denies the consequences of those risks, they are headed straight for Stage 4. – Jim Collins

There has been consistent denial from various key stakeholders involved with rugby league, who argue that the game is in an extraordinarily strong position. This includes recent comments from former CEO, Todd Greenberg; David Trodden (CEO NSWRL); former chairmen John Grant, Peter Beattie, and Peter V'landys in relation to the code's strength and popularity. But looking more closely across the code, there are worrying signs and trends. These include key metrics, such as the demise of country rugby league in certain regions in NSW and Queensland, with many clubs folding and others struggling for playing numbers. There is also the matter of Sydney's declining TV ratings. The 2019 and 2020 NRL Grand Final national ratings were the lowest on record. Male participation numbers declined at all levels, and at an alarming rate. There was no domestic growth or new infrastructure established in heartland Australian Rules territory. And, of course, there is rugby league's poor financial base and lack of assets. There has been a decline in top-end corporate sponsorship, with many of these companies backing other major sports. Continual player misbehaviour has hurt the code's reputation. There has been little or no crowd growth over an extended period, especially in the Sydney market. There has not been any expansion into new markets, such as Western Australia, despite the demise of the Western Force Rugby Union team pre-Covid. There are no new teams in New Zealand, or even a second Brisbane franchise to challenge the Broncos' monopoly before Covid. Fans have also become disillusioned with the current on-field 'product.' Officiating seems to be discussed every weekend, often overshadowing the actual game, with no real solution coming from NRL HQ. The continual rumours of a divide between the NRL HQ and NRL clubs, state bodies and players are not conducive to change. NRL leaders continually deny or ignore these signs by issuing positive public relations statements about how well the code is performing.

Ask anyone involved with bush footy, and they will confirm the code is struggling. But the NRL leadership denies the truth. They wax lyrical about how they sent a development representative or ex-player to a school or region, and "It's all going wonderfully well" and the next generation of stars will soon be found. The NRL have been continually blind and inactive, despite the AFL's aggressive expansion into rugby league heartland. Most regions in traditional league heartland now have an AFL team that includes junior, men's and women's teams. Many regional areas have had no support, until recent times, to fight the cashed-up "Southern Game powerhouse," and the NRL blindly believes the recent merger between the Country Rugby League and New South Wales Rugby League will resolve the issues.

The game's HQ has been called out by many, with regard to the weak financial position. Despite billions of dollars falling into their hands, the game's leaders have kept spending the money as fast as it came in, and, as a result, there are limited cash and assets on the NRL balance sheet. Over the last few years, the loose financial controls have come under much criticism. Former chairman Peter Beattie and current chairman Peter V'landys have made it clear the game needs to have a "rainy day fund," and, with that in mind, they have started on an asset plan to build the game's finances, something which will be the focus of ARLC Commissioner Gary Weiss.

The game's past and present leaders have seemed unable to grasp the reality of the many issues the game faces. They seem to have a belief that the game made two recent profits before Covid and that all will be good. But they are blind to the many challenges that must be faced.

Denial has been a consistent response to questions about the code's health, on and off the field, and the challenges it faces for its long-term future. Some parts of the game are in a healthier position. There have been strong Foxtel television ratings figures and increased membership numbers for clubs and State of Origin, female participation numbers have risen, and there has been stronger fiscal control in the NRL's head office after the initial outbreak of Covid.

Some metrics of the code are in the denial of Stage 3, as outlined by Collins, whereas other functions are just clinging to life, and have moved to Stage 4.

Stage 3 markers

- *Amplify the positive, discount the negative*
- *Big bets and bold goals without empirical evidence*
- *Incurring huge downside risk based on ambiguous data*
- *Erosion of health team dynamics*
- *Externalizing blame*
- *Obsessive reorganisations (restructures)*
- *Imperious detachment*

– Jim Collins

Stage 4 - Grasping for Salvation

> *The cumulative peril and/or risks-gone-bad of Stage 3 assert themselves, throwing the enterprise into a sharp decline visible to all. The critical question is, How does its leadership respond? By lurching for a quick salvation or by getting back to the disciplines that brought about greatness in the first place? Those who grasp for salvation have fallen into Stage 4. Common "saviors" include a charismatic visionary leader, a bold but untested strategy, a radical transformation, a dramatic cultural revolution, a hoped-for blockbuster product, a "game changing" acquisition, or any number of other silver-bullet solutions. Initial results from taking dramatic action may appear positive, but they do not last. – Jim Collins*

If you said that rugby league could face the real possibility of Grasping for Salvation, you would be laughed at and mocked by many. But the game has real issues, underneath the record television deals, solid televisions ratings, the large core fanbase that dominates two states, and extensive media coverage. If rugby league does not improve its operational performance, it will face severe challenges in the near future. The game has become addicted to money and all the things that go with billion-dollar television deals and sponsorship. Money is just a magnifying glass and simply makes you more of what you already are! Money can't fix all the problems. It will require determined leadership, brains, and courage to navigate the game's problems and challenges.

The transition from Stage 3 Denial to Stage 4 Grasping for Salvation can happen rapidly or via a slow decline. I believe some functions of the code have entered, or are about to enter this phase. Numerous country rugby league clubs have folded during the last decade, while others are struggling to survive. Some of the leading sports in Australia are currently fighting for their own survival, including A League soccer and Rugby Australia.

In March 2020, new Chairman of the NRL Peter V'landys was asked – by Danny Weidler of Nine News – about rumours of a divide between

NRL clubs and former CEO Todd Greenberg. V'landys was honest. He acknowledged that some clubs found Greenberg to be arrogant, but that his relationship with him was fine, and that he and the NRL Commission would look to improve this and have further discussions. Greenberg stepped down as CEO on April 20, 2020. V'landys has backed the clubs and players on most matters during his tenure.

Talking to Danny Weidler before Covid, V'landys said the code badly needed to improve its financial asset base, to defend against possible emergencies. He later went on to mention that with the impact of the Covid pandemic, we have seen why the game needs to be prepared for all emergencies.

Rugby Australia and A League are currently in Stage 4 in their respective sports, fighting for survival. After passing through the first three stages, they face challenges, on and off the field, financially and operationally, as well as trying to win back the hearts and minds of fans and sponsors. While striving to bring attention back to their sports, time will tell if they will recover, or fade into the death or irrelevance of Stage 5. Their current position and struggles are an important warning to rugby league.

In 2003, Rugby Australia was surging with momentum. They hosted the Rugby Union World Cup, with great success, including record attendances, worldwide media attention and over four million Australian viewers watching the final between Australia and England. Rugby union looked to be a major threat to the NRL and AFL. But over the last decade, the code has lost supporters, was nearly declared insolvent and required an emergency loan from World Rugby to survive, while Super Rugby is at a loss about how to move forward and reinvigorate itself in the eyes of the public. With poor and declining television ratings, they are in deep discussion with broadcasters for future television rights. But there may be light at the end of the tunnel: as Rugby Australia agreed to a 12-month deal with Foxtel for 2020, after Covid meant an Australian-only domestic season, with five teams.

Rugby Australia announced in November 2020 a 5-year deal with Nine and Stan to show Super Rugby and test matches, leaving Foxtel after 25 years.

Super Rugby had seen solid 2021/2022/2023 ratings on Stan and Nine for internationals.

The A League commenced in 2005 and made an immediate impact. It seemed, after many years of struggle in Australia, the game was ready to follow its European and world colleagues and make an impact on the Australian market. After many years of being in the shadow of other sports, such as rugby league and AFL, the new A League national model quickly gained attention, and built teams all around the country and in New Zealand. This included popular derby matches in Melbourne and Sydney. Crowds, sponsorships, media attention and ratings were encouraging, but, over a noticeably short span of time, things have quickly declined. With terrible ratings on Foxtel, sponsors leaving, crowds declining and internal politics dividing the game, the A League has major hurdles to overcome if it is to remain a major sporting code in Australia. It will have to fight hard to return to the strong period of growth and excitement of A League's early days.

In May 2021, the A League with the W League announced a 5-year $200 million dollar deal with Channel Ten and streaming service Paramount.

In a story of hope, the NBL had been in Stage 4 and grasping for salvation for an extended period, after enjoying much success in the early 1990s, before falling on hard times with the sport nearly dying, and the game of basketball being at an all-time low in Australia. But new leaders and owners, with great drive and determination, have restructured the league and turned the sport back from this near-death experience, or Stage 5, which Collins identifies as death or irrelevance. On the back of many Australians plying their trade in the NBA, as well as NBA superstars such as Lebron James and Steph Curry influencing a new generation of Australian kids, the sport's popularity has surged again, in a 'second coming.'

In 2017, leaders restructured the NBL competition, and each year the game has grown, with increased attendances, ratings, sponsorship and media awareness across the sporting landscape. All signs look positive for the NBL's continued development as a sport, as they fight their way back to better days.

In summary, the NRL has been in denial about the many challenges the code faces and there is a real chance the code could be grasping for salvation in the near future. While some functions of the game are still performing well – media attention, television ratings, female participation, State of Origin – there are other functions in the areas of Stage 3 and 4 that will require attention. Time will tell, under Peter V'landys' leadership, how the game will respond and move forward. V'landys has a reputation as being a 'go-getter' and moving fast from his time with Racing NSW, and many have huge faith in his abilities to do the same with rugby league.

Stage 4 markers
- *Series of silver bullets*
- *Grasping for a leader-as-savior*
- *Panic and haste*
- *Radical change and revolution of fanfare*
- *Hype precedes results*
- *Initial upswing followed by disappointments*
- *Confusion and cynicism*
- *Chronic restructuring and erosion of financial strength*

– Jim Collins

Stage 5 – Capitulation to Irrelevance or Death

The longer a company remains in Stage 4, repeatedly grasping for silver bullets, the more likely it will spiral downward. In Stage 5, accumulated setbacks and expensive false starts erode financial strength and individual spirit to such an extent that leaders abandon all hope of building a great future. In some cases, their leaders just sell out; in other cases, the institution atrophies into utter insignificance, and in the most extreme cases, the enterprise simply dies outright. – Jim Collins

Many would say there is no way that rugby league could ever become irrelevant or die, but history says this is not true. History is littered with many former empires, big businesses, and sporting teams which were once powerhouses, and are now irrelevant or dead. Let us name a few:

- Persia
- Greece
- Babylon
- USSR
- Ancient Rome
- British Empire
- Kodak
- Enron
- Lehman Brothers
- Blockbuster
- Borders
- Toys R Us
- Sears
- Seattle Supersonics
- Fitzroy Lions
- Bradford Bulls Rugby League
- French Rugby League – World Champions in 1978
- Widnes Vikings Rugby League
- West Indies Cricket

Rugby League in Australia has a long history of once famous clubs becoming irrelevant or folding, or having to change with the times:

- Gold Coast Giants
- Gold Coast Seagulls
- Gold Coast Chargers
- Western Suburbs Magpies
- Balmain Tigers
- North Sydney Bears

- South Queensland Crushers
- Illawarra Steelers
- Hunter Mariners
- Adelaide Rams
- Western Reds
- Northern Eagles
- Newtown Jets

American founding father Ben Franklin famously said during the American Revolution, when asked by a member of the public in 1787, "What do we have?" After helping prepare both the Declaration of Independence and the Constitution, he replied: "You, my friends, have a republic. The question is, can you keep it?" Franklin and the co-signers of the American Declaration of Independence knew that the biggest battle would come from within, and history has proven this to be correct, for all empires and organisations. The founding fathers of America were not fools, and had studied the rise and fall of many empires throughout history to design America's governance model, including the Persian Empire, Greece, Alexander the Great's empire, Rome, the Holy Roman Empire starting with Charlemagne, France during the French Revolution, and the British Empire, and how they each become giants, and then fell away from within.

Rugby league's greatest threat is from within. It has always been that way. The key questions are:

- Where is rugby league heading?
- Where will it be in 1, 3, 5 or 10 years? Can rugby league leaders unite, or will they continue to be a house divided on key matters that will continue to hinder the code?
- Can they fight off the AFL's aggressive push to dominate Australian sport?
- Can they meet the challenges and threats and become Australia's number one sporting code again?
- Can they set the code up for the next generation?

Stage 5 markers
- *Death*
- *Irrelevance*
- *No cash*

– Jim Collins

CURRENT ASSESSMENT - QUICK OVERVIEW

PRE-COVID IN 2020, rugby league had a mixture of positives and negative outcomes, across all levels.

The strong positives include television ratings on free-to-air, streaming and Foxtel, with State of Origin and the NRL Grand Final among Australia's highest ratings programs, every year nationally, with Origin continuing to be one of Australia's biggest sporting events, attracting huge media attention. There also has been the growth of the female game, at all levels.

The negatives include the decline in country rugby league in many parts of NSW and QLD, with many clubs folding or struggling for numbers; the decline at grassroots level, including male participation numbers; player misbehaviour over a long time frame; game product and entertainment; no expansion into new regions pre-Covid for either professional teams or the community domestic game; and minimal crowd growth, especially when compared with the AFL's exponential growth over the last 25 years. Sydney's small to flat decline in TV ratings continues to be of concern, as it is the heartland for the game. In addition, there is the poor financial position of the game, after billions of dollars have come and gone, with no real assets or investment to show for all that money.

The game of rugby league in Australia seems to be somewhere between Stage 3 and Stage 4 of Collins' matrix.

The professional game would be sitting around Stage 3, but worrying trends are mounting potential risks for the long-term future, and if the leaders of the NRL do not confront some of these issues, they will move into Stage 4 territory and will face more severe challenges as they try to reverse the trends.

The community and grassroots game would be placed between a mixture of Stage 3 and Stage 4 as their current position. There are positives, with some clubs having strong numbers and being in a relatively healthy position. The growth in the female game is another positive, plus rugby league's association with touch football and Oz tag is adding strength to the game.

But many bush and city clubs are struggling or have already folded. Many are struggling for numbers to fill grades at all levels, and once strong regional and metropolitan leagues are in many cases much weaker than in their former glory days.

Grassroots and male participation numbers are of particular concern and need urgent attention, with the AFL and other sports and entertainment applying huge pressure on the code to attract boys and men.

There has not been any new growth, while the AFL has expanded its national footprint at all levels. The NRL has the opposite strategy, if it can be called that, content with staying within existing states and clubs.

The NRL, under V'landys, has made it clear that it needs to be in a much stronger financial position for the game to have security and long-term success. Large cuts have commenced across the game to make it more sustainable.

How the NRL's leaders respond to all the challenges they face will determine whether the game continues to have long-term success and growth in Australia. If it continues to be in denial of the many negative trends, this could soon lead to the code fighting for its life at all levels, as has been seen recently with rugby union, NBL and the A League.

Time will tell!

RUGBY LEAGUE SCORE SHEET - 2020

Strengths

2nd strongest winter sport in Australia, behind only AFL

State of Origin

2nd highest TV ratings on sport, behind only AFL

Strong history and culture with the code forming in 1908

NRL brand awareness

NSW and QLD's biggest sport

Extensive media exposure in northern states

Growing international game

Improved financial position from 2018-2020

Female game growing

Touch football/Oz tag

Weaknesses

AFL dominating all markets and getting bigger

AFL expansion into rugby league heartland markets

CROSSROADS

- AFL grassroots growth nationally
- Vision and strategic plans
- Male playing numbers in decline
- Country rugby league health
- ARLC performance
- Peter V'landys' performance
- Governance of code
- Finances of game
- Playing entertainment product for viewers
- Officiating
- 2020 TV ratings down
- 2019/2020 NRL Grand Final figures
- Last two NRL Grand Finals lowest rating grand finals in OzTAM history
- Middle management capacity
- Unity of game across key stakeholders
- Grassroots health
- Player misbehaviour
- Crowd flat growth – Sydney concerns
- No expansion
- No growth into new markets outside NSW/QLD
- Not growing the NZ market
- Inactivity of international game
- Integrity of code
- Political involvement
- Conflicts of interest in game

PART 2

The Issues (The Log List)
Leadership
Australian Rugby League Commission
Peter V'landys
Vision
Teams – Workplace Culture
Finances
Country Rugby League
Player Numbers
Politics
Integrity
Rules and Regulations
Expansion
International
World Club Challenge
New Zealand
Pacific Island Development
Media

LEADERSHIP

Winning starts in the front office – Jack Gibson

Everything falls and rises on leadership.

THE SINGLE BIGGEST issue affecting rugby league since the NRL era commenced in 1998 has been **LEADERSHIP.** The lack of strong results-driven leadership at all levels of the game has had an adverse impact on many issues that are plaguing the game, as mentioned in our opening section, from the top-tier National Rugby League, state leagues, country rugby league (now under the NSWRL umbrella), grassroots operations, expansion and new domestic community structures in non-heartland NSW/QLD regions, on-field entertainment product, officiating of the game, regular international competition and growth, school participation, player behaviour, the game's finances and just about anything else you could think of associated with the game. Without strong united leadership and direction, the code has stagnated or gone backwards in many metrics and needs courageous bold leadership with intelligence to turn things around across all areas of the game and not just with the top-tier professional NRL.

In March 2020 during Covid, the NRL advised they could not survive if the competition was stopped for 3 months with inadequate fund reserves to support the game.

From the mid-1980s to the early 1990s, Australian Rules Football (AFL) faced a fight for its own survival, with severe challenges to the code including struggling crowds and sponsorship, clubs struggling financially, identity issues, infighting over the future direction of the code with a Victorian-centric code divided, with interstate counterparts not wanting to expand the code nationally, and the future governance of the game. But over the course of the next 25 years plus, the AFL has powered up to become the number one sport in Australia, on the back of record television deals, huge television ratings, record crowds, a club membership surge, a strong financial base with large assets including the Marvel Stadium ownership, and many clubs having strong balance sheets, with some clubs such as Richmond, Collingwood and West Coast the envy of many sports and clubs in Australia, Auskick record participation nationally for grassroots junior numbers, large top-end corporate support and government funding, the AFLW initial success and growth for the female game, national expansion well executed with a second wave of recent new teams from the Gold Coast and Greater Western Sydney after the initial mid-'90s expansion in Adelaide and Perth, alongside the Brisbane/Fitzroy merger and Sydney Swans entry, and growth into new markets, which has been the envy of every other sporting organisation in Australia.

When you consider in the early '90s rugby league was, in many experts' opinion, probably the number one winter sport in Australia, and now in 2023 AFL has become the clear number one sporting code in Australia, with rugby league slipping back to number two nationally with quite a large gap now between the codes on many metrics, what was the key difference and how did AFL overtake rugby league and every other code? The answer is leadership!

The key difference between the codes has been leadership that drives a clear and compelling vision, strong professionalism with high output and the high standards that come with strong leadership. The AFL has been better led in this period, more definite and decisive in purpose. It executed its vision and mission; had strong performance from its people across all divisions in its business structure; marketed better to all demographics; developed AusKick to drive grassroots junior participation, interest and expansion; invested earnings better into real assets and reinvestment of the sport; drove deep into new markets across Australia for both the junior and the community level game, with strong middle management on the ground building a national footprint; ran better regional and grassroots competitions that stakeholders and communities enjoyed; got better government support for funding initiatives and infrastructure; and set up a sound asset base including the purchase of Marvel Stadium, to remain the dominant sport in Australia, even with the challenges of Covid to the sporting and entertainment industry.

In comparison, rugby league leadership in the same period has dropped the ball on many key matters, with no clear vision to aim for, often drifting aimlessly, being divided internally between key stakeholders and allowing the media to control the code's destiny.

The Australian sporting market is not a case of brand against brand, as many state (organisation vs organisation), but really is each organisation's leadership group vs the competitors' leadership groups. Each organisation is the people behind the brand name, at the end of the day.

People with strong leadership and united teams win battles in the areas of the military, politics, business and the sporting landscape. Underneath every organisation or business banner are still people, and they decide the future of each individual entity. Hearts, intellect, teamwork and the will and desire to win are still key ingredients to success for any organisation.

Ford vs GM, Boxing vs UFC, Nike vs Reebok, Coke vs Pepsi, Airbus vs Boeing are just a few of the great corporate rivalries.

Take the best 20 people out of any organisation and you would watch how its results would decline fast to quickly become an unimportant company. You see this on the rugby league pitch when key players are unavailable, and it is no different within the corporate environment.

After the departure and end of the ARL era of league statesmen such as Arthurson and Quayle, the NRL has struggled to find the right leaders to drive the game forward and has been divided internally amongst numerous stakeholders, both inside the NRL and the other key bodies.

This leadership void has also flowed downstream to other areas of the game, including the country game and grassroots functions, which have lacked strong management in many key roles.

In the NRL modern era, six leaders (CEOs) have led the sport between 1998 and 2023:

Neil Whitaker 1997-1999; John Ribot 1997 (Super League)
David Moffett 1999-2001
David Gallop 2002-2012
David Smith 2013-2015
Todd Greenberg 2016-2020
Andrew Abdo 2020-present

Four CEOs have been recruited from outside the NRL, with the last two appointments of Greenberg and Abdo winning internal promotion for the CEO role from within the NRL ranks.

Great organisations are always asking: Do we develop our own people internally or replace and bring in external talent from the outside? Each method/decision has its pros and cons.

Todd Greenberg was the former CEO of the Canterbury Bulldogs from 2008-2013 before taking an internal role at the NRL as Head of Football before progressing to the CEO role in 2016.

Andrew Abdo replaced Todd Greenberg as Interim CEO in May 2020. Abdo had been performing the role of Chief Operating Officer/Commercial Officer for the NRL before stepping up to Interim CEO in 2020. Abdo was appointed permanent CEO of the NRL in September of 2020.

Rugby league leaders have faced many challenges in the game's history, and the Arko/Quayle era was no different, with many challengers to be met head-on. This era faced many difficulties that the code faces today and their leadership style drove the game to new heights. Today's rugby league leaders will also need to deal with many challenges to keep the code in good health. With a few examples, we will see the leadership style shown by both men, with the ability to see and face the brutal truth and the ugly side of things in the game, having a bold vision for the code and thinking outside the box with smart marketing campaigns to draw a wider and new audience and markets.

The Arko/Quayle era was very definite in its direction and vision for the code, compared with the drifting and indecision that has plagued modern leaders of more recent times.

The '80s saw the game's leaders meet the growing concern from the public over thuggish and violent player behaviour, with many incidents hurting the code's reputation. There was an appeal to stop the violence and to bring more fans to the game from a wider demographic base, rather than its traditional male-dominated audience.

The game's leaders knew for the game to grow and prosper it had to change the reputation, DNA and makeup of the game and make it more appealing for sponsors, television audiences and for a wider audience such as children, families and females, with more focus on entertaining football and marketable players rather than ugly incidents on the field, which were killing its reputation and brand.

Violent player behaviour had always been associated with the sport, especially in the '60s,'70s, and early '80s, known for its tough no-nonsense style, with many ugly incidents often overshadowing the actual games being played. Many players in that era were known for their fearsome reputation such as Malcom Reilly, Dallas Donnolly, Tommy Raudonikis, Steve Roach, Les Boyd, and Les Davison, just to name a few.

The game's leaders decided to meet the player behaviour head-on and took a strong stance, with new guidelines and rules introduced in the 1980s to eliminate or reduce many of the thuggish incidents hurting the code. A new judicial system and committee were introduced to enforce the new rules and uphold the integrity and reputation of the game.

Players breaking the new rules and guidelines were handed fines and suspensions and had to face independent judicial hearings. Referees now also took a far stronger stance on player behaviour during matches. The league was committed to changing the culture of the code, with today's modern game still imprinted by these decisions to change the face and reputation of the game.

The judiciary system and referee power with clear rules and framework is still an institution in today's game from the implementation in the '80s to change the makeup of the game for a wider audience.

Arko and Quayle would not stop with wanting to change the game's reputation on the field. They had a bold vision of wanting to grow the game to a younger, fresher and much wider audience. The game went into new territory, with new marketing campaigns led by rock star Tina Turner in the late '80s and early '90s. The Tina Turner campaigns of that period were a huge success for the game, hit singles such as *What You Get Is What You See* and *Simply the Best* receiving wide praise. The mix of Tina Turner with star players, football montage of the game and great music was simple in essence but worked to perfection.

The Simply the Best campaign is still considered to be one of Australian sport's best marketing campaigns, alongside cricket's *C'mon, Aussie, C'mon* during the Kerry Packer revolution of cricket in the '70s, and the AFL's *I'd Like to See That* in the '90s.

The Arko/Quayle era was known for its boldness and clarity of purpose in knowing what it wanted the game's future to look like, with a clear vision set for the code. The game had long had a strong presence and history in QLD and NSW, with the two states being the heartland for the game, and the game's leaders were looking to grow the game to new audiences and become the nation's biggest sport.

After taking many pre-season and premiership games to new cities across the country in previous years, 1995 saw the game take some of its biggest risks, with four new teams entering the league: North Queensland Cowboys, South Queensland Crushers, Western Reds and

Auckland Warriors. Arko and Quayle believed in the game and entertainment product and knew, for it to grow, it had to reach new audiences, and also match the potential threat from its great rival the AFL, who were also in the process of expanding their competition outside the traditional Victorian-dominated league.

North Queensland Cowboys and Auckland Warriors (now New Zealand Warriors) have had a tremendous impact on the game since their arrival, with both clubs representing their geographic regions proudly and adding a strong fan base to the game. Both club brands are some of the most recognisable in the Australia and New Zealand sporting landscape today.

The Western Reds and South Queensland Crushers are sadly both no longer in the NRL, but could not be called failures. The axing of both clubs was more a reflection of the times, with the Super League civil war dividing the game with the dirty politics that followed when the code reunited in 1998 and deals were done to reduce clubs as part of the agreement between the ARL and Super League in merging with the new NRL introduced in 1998.

Many pundits still believe that if both clubs were alive today, it would have been a major success. The fact the game's likely next two expansion team leaders are Perth and Brisbane tells you the great opportunity the game has missed.

These are just a few small examples, but it does show you a leadership gap between that era and the leadership of the last 20 plus years. The game's leaders of recent times have had an inability to find solutions to many problems hurting and holding the code back, and have been very indecisive when setting the direction for the game's future. The lower levels of the game are now in far weaker shape than they should be and often found to be too reactive in operational practices and delivery. Many leaders have come and gone across the game, but few have left a great legacy in the last generation.

The fruits of great leadership include performance, longevity, impact and reputation. Success leaves clues, and it is no fluke that great success in rugby league always comes with strong leadership, whether it be leading a club, the head office or state leagues. There are many examples of administrators leading their clubs and organisation to great success on and off the field and making great contributions to the game.

Here are a few administrators who have made a great mark in rugby league:

- John Mcintyre was the driver/godfather of bringing the Canberra Raiders to life and was a major reason for the Raiders' great success in the late '80s/early '90s.
- Peter Moore was the godfather at the Bulldogs and was instrumental in the success of the club in the '80s.
- Ross Livermore was instrumental in the longevity and success of the Queensland Maroons.
- Ron McAuliffe drove Queensland Rugby League through controversial innovative and authoritarian practices.
- Nick Politis, also known as The Godfather, has been instrumental in the long-term success of the Sydney Roosters.
- Harry Sunderland was a visionary in his time, making a tremendous contribution to the international game and French Rugby League.
- Maurice Lindsay was instrumental in the glory years of the Wigan Warriors, making the club the biggest in the world at one time in the '80s and early '90s.

Whilst the game's overall leadership has been disappointing over the last 20 years, today, a number of highly ambitious and competent administrators lead the way for the code, including Blake Solly from South Sydney and Dave Donaghy from the Brisbane Broncos.

Making progress and getting great results does not just randomly occur, nor is there a magic pill to give you guaranteed success. Strong leadership is always one of the key factors behind any successful organisation. This is the leadership of driving people and resources to achieve the outcome they seek.

Leaders drive progress, standards and the values that hold any organisation together. For many reasons, the quality of leadership has declined since those glory ARL days under Arthurson and Quayle before Super League, and, as the quality has declined in leadership, so have the standards, vision, values and output of the game. The leadership sets the tone for the vision, values, standards and output, and, as the leadership capabilities have declined, so have those metrics across the wider game.

The quality of leadership affecting the game is not just an issue at the top of the game. The game is crying out for stronger and more capable middle management for all facets of the code in a variety of roles, both operational, professional and strategic-based roles for the NRL, grassroots and state rugby league bodies. Rugby league is facing stiff competition in the lower non-professional levels of the sport, and now, more than ever, it needs strong middle management to help it fight off other sports and entertainment.

Until rugby league appoints the right leaders and has the right people in the right seats across the whole game, from NRL Head Office, board appointments, international representative roles, country rugby league, state leagues, grassroots, club land, and professional management roles within the game, it will struggle to move forward. It is critical to get the right leaders, who have a deep passion for the game.

More Leadership Capabilities = More Horsepower
Leadership + More Leadership Horsepower (middle management) + Unity = Moving Mountains
Everything falls and rises on leadership

History has proven that everything rises and falls on leadership! You see this playing out every day in business and politics, as well as throughout global history. Many examples are available of once strong businesses or nations who are now a ghost of what they were. Only 25 of the top Fortune 500 companies in 1955 were still on the list in 2008!

All positions in life and business are temporary, and in the digital era, things are moving at even greater speed, and companies and organisations are even more susceptible today to greater threats and challenges.

Oliver Stone, in his book *The Untold Story of the United States*, stated that five empires had collapsed during the lifetime of a person born before World War Two, three more empires had collapsed earlier in the twentieth century, and that America today was at great risk of soon following suit. Empires to have fallen for people born before World War Two include Britain, France, Germany, Japan and the Soviet Union. The three earlier collapses in the twentieth century were the Russian, Austro-Hungarian and Ottoman Empires.

Much discussion continues about what skills and experience is needed in the CEO role of the NRL, with much debate about past and current CEOs.

People say that former CEO David Gallop was too much of a News Corp person after Super League, and this impacted on his ability to perform the role independently. Gallop was a former News Corp lawyer. He was perceived to be too reactive to the many challenges facing the code. Welsh banker David Smith was next appointed as CEO, with vast experience in the banking sector, but many argued that he did not know enough about rugby league. With his primary strength being the financial business (operational) side of an organisation, many in the media cited how Smith was unable to identify Australian Captain Cameron Smith during a press conference. He was also quickly in trouble after television rights negotiations with media partners fell apart, with News Corp owner and billionaire Rupert Murdoch taking digs at him and the code in the wider press via his own media outlets during this period. Murdoch stated arrogantly, after announcing a deal with the AFL in an AFL press conference, that he always preferred AFL over rugby league during the television rights negotiations. To be fair to Smith, Murdoch's huge ego and power was leveraging his media outlets for selfish purposes to harm Smith's reputation and capabilities during negotiations, after Smith had not given Murdoch preference in negotiations. Murdoch wanted to make Smith pay, for all to see. Smith still achieved the biggest television rights money for the game up until that point, but the end was in sight when Murdoch and News Corp became relentless in going for the kill.

Following Smith's departure, the game appointed former Bulldogs CEO Todd Greenberg as the next CEO in March 2016, many citing the need for more football knowledge in head office after Smith's time. Greenberg's tenure was disliked by many fans and clubs, with many believing he was too much of a politician and not authentic, and that the game had become too political under his leadership. Greenberg also had a reputation in some NRL clubs for being very egotistical and unwelcoming to new ideas within the game. Greenberg's tenure at the Bulldogs included a number of ugly incidents, including the salary cap rort and player misbehaviour, with such incidents as Coffs Harbour being hushed over in the media.

Greenberg was quickly moved on by Peter V'landys, once he had taken over the Chairman of the ARLC role in October 2019.

It was clear from the beginning of V'landys' tenure that Greenberg would not last long. Greenberg had lost V'landys' confidence early on, over the mismanagement of the finances of the game, and his relationships with key stakeholders such as NRL clubs left V'landys with little confidence or trust.

V'landys spoke well about Greenberg to the media, but actions are the best indicator, and V'landys' actions in supporting clubs on sensitive matters and openly criticising head office over fiscal mismanagement left no doubt that Greenberg would not remain CEO of the NRL.

South African-raised Andrew Abdo was promoted from Interim CEO to CEO in September 2020, after performing the role of Chief Operating Officer for a number of years at NRL HQ.

Peter V'landys had publicly supported Abdo from the beginning of his tenure as chairman, and it was clear when Abdo accompanied V'landys to America on a fact-finding mission for future television rights and investigating the streaming media landscape, that Abdo would be a leading contender for the CEO role. V'landys had publicly praised and supported Abdo in the media, stating that Abdo would be the best NRL CEO ever.

Abdo's initial performance as the CEO had already raised many red flags, contrary to praise from V'landys and the media for the South African. Already early into Abdo's tenure, a number of incidents had given cause for concern.

The NRL announced that the national anthem would not be played at Game 3 of the 2020 State of Origin. This caused wide criticism of the NRL for political correctness, and the NRL backtracked and later changed the decision. There was no doubt that the NRL and the commission made the decision to remove the anthem after much political debate about indigenous players not approving of the anthem, which had created a lot of attention in the media from both the 2018 and 2019 series.

Abdo and V'landys also approved a raft of radical new rules for the 2020 season, including no scrums, captain's challenge and six-again, aimed at faster play, with fans angry at the introduction of new rules. Many of the new rules still ignore the fundamental issues that many fans have with the game, including the video referee's impact on the game, and wrestling's imprint on the modern game, leaving many fans frustrated and angry.

The breakdown in 2023 between the Rugby League Players Association (RLPA) and the NRL over employment rights and entitlements with the Certified Agreement, is also cause for concern with Abdo, one of the senior leaders in negotiations, as each party blames each other in a long-standing dispute that continues to get dirtier. Mediation discussions continue between both parties.

Four of the past six CEOs and the past three chairmen have been appointed externally from outside the NRL, which raises the question about the inability for the code to build a strong cohesive culture and knowledge inside HQ that can lay down a strong foundation which will endure long after one leader leaves the organisation.

Appointing external candidates to these roles can have some benefits, with new knowledge and experience in other environments, but also raises risks, with consistent changes occuring internally that can result in no cohesion or community that can be built inside HQ, with each leader restarting and reinstating the culture and leadership style, which then ripples across the game.

In comparison, the AFL has fostered a culture of internal promotions with leadership development from within, built on understanding how the game operates from inside HQ and understanding its own culture and practices. Gill McLachlan and Andrew Demetriou, the last two appointed CEOs of the AFL, came with strong experience inside the game from senior roles at HQ, players association and the board of the AFL - a long apprenticeship before being appointed to the top role.

The AFL announced in 2023 that Andrew Dillion would replace Gill McLachlan, who will step down as CEO. Dillion will take the reins from October. This continues the AFL tradition of appointing an internal candidate. After Dillion had previously spent many years as a senior executive at the AFL, he became only the fifth appointed CEO at the AFL since 1986.

Rugby Australia, A League and Australian Cricket have undergone widespread change with their leadership roles in recent times, with all three organisations having rapid change at the top roles since the departure of stalwarts such as John O'Neill and Malcolm Speed, and, to a lesser extent, Sutherland, in their respective codes.

Peter V'landys has a strong reputation as a go-getter and of getting what he wanted during his time with Racing NSW.

Leadership is never easy in practice and even more so today, in this divided politically correct society we are living in, with extra pressures from the mob of social media and the need to remain firm against the pull and pressures of the crowd, as well as identity politics that has divided society and the world in a greater culture war across all society.

The game needs leaders to see both the forest and the trees today and into the future, a duality that can lead the NRL and the representative scene, but also to see the importance of grassroots and the community game so the game can remain healthy at all levels.

For the game to succeed, it needs a much better balance of knowledge and power between middle managers across the sport and senior leaders in the code. We have people with power in the game who have no knowledge or wisdom on key matters, and we have people with knowledge and understanding and no ability or power to make key decisions in the game.

People on the ground know the condition of bush footy or grassroots leagues well before HQ, but far too often, the CEO and senior leaders are too far away from the voices and staff to have any ideas or facts about the current environment and condition.

The blending of power and knowledge is a vital component to achieve unity.

Yet the leadership has been a vacuum inside NRL HQ, too often found not listening to key voices on the ground, and stakeholders warning of major risks ahead for the game.

In summary, everything rises and falls on leadership, and rugby league is dying for strong leadership, leaders who love the game and have its best interests first, leadership to drive the code forward across the whole sport, not just for today but to leave a legacy that will endure for many years to come. Statesmen are needed now more than ever to keep the game in safe hands for future generations. It needs inspired leadership that can set and achieve a grand vision, and build a strong team and culture that represents the sport with excellence and integrity, and drive discipline throughout the sport.

Core values are the foundation and bedrock for any long-term success, and the game's leaders must make values the foundation for the code at all levels. Without strong and united leadership, the game cannot succeed, and if rugby league doesn't want to improve its leadership and not change, then it should look behind, because that will be its future ahead repeated, with more of the past in its future!

AUSTRALIAN RUGBY LEAGUE COMMISSION

Many boards are asleep at the wheel. It's called Absentee Ownership.

Is the ARLC a sporting body or political body?

Aristocrats have taken over the game.

WHEN THE AUSTRALIAN Rugby League Commission (ARLC) was formed in 2012, it was hoped by many it would be the saviour for the code after the relinquishment of News Corp ownership (50%) of the game in 2011 led by Former News Corp chief executive John Hartigan. Finally, to many of the code's supporters, the game was getting its house in order, with an independent commission at the steering wheel with no conflicts of interest overseeing the greater game, similar to what was already in place for AFL and many other sports, both nationally and internationally.

Many in the media were glowing about the introduction of the commission, stating the game would now have the off-field professionalism and independence to fight the AFL with fire.

Finally, after the long-term negative effects of Super League, the NRL could deliver on its untapped potential.

But less than a decade into the life of the ARLC, those early hopes have been dashed by the brutal reality that the commission has been a major disappointment in its short existence and has failed to deliver anywhere near the hype hoped for at its inception. It has now become its own animal and is a threat for the long-term success and health of the game.

At the completion of the Super League war, the ARL and News Corp (Super League) reunited in 1998, after separate competitions in 1997, rebranding with the new trademark of the NRL (National Rugby League).

From 1998 in the new NRL era, the game's ownership was equally shared between the Australian Rugby League (ARL) and News Limited. This led to major governance issues within the game. One of the main challenges was the conflict of interest for the game, with a major media company (News Limited) owning half the game of rugby league (NRL). News Limited was renamed News Corp in 2013 and is Australia's largest media outlet, with ownership of both major newspapers and pay television giant Foxtel in Australia.

The NRL was in a position of negotiating television and media deals with News Limited, which owned half of the NRL, and media outlets such as Foxtel, for which rugby league is the highest-rating sport program. News Limited owned major newspaper publications such as The Daily Telegraph in Sydney and The Courier Mail in Brisbane, which were the leading newspapers in NSW and QLD for covering the game, causing a huge conflict of interest and lack of independence when reporting on rugby league matters. In addition, Victoria's leading newspaper the Herald Sun was also owned by News Limited.

News Limited's equal ownership with the NRL after Super League in 1998 caused major governance issues for rugby league including:
- Conflicts of interest
- No independence for governance of sport
- Inside information held by stakeholders

- Negotiating key matters with owners of the game
- Devalued TV and other media rights
- News Limited's ability to leverage its media outlets for selfish reasons
- Biased public relations from media parties
- News Limited could control narrative in media
- News Limited owning NRL clubs such as Brisbane Broncos, Melbourne Storm, North Queensland Cowboys
- Perceived bias towards News Limited's own corporate agenda
- NRL clubs getting preferable treatment
- Corporate profit vs community agenda
- Media guidelines and laws
- Potential legal disputes
- Government grants
- Grassroots and community game compatibility with corporate ownership model

News Limited had long wanted to get out of this shared model, with many believing the model could cause potential legal disputes, with the clear conflict of interest with the NRL, plus the media giant had spent a fortune on the game during Super League and had now set up Foxtel across Australia.

From 1998 until 2012, the dual ownership of the NRL was always a brake on the game moving forward after the civil war of Super League had ripped the heart out of the game. Having a major media empire own half the game did not allow the game to be governed independently, with sound foundations and integrity. The governance issues which held the game back between 1998-2012 resulted in far weaker results both on and off the field and enabled AFL and other sports to make up ground fast on rugby league, their governance operating models being far superior than that of the NRL.

In 2012, John Hartigan announced that News Limited would relinquish ownership of the NRL, stating that it was in the best interests of all parties that the media company sell its ownership stake. This announcement was a big shock to some in the sporting and media landscape, especially when you consider the costs and time spent on rugby league during the Super League war. But to many with their prime focus on media rights, it was not a surprise.

After News Limited relinquished ownership in 2012, a new governance model was designed. The ARLC would now sit at the top of the game, overseeing all facets of the code from the top-tier professional NRL to grassroots rugby league. The commission was formed to provide overall management of the game as an independent body, and gave clear strategic direction to the code, with executive power on key decisions across the game.

The NSWRL and QRL state bodies would still remain, and administer rugby league in each state, with the NRL providing annual funding to each state rugby league body to operate.

Country Rugby League (CRL), which had its own independent body in NSW, merged with the NSWRL in 2019, and grassroots would be served by both the state bodies and the NRL, with state bodies receiving annual funding allocation from the NRL.

Game Structure

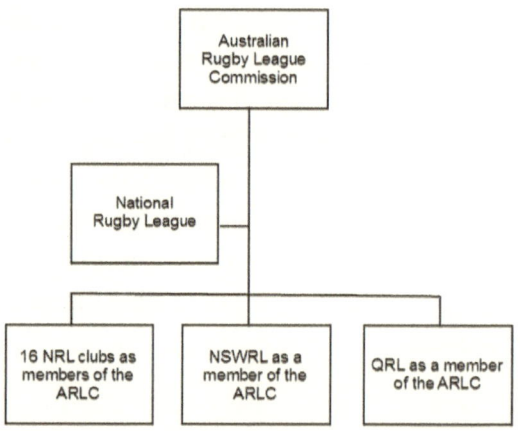

The Commision in 2012 was initially made up of commissioners and a chairman:

John Grant (Chairman), Catherine Harris AO PSM, Ian Elliot, Peter Gregg, Wayne Pearce OAM, Gary Pemberton AC, Jeremy Sutcliffe and Dr Chris Sarra.

Initial and current appointed commissioners were from diverse backgrounds including business, politics, government, education, academia and rugby league. Many involved with the game, including outsiders, believed the new commission needed much more business and corporate knowledge and experience within the governing body to lead the game forward.

The initial members were mandated that commissioners must have had no conflict with rugby league during the last 3 years.

Many thought the commission would provide the independence, knowledge and business capabilities the code badly needed after the complications of a shared ownership model with a media company, and would enable the code to govern independently, much like the AFL, cricket and other sports. But this hope quickly turned to concern when deep financial problems arose inside the code in the early years of the commission era, with concern over fiscal sustainability and internal conflicts between the new body of the ARLC and existing stakeholders, in particular, former chairman John Grant's working relationship with existing game stakeholders and clubs.

Following the code's two record television deals, valued at over one billion dollars, the game was quickly in financial despair, which still plagues the code today, even before Covid caused worldwide chaos.

Following the television deals with media partners since 2012, the NRL had spent all of this money and was looking for an overdrawn loan from a major bank to survive (which was later declined), and needed forward payment loans from its media partners to survive. The game also had funding allocation disputes with NRL clubs. In 2015, after former Chairman John Grant had promised all NRL clubs a set club funding allocation of 130% of salary cap, Grant had to go back on his word, saying that this could no longer be honoured, as there was not enough money left to fund this and the funding was unsustainable long term for the whole sport, with the clubs wanting too much of the game's money. Eventually, the clubs and NRL agreed on a funding allocation after much back and forward dispute, but cracks and trust were visible for all to see again, and division and infighting were again plaguing rugby league.

Rugby league media personalities such as Phil Gould, Phil Rothfield, Paul Crawley, Paul Kent, Ben Ikin and many more asked questions about this mismanagement of financial resources.

Questions to this day include:

How did the code spend all this money?

Where did the money go?

Why were NRL clubs and players getting so much of the game's funding allocation?

Why did the code not prepare an emergency fund?

Why does the code have no assets?

Why was there no greater funding to grassroots and country rugby league?

Why was there no expansion?

Why did NRL HQ have so many staff?

What were the plans for the NRL digital media division?

Many of these questions have still not been answered to this day, and many continue to raise concerns about this today. There were strong rumours the ABC Four Corners investigative program was going to do an investigation in 2020 but it did not go ahead, as none of the parties involved would speak to the ABC on the matter.

The Covid epidemic of 2020/2021 further highlighted concerns about the past mismanagement of funds, with the virus placing the NRL in a precarious and dangerous position with a potential lockdown and stoppage of games, which would lead to funding from all media partners being halted. The lack of saving and emergency funding made it very hard for the game to deal with any crisis.

Peter V'landys stated in early 2020 that if the game was stopped for more than 3 months, it could not survive. V'landys was immediately pushing for government funding to help the code through Covid in the early days of the virus in 2020.

The ARLC's poor record extends far beyond fiscal mismanagement and infighting between the commission and key stakeholders such as clubs, players and state bodies, a longstanding theme for the modern game.

The DNA of the game has fundamentally changed under the commission, and not for the better. The code has now become far more political, involved in social matters outside the traditional sporting parameters, with many non-rugby league stalwarts who are not members on the commission. Seats on the board have been filled by many folks who come from non-rugby league backgrounds and have leveraged their roles on the board to support such social matters as Black Lives Matter, LGBTQ and women's rights, national anthem disputes, domestic violence issues, mandatory vaccinations, the Voice Referendum and other political matters.

It seems the ARLC has put more focus on these social and political matters than the actual game, with grassroots and country rugby league often being forgotten, in favour of more mainstream social and political matters.

Going down the political or social road is a lose/lose (no win) situation, no matter which way you go. No matter which cause the game supports, there will be detractors, and it will lose fans and sponsors, due to their political and social views. A large core base of the game's long-time fans do not support many of the agendas the ARLC and NRL are currently advocating and supporting.

The commission era has not improved the grassroots level, and no growth has been seen outside heartland NSW and QLD, despite lavish praise for chairman Peter V'landys.

The commission membership seems to be moving more towards an aristocracy of elites who leverage the game, and have an influential board position, enjoying the status that comes with it, while true rugby league stalwarts have no voice or opportunity to join the commission. Seats on the board since inception seem to be only available to people from high status backgrounds such as in politics or business, or having the right contacts to get a seat on the board.

Ex-Queensland Labor representatives such as Peter Beattie and Kate Jones are currently sitting on the board. This follows on from ex-Queensland Labor treasurer Andrew Fraser formerly holding a senior management position in the NRL Head Office.

The election process for vacant board positions is not available or open to the general public wishing to apply, with a direct appointment process going to rugby league outsiders or people with key contacts such as politicians and corporate businessman, with only ex-Balmain Tigers player Wayne Pearce and former chairman John Grant from rugby league backgrounds holding seats on the board.

Pearce has had a seat on the board since inception, and his role and performance should have gained far greater spotlight after overseeing many of the issues that still plague the game.

The commission has not been the success many hoped it would be for a variety of reasons. Let's look at a few key issues holding the governing body back.

- <u>Knowledge</u>

Many of the past and current commissioners elected have little rugby league knowledge, with past chairman and former Queensland Premier Peter Beattie unable to name the Cronulla Sharks when interviewed by Phil Gould on Nines 100% Footy. After taking over the chairman's role,

Beattie's lack of rugby league knowledge was apparent for all to see and a common theme during his chairman reign when speaking with fans and media. Many, myself included, question the passion of past and current commissioners for the code, when many have come from outside the game's corridors with no prior involvement or interest in the game. Many board positions in Australia are seen as prestigious places to further your CV and career. Being on the board of one of Australia's most high-profile sports is a sure way to gain attention, stay relevant or advance your career aspirations.

Many high profile board members across both the sporting and corporate landscapes today are now on multiple boards, which makes you question how an individual can focus on serving an organisation when they have multiple commitments.

The commissioners on this board are responsible for making strategic decisions for the whole game and many do not have the experience and knowledge to make sound rugby league decisions. They may have extensive business, academic and other experience, but the game still needs acute inner knowledge of rugby league, both historically and in the present, combined with commercial/operational and financial acumen, in order to make sound decisions.

How can we grow and expand the game, improve player numbers both in juniors and seniors, restructure grassroots and country rugby league and face all the challenges from a changing world when some of our commissioners' knowledge of the game is very questionable and very limited? It takes more than just reading a monthly board report and attending a meeting to gain an understanding and awareness of the many issues across the greater game. Rugby league IQ takes time to develop, not just on the field but also in the boardroom.

Another concern is how and from whom the ARLC is receiving information to make key decisions. In my experience, many elected boards do not have sufficient information when making such decisions. Often, the only form of information they receive is from internal senior employees such as a CEO or senior management within a company setting providing feedback and updates. It is quite common for a CEO and internal staff to withhold information that may result in pressure for their own roles within an organisation.

Have NRL Commissioners been receiving sound information for decision making? For many years, the game has been struggling in certain functions. One has to question how information has been moved up and down the communication line at NRL HQ and within the ARLC. One of the key differences in my eyes and why the AFL has overtaken rugby league during the last 25 years has been its superior middle management capability and the ability of the AFL Commission to make better, wiser and faster decisions compared to the ARLC.

Graeme Samuel, the only person to have served on both the AFL and NRL (ARLC) Commissions stated in April 2020 that the AFL Commission was far superior to the ARLC and operated in a far more professional manner and was in a much better position to withstand the challenges of Covid. Samuel was critical of the lack of true independence during his time with the ARLC and was critical of NRL clubs' control of the game, particularly the funding allocation.

For any organisation to be successful, there has to be a blending of knowledge and power. For far too long, rugby league has lacked this blending and balance to enable the code to succeed. Past senior management have had the power but lacked the knowledge and wisdom to make wise decisions, while some in the code have the knowledge to improve the game in a variety of positions but lack the power to make any real and necessary change.

The winds of change are often seen by people on the ground first, like a farmer noticing drought before Canberra politicians start talking about it, or a sales rep knowing the numbers and monthly reports long before a CEO sees the monthly figures. A police officer on patrol will notice crime well before senior officers or ministers start making statements to the public about crime figures.

Rugby league badly needs the better blending of the two (knowledge and power) and for the ARLC to be more open to more sources of information rather than just internal management, to improve decision making and gain a wider awareness and understanding of the game.

The source of the truth is unimportant, only the finding of it!

The commission must also be open to getting open, transparent and independent people providing feedback who are not associated with the game or work with the NRL. Far too many companies are solely depending on one source of information, and this seems to have also impacted the ARLC. Rugby league commissioners need the best available information. The source of the truth is unimportant, only the finding of it.

With knowledge comes potential power

Awareness + understanding = wisdom

Wisdom + application = transformation

- Election Process and Representation of Stakeholders

When the NRL commission was formed in 2012, it was made up of seven commissioners and a chairman, as named previously in this chapter. As mentioned earlier, the game's initial and current membership was made up of members from backgrounds such as business, academia, legal, government and rugby league. Wayne Pearce and John Grant were the only commissioners with a strong rugby league background.

NRL clubs have often clashed with past and present chairmen over the appointees on the ARLC. Some club representatives have made threats in the power plays between the stakeholders, with contention generally surrounding club funding allocation, licensing agreements and power within the game.

Entry to become an NRL Commissioner was based on direct appointment in 2012, which is still the case today. The focus on a more business oriented committee has not allowed the game to have a far wider representation of the code, which has hindered grassroots, international and state leagues. Their voices have not been included in any of the top-level discussion or decision making processes, which has hurt the code significantly.

Whilst the board has been heavy with business and corporate experience, it has badly lacked rugby league intelligence across various stakeholders outside the NRL to navigate the game's future. The blowout of costs and fallout with clubs was evidence of this. Too often self interest hurts the game's best interests and long-term future.

The initial board and current commission still does not have adequate representation across the total game. The game has no representatives from country rugby league, grassroots, international rugby league and state leagues, and this is a cause for concern when key stakeholders and decision makers are not part of the representation of the game. Outsiders and business reps can be a healthy independent addition to any organisation or board, but, as discussed before, there needs to be a healthy blending between knowledge and power in rugby league for the governance to succeed.

The QRL Board is designed with one representative nominated from each region of Queensland to be on the board plus independent members. In total, there are eight members plus the chairman position. The QLD model is a far more representative mix of key stakeholders and is one of the reasons QLD remains a rugby league stronghold and continues to remain in a strong position across the diverse geographic state from the metropolitan south east of Brisbane to regional areas across the state such as Townsville, Mount Isa, Rockhampton, Toowoomba, Mackay and Bundaberg.

The New South Wales Rugby League (NSWRL) is made up of members associated with the sport. It does not have a regional-based governance model like interstate counterparts QLD, and has seven members plus the chairman position, including mostly those who have strong experience in business and rugby league, but there are no grassroots or country representatives.

The NSWRL and CRL merged in 2019, with NSWRL now the one body overseeing all aspects of rugby league in NSW.

- Application Process

The application process for a seat on the board is also of concern. A direct appointment process for existing and potential board members is taking the power and future away from the people who love the game. Looking at current board members, it is clear that the pendulum has swung to entry only through key contacts and has created an aristocratic elite. All people from all backgrounds should be able to apply for a seat on the commission. Rugby league stalwarts and statesmen are now not having the opportunity to apply for a board position. The governance model is now more like a political party movement or top-level corporate entity, with direct appointment rather than an independent election process.

Term Limits are another option that should also be considered for any board appointments. Many board members stay far too long on the commission and yet add very little value or contribution to the sport. A 3-year maximum appointment period would be consistent with many governing bodies from other sports and industries.

In summary, for rugby league and the ARLC to succeed, it needs the highest form of independent governance in Australian sport. For this to occur, far more care must be undertaken in the recruitment process for potential commissioners, and the direct appointment governance model the ARLC uses should be removed. A genuine love and passion for the game is a necessity but also brains and the courage to confront the challenges that need to be faced. The game needs a stronger representation of key stakeholders and independence within the code rather than an elite aristocracy made up of ex-businessmen, ex-Labor politicians, academic and corporate folks. There must be a far greater blending of knowledge and power for the commission to succeed.

The commissioners must not just limit their advice to that from NRL HQ and senior management but be open to outside independent voices who have no conflicts of interest and who give the code the brutal facts and truth about the game.

PETER V'LANDYS

In Peter we trust – Channel Nine

Australia's greatest sporting administrator – Media

Man of the Year - Peter V'landys – The Daily Telegraph front cover

PETER V'LANDYS HAS become the new favourite of the sporting media landscape in rugby league heartland. Throughout his short time as chairman of the ARLC, he has been flooded with praise and adulation as the man who saved rugby league. V'landys is seen as a fearless leader who saved the game in 2020 from Covid and became the darling of the media, with the Nine network and its high-profile staff such as Phil Gould, Danny Weidler and many others all in awe of the new chairman's performance and leadership. FOX Sports (News Corp), the code's other media partner, has also been a huge vocal supporter of V'landys during his tenureship with its newspapers The Daily Telegraph and The Courier Mail, full of public praise, with television programs on Foxtel such as NRL 360 calling him the saviour of the game after the Covid pandemic and the game's restart in 2020, with host Paul Kent stating V'landys is the game's best leader since Arthurson and Quayle.

When Covid struck early in 2020, it looked like the season would be cancelled, with most of the public stating that there was no chance the NRL would be able to play the 2020 season. With lockdowns, border closures, no flights/travel allowed for teams in multiple states and in NZ, no crowds allowed and many other challenges, there seemed no possibility that the 2020 NRL season could be salvaged. But V'landys and his team were defiant to the media, state and federal governments and the general public, stating they would do all that was possible to ensure the NRL season was completed to keep the game a showpiece for fans, whose lives were becoming altered drastically by the pandemic, with new Covid guidelines and rules, including border closures and lockdowns across the globe.

V'landys defiantly stated that Australia without rugby league was un-Australian!

With Churchillian-like resolve, early into the Covid outbreak, V'landys and the NRL did indeed save the 2020 NRL season. Through persistent and strong leadership, tight Covid guidelines for players and staff, player hubs, relocation of the NZ Warriors and the Melbourne Storm to new locations, and government support, the NRL salvaged the 2020 season. Much of this was off the back of V'landys' strong leadership during the initial virus outbreak. The season was saved, along with strong support from code stakeholders and their commitment to ensure the season was completed.

The reality was, V'landys and the NRL had no option but to save the season. Had the 2020 season been cancelled, the code would have been in a dire economic condition. The game had little money and few assets saved for a crisis of this magnitude, and everyone from players, coaches, clubs, employees, media, staff and other stakeholders would be the big losers, should the season be cancelled.

Media outlets such as Foxtel/Kayo were also at huge risk of bankruptcy if the 2020 season was not completed. Had the AFL and NRL, its two leading subscriber drivers and other sports not played games in 2020, it was at huge risk for a run on cancelled subscriptions, with no cash flow coming into its business. Foxtel needed the NRL and AFL as much as both sporting codes needed Foxtel's money!

When the code got the green light to continue with the 2020 season with tight protocols, V'landys was hailed as the greatest sporting administrator in the nation, with front page articles in The Daily Telegraph. V'landys was even taking pot shots at the AFL and CEO counterpart Gill McLachlan when taking the early lead to restart its competition. The AFL was caught out on a rare occasion to be behind the NRL in managing the Covid outbreak and restarting its own league.

The praise and adoration for V'landys from fans continued right through the 2020 season, with the consensus being that he had saved the NRL and rugby league in 2020. Newspapers and sports programs echoed this sentiment.

Whilst there is no doubt V'landys did a superb job in supporting and leading the code's survival through Covid for the 2020 season, many other matters and decisions under V'landys tenure have not been scrutinised or questioned adequately by the media. Whilst V'landys is praised and adored by the media and many fans, is he really the saviour of rugby league they proclaim him to be?

Since V'landys wrested power from Todd Greenberg, total power of the game has sat with the Greek-born V'landys, who rose to fame in his role as CEO of Racing NSW (a role which he still performs), with the success of mega racing events such as The Everest becoming one of Australia biggest horse racing events, taking the spotlight away from the powerful Victorian racing calendar, the long-time traditional powerhouse state for racing in Australia.

Rugby league's environment and culture is far different than racing and is on a whole new level for media coverage and stakeholder management. The fans and sponsors have many key differences to horse racing, along with the extra media spotlight for the winter football codes.

V'landys' negotiations and decisions on key matters should be a great concern for all rugby league fans. His performance has received virtually no coverage and has been very biased from media outlets. A number of key decisions and trends for the long-term future for the game signal the game is moving towards a new trajectory in the V'landys era.

V'landys' relationship with media partner Nine should have attracted far more scrutiny from the media. During the initial outbreak of Covid, Nine CEO Hugh Marks played hardball with the NRL and wanted the season to be cancelled, as he believed playing on would devalue the rights of his network. Both the NRL and Nine and its media outlets leveraged their staff to push their own agendas about the television rights discussions. The possibility of Nine not showing rugby league was never going to happen, but Nine wanted a discount and pushed hard, and used the opportunity of Covid to pursue this strategy.

The Nine network, which had been hemorrhaging money for years under mismanagement, now wanted the NRL to discount the TV rights, should the game continue for the 2020 season.

V'landys and Marks were involved in a back and forth negotiation played out in the media, with the Nine network pushing its own biased agenda through outlets such as The Sydney Morning Herald, The Age and its extended digital networks and big name media personalities. Eventually, it was agreed that the 2020 season would continue as expected and Nine would provide full coverage, but the biggest surprise was that for the 2021 and 2022 seasons, the NRL would provide a discount of $27.5 million per season, totalling $55 million, to the Nine network.

The NRL provided a huge discount when ratings would not be affected by Covid, as viewers would now have more leisure time to watch the game, with many people unable to work during the virus outbreak. There was no sign, trend or empirical evidence that the game's viewing numbers or rights had been devalued, and yet V'landys, the lead negotiator for the NRL, panicked and signed a reduced deal, providing the Nine network with an outrageous discount to the game's media rights after the Nine network had run a smear campaign against the NRL.

$55 million was money that many in the game would have died for. It could have gone to the game day experience of three grades, junior development, grassroots, savings, investment, expansion and much more, but instead the cash went to the coffers of Channel Nine.

Even more outrageous was that later in 2020, it was announced that the Nine network had won the rights to rugby league's arch rival, rugby union's Super Rugby competition, with rugby union leaving FOX Sports after being with the network since its conception. Rugby was now moving to free-to-air on Nine and its digital arm Stan. The NRL's discounted TV rights had supported the Nine network to purchase the Super Rugby rights after V'landys' $55 million discount for both the 2021 and 2022 season. Marks stated that Nine could not afford the NRL rights in early 2020, and before the year had finished, had announced a new deal with Rugby Australia for Super Rugby. Nine reportedly paid $100 million over 3 years to show rugby on Nine and Stan.

The AFL also faced similar pressures with TV rights but stood firm for the 2020 season with its media partners Seven and Foxtel, and offered no discounts during the Covid lockdown. The AFL's TV numbers were up 4.3% in 2020 and justified its belief in the value of its product nationwide.

Nine didn't just stop at pressuring V'landys with renegotiation of discounted television rights. It publicly went on a PR exercise in early 2020, trashing the code in the media and outlining that the game was boring and needed drastic rule changes. V'landys again submitted to Marks and agreed to a raft of new rule changes for the 2020 season without any testing phase, including the six-again rule to the disappointment of many fans. This has continued for the 2021 and 2022 seasons, with even more new rules, including two-point field goals, captain's challenge, head-high crackdown and new restarts, all rules that seem to have the Nine network's support and influence for proposed faster, more open rugby league.

The new rules such as six-again and head-high crackdown, all approved by V'landys, resulted in the 2021 NRL season being one of the most lop-sided competitions in the history of the code. The product as a whole has been seen by many fans as the worst ever in the game's history, with many games unwatchable, with the touch footy-like viewing of many games, and lopsided scorelines.

Early in V'landys' tenure as chairman, he publicly spoke about the game having to grow to survive. As ex-chairman Peter Beattie had also stated, long term, the game would have to look at expanding into new markets such as Perth, Adelande and New Zealand if it was to grow and compete with AFL and other sports. But under V'landys' direction, this has now taken a dramatic shift from long-term grand strategic plans to appeasing stakeholders.

The Nine network was again calling the shots, demanding of V'landys that the next expansion team would not come from a new market such as Perth or Adelaide to compete with the AFL but would have to come from the league's heartland base of South East Queensland, as that is where Nine and Foxtel gained much of their television ratings, subscriptions and advertising revenue from. V'landys again folded and made it clear in an announcement that the 17th team from the NRL would come from the South East QLD region, with Redcliffe Dolphins later being the confirmed new NRL franchise.

The Nine network wanted another Queensland team to boost ratings and advertising. The on-field performance of the QLD clubs in the 2020 season was poor, with no QLD team making the finals, causing a significant drop in ratings for the Nine network. Nine needs the QLD teams to perform strongly on the field for ratings and advertising, and the more QLD teams allows more chances for this to occur and provides more regular QLD derbies.

V'landys had again appeased Nine with short-term thinking, and the game would not conduct any due diligence or go through a proper open tender process for expansion. The NRL would appease Nine's agenda for yet another QLD team.

Brisbane and the South East regions had very strong legitimate claims to be the next franchise to enter the NRL, but the fact that no due diligence, open tender application or long-term planning was discussed was confusing. It was apparent Nine were again driving and influencing key decisions within the game, when decisions should have been made independently by the ARLC and not the Nine network.

After discounting the NRL rights for 2021/2022 to Nine, V'landys also extended the TV rights with the game's other media partner, FOX Sports, during the middle of the Covid pandemic. FOX Sports funding provides the largest cash flow for the game, with all eight games being shown live weekly during the regular season and finals.

The code's weak financial position and limited cash reserves, along with V'landys' premature and rushed rights negotiations during the Covid outbreak, again left the game with a poor deal with FOX Sports. Going early in media negotiations was the strategic plan from V'landys, but the outcome was average or poor to many in the media industry. The AFL waited patiently and allowed the NRL to lead negotiations with media outlets early, and, after the NRL had struck a deal, the AFL executives went to the table later in 2020 and negotiated a deal far exceeding the NRL, with its media rights believed to be worth $155 million more per season than the NRL, and up to nearly $250 million per year after the 2022 extension. The NRL's annual financial report released in early 2021 was missing key information, with many stating the NRL were hiding how poor the financial deals were from both media partners, to disguise the poor deals from public and media scrutiny. Again V'landys escaped scrutiny, despite terrible media deals!

Under Greenberg, the NRL had invested heavily in its digital department with the move from traditional media to digital streaming platforms, but V'landys has taken a completely different approach, pulling back on pushing internal digital rights and NRL-owned content, thus reducing the chances of the code succeeding independent of broadcaster money.

V'landys has stated that the digital inhouse production is not financially viable for the NRL.

Whilst rugby league has backtracked on its digital content, stating it's not financially viable, many other sports are pushing forward to control their own destiny with their own content, production and special features. Both Foxtel and free-to-air networks such as the Nine network are against the NRL processing its own digital media department, as they become potential competitors of the old media landscape such as Nine and Foxtel rather than the new streamers and independent providers, which are growing exponentially in the digital age.

V'landys' role as CEO of Racing NSW should also have received far more of a spotlight. A clear conflict of interest is apparent when juggling both his long-term role as Racing Chief for NSW and Chairman of the ARLC. Racing NSW has a close relationship with rugby league media partner News Corp and the NSW Government. The major newspapers (Daily Telegraph/Courier Mail) owned by News Corp have a close business relationship with the racing industry through advertising, paper sales and subscription to digital services. The NSW Government also supports events for both rugby league and horse racing to attract tourism and events to the state.

News Corp, the owner of Foxtel and leading newspapers, and rugby league's major partner, was also considering acquiring FOX Bet, a new betting agency, which would pose a major conflict of interest for V'landys with Racing NSW and the prior TV deals done between the NRL and Foxtel.

V'landys is representing two large organisations – the NRL and Racing NSW – which have large financial business transactions with both News Corp plus state and federal governments, and this relationship is a clear conflict of interest for rugby league, due to the racing industry's close relationship with News Corp and deals conducted by all parties. The NRL extended discounted media deal with Foxtel barely received any attention, and V'landys should have been held more accountable for the rights deal compared to the AFL and his role in dealing with the same stakeholders with Racing NSW.

This conflict of interest has barely received any attention from rugby league pundits and the greater media.

News Corp media personalities such as Paul Kent, Phil Rothfield, Brent Read, Matthew Johns, James Hooper, David Riccio, Michael Carayannis, and Paul Crawley have been huge supporters of V'landys, with virtually no mainstream criticism coverage for discounted television deals, the 17th NRL team tender process, and the introduction of new rules.

Is it any wonder media corporations such as Nine and News Corp adore Peter V'landys and publicly glorify him in the various media outlets they own? The new chairman seems to be their puppet and the fruits are for all to see: television rights at reduced prices with no empirical evidence to support this, rule changes to suit media partners who trash the game in the public, and now media outlets deciding which will be the next expansion teams and halting the digital revolution, which possibly is a huge threat to both Nine and Foxtel.

Is V'landys looking out for rugby league or his media mates? It all smells very rotten!

Whilst V'landys is now the darling of the media, who stroke his ego after favourable support for media partners, the game suffers with poor decisions that will have long-term consequences for rugby league.

Fundamentally, under V'landys and the ARLC, the game has changed. V'landys is leading like a dictator not answerable to anyone. He is acting as both chairman and CEO of the game and has executive power on all decisions within the game, from TV rights negotiations, digital closure and expansion, to rule changes on the field and even becoming chairman of selectors for the Kangaroos. His close relationship and deals with Nine and Foxtel have been a disaster and yet have received no real independent scrutiny.

The game is now led by outsiders who are now the insiders holding power and making key decisions on the future of the game, appeasing key stakeholders with dangerous corporate relationships and having no real interest in the long-term health of the code.

VISION

Without a vision you will perish!

*You read a book from beginning to end;
in business you begin with the end in mind!*

What is it that you want!? Decide, then!

WHAT DOES RUGBY league want? What does the code desire in 1 year, 3 years, 5 years and 10 years?

What will the competition look like in that timeframe?

How many clubs will be in the NRL in 5 to 10 years?

What structures need to be in place across the game for long-term growth?

Do we introduce a player draft?

Grassroots playing numbers?

Plan for growth into new markets?

How do we halt and challenge AFL as the number one sport in the nation?

How do we get more kids into the sport?

How do we make bush footy strong again?

What are the biggest challenges to the game?

What are the biggest opportunities?

What is the digital and media plan to reach more people?

How do we grow the international game?

How will proper rugby league international tours return?

Some simple questions – but many that rugby league has not defined since Super League.

The game's leaders and the commission can talk about strategic plans that are presented for all to see on the NRL website, such as the 2018-2022 long-term strategic plan for the game, but in the end, it is results that matter, or, as the Bible says, *By their fruit you shall know them*, no matter how much you talk about strategic plans on your website or talk them up via the NRL Commission, CEO and digital media arm.

Everything is a matter of opinion but results are real!

The game has been hampered by indecision, procrastination, and division, and found to be drifting far too often. The game's internal structures have been allowed to decline and this has provided AFL and other sports opportunities to expand geographically and strengthen their position across all markets.

The fact that it took so long for any strategic long-term plan under the ARLC shows you how rudderless the code has been at the top during the NRL era. Even with its current strategic plan, the code still seems adrift compared to other sports, if it ever wants to be the leading sport in Australia and maximise its potential.

One of the main reasons AFL has become the number one code in Australia is simply its ability to set short and long-term objectives and use its financial and people resources, and have total focus and discipline to implement and achieve those objectives.

Such achievements include:

- National competition across Australia
- New teams on the Gold Coast, Western Sydney (18-team national team competition)
- Tasmania approved as new 19th team from 2028
- Grassroots development across Australia
- Targeting the top end of the town market and taking a strong market share base off rugby union, especially in the upscale Northern Sydney market. Many former NSW Waratah rugby union fans are now Sydney Swans supporters
- Auskick implementation across Australia
- Government funding to grow game
- Marvel Stadium ownership (asset)
- Governance reform
- Sponsorship growth
- Membership and crowd growth
- AFLW League

Whilst rugby league was indecisive, the AFL had clearly defined objectives and goals that were set and achieved. Rugby league continued to get bogged down in dirty infighting between stakeholders such as clubs, players, state bodies, the commission, media partners and NRL HQ.

The game, for whatever variety of reasons, can never seem to get its act together, have complete unity between stakeholders and be in total agreement on what it wants the game to look like in Australia and what it wants to move forward and achieve in any given timeframe.

The game is still in disagreement about core matters such as what the NRL should look like, if expansion should occur and where new teams would be placed, what should be the international program, how the governance model should operate, what power clubs and state bodies have in the governance of game, what the funding allocation is to key stakeholders, or how the NRL HQ should operate, etc., etc.

The game needs key leaders to be far more ambitious for the sport, both short term and long term. It needs to believe in its product and take the fight to the AFL and other sports, but, more importantly, it needs people and leaders who can help achieve its grand objectives for the future, not just talk about its strategic plans and goals but actually deliver with real results in an industry which is becoming more challenging by the day in the digital age, with a saturation of competitors.

The promise of the future is an awesome force – but you have to know what you want and take massive action with dogged persistence for this to become a reality. This is something rugby league has not done!

TEAMS - WORKPLACE CULTURE

More horsepower equals better results

More leadership equals more horsepower

THERE IS A quote that is told often and it goes:

People are your most valuable asset.

It's not quite true. They would have been closer to the truth if they had said:

The right people are your most valuable asset.

The sports and entertainment industry in the digital age is probably the most competitive and saturated it has ever been in the history of professional sports and entertainment, with every sport in Australia and the world fighting for their share and profit in both national and global markets. The sports market has never been so saturated from existing and new professional sports and leagues such as the NRL, AFL, Cricket Australia, Super Rugby, A League Soccer, NBL, Big Bash, new women's sport leagues and international brands such as the NBA, NFL, NHL, MLB, EPL, UFC, plus other entertainment options like social media, podcasts, entertainment streamers like Netflix and Amazon all fighting for their share in the entertainment market.

People often talk about a brand name against another brand such as AFL vs NRL or NBA vs NFL vs MLB, but at the end of the day, it is basically one organisation's group of people against another group of people inside an organisation, as stated in the previous chapter on leadership.

Behind all these famous brands are people, who, on a day-to-day basis, perform functions to better grow their brands and sports, not just in their own traditional core market but now worldwide.

Famous World War Two Leader George Patton said it best: *It's not weapons but people who win you wars*. This definitely applies to the business and the sports world as well.

In the Australian sports market over the last 25 years, the winner has been the AFL. The AFL's move from a Victorian-centric league in the early '90s to a high-level national league with a national footprint and structure, independent governance, high-level of professionalism and standards and ability to achieve clear and focused objectives has left the NRL and other sports for dead, and now all sports in Australia are playing chase.

For far too long, rugby league did not have enough of the right people in key seats driving the game in key functions from grassroots to the NRL. We mentioned issues surrounding leadership and the ARLC in earlier chapters, but it flows on down from senior leadership roles within the game to all key roles associated with the sport, including the vitally important mid-management roles that drive results on the ground and do much of the grunt work from the strategic vision.

Rugby league needs the best and most passionate people involved in running the code if it is to challenge AFL and other sports. If the code doesn't have the right people, it has no chance to move to the next level and will continue to fight gravity like it has over the last decade and more.

The competition has never been bigger, stronger and better, and only the best will survive. The digital revolution in the media has leveraged this even more, to execute well for markets to thrive and exist.

The bigger will become bigger and the poorer will get poorer (smaller get smaller) even more so after Covid.

There are some great people working for the code, who love the game passionately – let's be clear on that – but in some areas of the game, the results have been poor, and these results must be examined as to why the decline in results and standards in comparison with past results and competitors' expanded position or dominance in the market.

Since 1998 and the unification of the code after Super League, it seems that no leader has had the ability to build an A Team for the code, either in the NRL Headquarters office or other key business units and functions of the game nationally, including grassroots, bush footy and domestic leagues, in both new and existing structures.

The fact that four of the game's past leaders have come from outside the game and the last three chairmen appointed to the commission have also come from outside shows the head office has experienced much change during this period, with no inner promotions to senior roles, with the exception of current NRL CEO Andrew Abdo, and Todd Greenberg.

When you have a revolving door of leaders, you have a culture on the ground that is continually changing and has no cohesion or consistency, which impacts the culture and environment of the workplace from top to bottom. It becomes even more complicated with the two-state leagues getting funding allocation from the NRL and delivering services from top to bottom in each state.

It is impossible to have a great culture that promotes trust, ethics and teamwork when you have the continual change that comes with every new leader appointed, who will have a different style and temperament of leadership.

An outsider can be great when internal resourcing does not have the capacity (capability) to perform the roles needed or there are deep-rooted culture and performance issues inside the organisation that need addressing, but the game must build better teams and a stronger culture that ensures a strong foundation for the game.

The game needs the best talent in a range of professional and operational roles for not just the NRL, but across grassroots, country rugby league, the NSWRL, QRL, media roles and in a variety of other professional and operational roles.

AFL and other sports are all fighting for a bigger share of the pie, and this is now occurring at all levels of sport. The competitiveness in all markets is likely to increase greatly into the future, with every sport fighting for the hearts and minds of supporters, from 5-year-olds to grandparents.

The AFL middle management has essentially driven better domestic leagues, the Auskick grassroots program, greater participation numbers and expansion into new regions across Australia, with ever improving infrastructure and systems. This has been accomplished via clear strategic plans and goals, strong leadership in the middle management, higher professional standards and measured metrics from key senior figures within the game.

These have been some of the key reasons why the AFL has had tremendous growth over the last 2 decades in comparison to the NRL.

Rugby league has to have a complete change in philosophy surrounding appointments for the code, especially in critical middle management roles. The AFL's professionalism has left other sports behind, including rugby league, and all sports are now playing catch-up. Rugby league and many other sports are still in many ways running the operations of the domestic game in an amateur fashion compared to professional operations like the AFL, which have been heavily influenced by European and American sporting leagues in moving into the professional arena at all levels of the game.

The game now, more than ever, needs the right people in the right seats and the wrong people removed. We need people with brains, courage, character, and intelligence, who are great team players and have a deep passion for rugby league, to be involved in all levels. If we get those people on board, the game can only prosper, but if we have the wrong people in the game, we will continue to struggle.

The right people are your most valuable asset, not all people.

FINANCES

Money is just a magnifying glass. It simply makes you more of what you already are.

If you're a drunk, you will just drink a better brand; if you're generous, you will give more away.

SINCE THE FORMATION of the ARLC, the game's finances have been a hot topic, with many stakeholders involved in the code and outside voices all holding strong views. The game had been flush with cash from record-breaking billion-dollar television deals with media broadcasters, but only a few short years later, the NRL was in deep trouble, with few cash reserves and no assets to support the game.

The game's precarious financial position has again been highlighted by the outbreak of Covid in early 2020, which was still an ongoing matter in the 2021, and, to a lesser extent, the 2022 season, which has further put the NRL and code under intense pressure to survive.

Whilst other codes had ceased playing early into the Covid outbreak, in 2020, rugby league was the frontrunner in needing to continue playing, in an attempt to save the code from financial ruin. Such is the dependency on cash flow from TV broadcasters and sponsors, due to limited reserves to cope with any emergency.

The relocation of all NSW clubs plus the Melbourne Storm and New Zealand Warriors to Queensland in July of the 2021 season cost the NRL tens of millions, this on top of the extra costs and relocations to keep the 2020 season going. But the NRL had to do this or the cash flow tap would have been turned off.

NRL Chairman Peter V'landys stated to the media in March 2020 during the initial Covid outbreak that the game could not continue without the cash from broadcasters and it may need support and funding from the government stimulus package to survive the pandemic.

The warning signs had been flashing long before Covid hit the entire globe in early 2020. For years, the code had been living the high life, with spending far exceeding revenue and no long-term plan for the game's financial security or preparations for a rainy day emergency fund.

The game had seen money pass through like never before in the history of the code in Australia that dates back to 1908.

The revenue during the ARLC era pre-Covid was enormous. The NRL was behind only the AFL in total revenue. The AFL earned a whopping $794 million for the 2019 season alone.

NRL Total Revenue 2012-2022

2012 - 181m
2013 - 303m
2014 - 324m
2015 - 334m
2016 - 350m
2017 - 354m
2018 - 496m
2019 - 528m
2020 - 417m
2021 - 575m
2022 - 594m

In 2020, the NRL announced a full year deficit of $24.7m. The deficit excluded the 2020 State of Origin series, which was played in November instead of the traditional mid-year slot. Had Origin been counted, the deficit would have been $3.7m. This was on top of harsh spending cuts across the game, including a reported 25% cut at the NRL head office.

The NRL was an undisciplined organisation which spent recklessly and lavishly on consultants, executives, programs, NRL clubs, state bodies, employees, players and other aspects associated with the sport. What is most disappointing is that with all this television money and other sources of revenue, the organisation never looked after the game or built a stronger foundation to endure the changing cyclical seasons of business and life and ensure its long-term future.

No expansion has occurred either domestically or professionally up until 2023, with great opportunities being missed for a second Brisbane team years ago and other options like a new team in Perth that would give the game a greater national presence. The Toyota Cup, the old U'20s national competition, has been canned, which was the premier youth pathway program in Australian junior sport. Some pundits believe the poor standards and quality of the 2021 and 2022 NRL seasons are due to the lack of development pathways. Clubs like Penrith Panthers and Melbourne Storm, which have strong pathways, revealed the apparent gap between the strong and weak clubs in 2021. Many of the NRL games in 2021 were of a very poor quality, with many high-scoring fixtures more reminiscent of the English Super League or the Toyota Cup, with both of those leagues having a reputation for high-scoring games and mediocre defences.

Country rugby league in NSW and QLD has continued to decline, with no new operating models or extra support being implemented to bring in more professionalism to strengthen and fight off other codes. Grassroots pathway and junior programs which have received central funding continue to come under scrutiny about the long-term benefits of the cash outlay, with the return on investment very questionable, despite positive media statements from the NRL head office.

Whilst most attention goes to the top-tier elite NRL, the real battle of the codes is for the hearts and minds of youth across Australia. Whoever dominates this market of the sporting codes will have the inside running for future trends and demographics and potential growth. Turning kids into players then supporters then to lifetime fans is a key for any sport organisation for long-term growth, as it can lead to generational growth with a sporting code.

Former South Sydney CEO Shane Richardson was brought into the NRL head office to look at the sustainability of the game and plan some strategic models to take the game forward.

He was quite blunt in his assessment when speaking with Ben Ikin on NRL 360 in 2020, stating that the game could not afford its current expenditure. He was highly critical of the money being spent on clubs and players and not enough funding and resources for grassroots development.

In 2021, each player's payments for each NRL club was operating on an allocation of $9.02 million, down from $9.6 million under the original players CBA agreement. Players would receive $9.11 million in 2022 from a planned $9.7 million. All 16 NRL clubs receive annual grants of around $13 million each year from the NRL, which has been reported to be upgraded each year.

The NRL announced in late 2022 that the 2023 NRL salary cap would increase by an incredible 25% to $12.1 million per club!

All NRL players took a pay cut of 6% for the 2021 and 2022 NRL seasons after the Covid outbreak.

The NRL announced in September 2021 another $7 million in support to clubs to help them after Covid had canned most clubs' home game revenues for 2021.

Original ARLC Commissioner Gary Pemberton said the code should save $50 million per year in an emergency fund, to be prepared for any unexpected event. The last two chairs of the commission, Peter V'landys and Peter Beattie, have both stated it was essential the code have an emergency fund to support the game in times of crisis like we saw during Covid. Why Pemberton's plea to bank $50 million back in 2012 for a rainy day fund was not acted upon is still a mystery, as he was on the commission and had a voice with other senior stakeholders on the commission.

Paul Kent from The Daily Telegraph has stated many times on Fox's NRL 360 that no one from the code has been able to provide an explanation of where the money has gone. The NRL, like the AFL, has tax exemption status from governments and has received large funding from all levels of government, which should have involved more scrutiny on the code's fiscal mismanagement or potentially more serious consequences for misuse of funding.

An astonishing amount of revenue has passed through the code since 2012, with very little to show for it and no accountability for those involved in the waste, with no cash or assets on the books or fundamental structural developments for the game until recent times. The fact that the NRL was declined a loan from major banks and had to request a forward payment from broadcasters to survive is embarrassing, and outlines how the commission and NRL senior management have mismanaged the finances of the code. Some would say what has occurred over the last decade was near criminal when you factor in tax exemption status and a lack of transparency about financial records.

Many have blamed the code's poor finances on the huge number of staff employed at NRL head office, whilst others, such as Shane Richardson, blame the NRL clubs and players for being too greedy and taking too much of the code's income as being unsustainable. Phil Rothfield reported that between 2010-2020, NRL clubs had squandered almost $400 million in mismanagement, with an astonishing turnover of 116 different chief executives and chairmen at the 16 NRL clubs.

Peter V'landys stated in March 2020 that he could not comment on past financial issues with the game but in his role as chairman, he would build an emergency fund. This was a weak response from V'landys, and more spotlight should have been on the ARLC and individual commissioners and other stakeholders such as the clubs and players.

The more money the game made, the more was spent. The NRL did not have the right people or maturity to control and handle the billions that have passed through the code in the last decade.

The Covid outbreak just brought it to life for all to see. As Warren Buffet famously said: *When the tide goes out, we soon find out who is swimming naked.*

Warning signs were apparent as far back as John Grant's tenure as chairman, when he advised all clubs that he could not honour his promise of the annual grant allocation to NRL clubs. When this all fell apart with clubs and players and his position was on the line, he changed tack and offered the clubs more money, which the game could clearly not afford, nor was it sustainable.

Whilst Covid was to some the black swan event and took most by surprise, there were clear warning signs long before the outbreak of the virus of financial mismanagement of the game and the likely scenario of cash flow problems ahead for the NRL.

The movement from Stage 3 – Denial to Stage 4 – Grasping for Salvation, as outlined in earlier chapters, can be a slowburn or happen virtually overnight. Rugby league now knows how close it is to being insolvent, with no income or cash flow making its way to the NRL.

Staff cuts at the head office and reduction in player payments are potentially only just the beginning to make the game more sustainable. State leagues and grassroots could also be greatly affected in the future. No stakeholders in the game are immune to future funding cuts now after Covid. The whole game allocation and funding model will be a delicate and disputed process between stakeholders and management, moving forward.

Peter V'landys had already signed reduced television deals with both Foxtel and Nine, which provide the largest cash flow to the game, and clubs were hurting even more so with lower crowds or no crowds in attendance during Covid. The league's clubs behind many of the NRL teams have had massive damage from Covid, with the bottom lines from gaming and hospitality significantly reduced over the last 2 to 3 years.

The current agreement between the players and NRL allocates around 30%-40% (higher for 2022 - 282m, 47.5% of total earnings) of the code's total revenue to the players and clubs. Richardson believes this is unsustainable, and with no or less crowd revenue during Covid and a lesser television deal and potentially less corporate support, this may support his assessment.

The current NRL/Players part-ownership model based on players receiving a percentage of the game's total revenue would have to be questioned! This agreement is an industrial agreement between the NRL and players association and would need to be renegotiated in future deals.

A dispute broke out between the Rugby League Players Association (RLPA) and the NRL in mid-2023 over working rights and contracts. RLPA President Clint Newton says the dispute has nothing to do with money. NRL CEO Andrew Abdo says the NRL will not be bullied or held to ransom by the players association, as mediation continues between both parties.

New financial models that are more sustainable long term will now need to be designed, but getting the stakeholders all in agreement and doing what is best for the code will be a huge challenge. That is a delicate and difficult process and looks highly unlikely, with the salary cap growth for 2023 and the ongoing player dispute, which may head to the Industrial Relations Commission, with further division between players and head office.

The current governance model of the ARLC is a huge threat to the code's financial future. Many stakeholders in the game, such as state bodies, clubs, players, grassroots, non-heartland and international reps, have no representation on the commission, with many current decisions impacting them all greatly, for which they have no voice. The commission has been terrible in its short existence and many of the commissioners are unqualified to be making decisions on key matters for the game.

NRL clubs still have huge power in the game, despite the fact they have no seat on the commission. Clubs have always put themselves before other areas of the greater game, especially when it relates to funding. The John Grant dispute is an example of this, with the NRL announcing in July of 2021 that Australia would not participate in the 2021 Rugby League World Cup to be held in England without discussions with the players association. This was again the NRL clubs being selfish and not allowing players to represent nations, with fears they could get injured, and where clubs would not be financially reimbursed.

In summary, the code needs much tighter financial control measures with more accountability and transparency to stop a repeat of the dire financial situation the sport has witnessed and should have never been in. A new sustainable funding model representing all stakeholders, not just the players and NRL clubs, from under-sixes to the international arena, must be designed for the code's long-term health, with tough calls being made to ensure the code's future at all levels.

Key stakeholders need representation and a voice on key matters, rather than the current direct appointment process on the ARLC that is an anchor on the ship of progress to the game's future and prosperity.

Reduced deals from poorly negotiated past television rights and the likelihood that media revenues may have possibly peaked from the game's 2019 highs, added to the far tougher economic conditions that are currently present within the global and national economy post-Covid and strong inflation and deflation causing a stagflation like effect, will make things much harder to navigate and leave the code with many future challenges.

More than ever before in the history of the modern game, rugby league stakeholders need to work in unity, and changes must occur fast!

COUNTRY RUGBY LEAGUE

If you know Bourke, you know Australia – Henry Lawson

ASK ANY PERSON who has been involved with country rugby league for an extended period of time in the bush how the game is going and they will bluntly respond that the sport is struggling and facing some serious challenges to its long-term future. The sport in the bush has been on a declining trend since the Super League war and it seems to be heading downward fast unless changes are made.

Many involved with the game in the bush will have different reasons as to why the code is dying or struggling, and each individual club and region will have specific reasons, but the bottom line is the code is struggling or in decline in regional Australia, specifically, in heartland areas in NSW and some parts of QLD that need drastic attention to turn it around.

The reasons for the decline since the '90s civil war of Super League include:
- The Super League war had a major impact on bush footy, which started a downward trend, turning fans off the game with greed, big egos, and selfishness
- The NRL took its eye off bush footy and took things for granted

- Lack of resources
- Culture of the game and the perception by women, parents, families, members of the public
- Lack of leadership and accountability
- Lack of transparency from head office on real data
- Wrong structure and governance model
- Wrong people involved in running the sport
- Lack of professionalism
- Middle management capabilities to run local competitions
- Lack of funding
- Lack of adequate code of conduct enforcement across the game
- Poor infrastructure of some local clubs
- Poor player and crowd behaviour
- CRL's poor performance never questioned for many years
- NSWRL
- Job losses in regional communities
- Towns declining in population and finding player numbers
- Lack of funding to support clubs
- Regional economies
- Other sports: AFL, rugby union, basketball, soccer
- Digital and social media age (Netflix, Facebook, Instagram, Twitter)
- Rich clubs raiding poorer clubs

In 1999, I played under 18s in the Group 4 competition, located in north west New South Wales. This area is known for being a heartland farming agriculture country. The north west has always been a strong rugby league area, with a deep history of rugby league. The group has had famous players: Jamie Lyon, Clive Churchill, Ewan McGrady, Dallas Donnelly, Tom Learoyd Lahrs and many more learn and play their trade in the region.

The 1999 Group 4 competition consisted of nine teams all fielding three grades: an under 18s, reserves and first-grade team. (The women's competitions had not yet been formed.) This was a strong and vibrant regional competition made up of the teams below, all fielding three full-grade squads with a strong local following and proud history deeply woven into the north west community, with a strong local media covering the zone.

Group 4 Teams 1999:
West Tamworth Lions
North Tamworth Bears
Werris Creek Magpies
Manilla Tigers
Coonabarabran Unicorns
Gunnedah Bulldogs
Narrabri Blues
Moree Boars
Wee Waa Panthers

In 2019, the competition was made up of seven teams:
North Tamworth Bears
Narrabri Boars
Gunnedah Bulldogs
Werris Creek Magpies
Dungowan Cowboys
Kootingal Roosters
Boggabri Kangaroos

In 2 decades, this Group 4 competition has gone through many changes, with many ups and downs in that timeline, with new teams entering the competition and old teams exiting or joining other rugby league zones in close proximity. But it runs far deeper than just who was a member of each competition; in that 2-decade period, much more had occurred, if you look deeper at the issues, and this is occurring regularly across the regional sport.

This example of Group 4 has been happening in numerous other regional competitions across the sport.

Last 20 years consistent trends

- Clubs folding – Wee Waa Panthers, West Tamworth Lions, also Werris Creek Magpies for a period but back in Group 4 in 2019, Coonabarabran Unicorns, for a period of time and now in a new zone.
- Clubs unable to field three full grades, most clubs would have had trouble at one point in time; some clubs have serious issues for extended periods of time.
- Lack of match officials.
- Minimal support or no support from CRL, NSWRL and NRL.
- Major sponsor Wests Tamworth Club removed sponsorship due to 2 years in a row of on-field player incidents in grand finals, including player attacking referee in 2016 grand final. One player received a 20-year ban from the NSWRL.
- No middle management professional support to committees to run code more ethically and professionally.
- Poor culture and non-family environment turning people away (violence and poor behaviour).
- Code of conduct is not enforced well.
- Rich clubs raiding poorer clubs.
- Lack of committee members to run clubs and groups, lack of resources.
- Conflicts of interest and lack of true independent decision-making power on key matters across zones.

These are just a few examples of why the game is in decline in the bush and what occurred in Group 4 between 1999-2019, which could be applied to any other group or zone across country rugby league, as most local clubs have or are facing similar challenges of similar nature.

It should not be seen as all negative; there are still many positive stories and many clubs are still doing great things for the game and their local communities, despite limited support, and are continuing the proud tradition and history the game has with regional Australia. Many club stalwarts, committee members, volunteers, coaches and players are the backbone/bedrock of the game and do it all for love.

In contrast, 20 or so years ago in 1999, there was little AFL in the north west of NSW or the Group 4 rugby league zone.

Twenty years later, the 2019 North West NSW AFL competition consisted of the following clubs:

- Gunnedah Bulldogs
- Narrabri Eagles
- Inverell Saints
- Tamworth Kangaroos
- Tamworth Swans
- New England Nomads
- Glen Innes Celts
- Moree Suns

In less than a decade since conception, the AFL in 2019 had an eight-team senior competition deep inside rugby league heartland, which also includes juniors and female teams with their own local committees, and clubs growing the game with the assistance of each state AFL body. It's an incredible story of growth within such a short period in rugby league heartland, built on the AFL starting the ball rolling from nothing but hard work, with key strategic plans implemented to expand the game, especially in the northern states market, raising awareness of the game and its opportunities, regular player development visits to schools and clubs, and then individual clubs and volunteers growing it to what it is today with passion and commitment.

In the same period, Group 4 rugby league, which had always dominated this local market, with rugby union as the other local powerhouse, were now struggling and facing many challenges for the game's long-term future in a local market that had never been this competitive. These challenges would include junior participation, local community support, sponsorship and local media attention.

Many would argue that some regions and regional towns are in decline and this is a strong factor in the game's decline and that there are possibly fewer jobs or opportunities in some regions. This may or may not be true, but one thing I will argue is: rugby league could have done a much better job of running and maintaining the game if the right models and people were involved. The eight-team implementation of the AFL is a great example of what hard work and a bold vision can achieve from next to nothing, though it is one thing starting a league; it is another challenge to keep it strong for longevity. Rugby league, however, would die to have implemented local comps so fast in AFL heartland such as Victoria, Tasmania, Northern Territory, Western Australia or South Australia.

Regional and bush footy sat under the umbrella of Country Rugby League in NSW for many decades until a merger with NSWRL in 2019. CRL completely dropped the ball in administering the sport in NSW and was never called out or held accountable by the NRL for the poor performance over such a long period of time. Many clubs in the bush often complained about the lack of support from the CRL, but those pleas and complaints fell on deaf ears.

QLD has dominated State of Origin, winning 14 of the last 18 series since 2006, with many praising the Maroons' dominance. The opposite side of the coin that does not get discussed often is it shows the decline of rugby league in NSW in both the city and country regions.

Under the new governance model of NSWRL taking over Country Rugby League in NSW, it is probably too early to see what difference they may make to the game. They have done a lot of work in fundraising for good causes, but the actual running of competitions, growing sustainable and strong regional competitions, building better systems and improving leadership and culture of the game is the big question and has seen little improvement to date.

The early signs are not good. NSWRL is well aware of the many challenges and the decline of the game in playing numbers, quality and overall health, and faces a huge test to turn this trend around.

In summary: rugby league in the bush has some major issues and it needs to confront these challenges head-on and really think long term about the sustainability and success of the code in the bush. Too many clubs are in decline or have died. General Douglas MacArthur said almost all failure can be summed up in two words: *Too late!*

The game cannot delay and lose the next generation to other sports and forms of entertainment.

Country rugby league is the backbone of the game. It has produced some of the greatest players the game has ever seen, and the game itself has a deep history in communities across Australia. The game must protect and defend country rugby league at all costs!

PLAYER NUMBERS

Numbers give meaning!

THE SYDNEY MORNING Herald ran an article in May of 2021 with the headline stating NRL power brokers were concerned about recent data released for playing numbers across the game.

The game has long sugarcoated the real playing numbers, often inflating true figures and data, so you often have to look far deeper for the true numbers and health of the code.

All professional sports in Australia are guilty of using their PR teams to make things sound far better than they actually are, especially with junior participation and player figures. Sporting organisations do this for positive media attention, public perception, sponsorship opportunities, branding strength, infrastructure development and government funding. The data released is often misleading and not a true reflection of the real playing numbers.

The NRL has been as guilty as any other major national sport, often releasing positive PR statements, bragging about participation growth or using its own NRL media to push positive statements to the public about participation and playing numbers.

The metrics for playing numbers data is very grey, and Australian sports are not reporting data and numbers using the same model or from the same source to provide an honest comparison.

Often sporting bodies will push out positive press statements using data that could include school programs, one-off school visits from development officers, a sports carnival, an online program or many other programs national sports are now utilising.

A student competing in a one-off school visit by a major Australian sport which has no other involvement with this sport is not the same as a student who plays for their local sporting club every Saturday throughout the winter months.

The 2021 report stated that nationally, rugby league had 144k men playing the code. This figure includes both men's seniors and juniors. The women's game had 17k playing the code, including seniors and juniors.

The women's game, which is in its infancy, has seen positive growth, which is expected, considering how young the women's game is. Since 2016, it has more than doubled in participation numbers, starting with over 7k from first records in 2016.

The men's game is a different story, with the game seeing a flat to small decline in playing numbers. Such is the state of country rugby league. The game's health and playing numbers vary from region to region, with weak and strong districts both regionally and in the metropolitan areas.

Whilst the NRL and its own media department have pushed out positive stories relating to playing numbers and junior participation, those in the know who have been involved in the game in some capacity for a long time know the real truth, or, as Bob Dylan famously said in his song Subterranean Homesick Blues: *You don't need a weatherman to know which way the wind blows!*

The truth was bared for all to see, without the fake or unofficial misguided data or NRL media statements: clubs folding, fewer teams in competitions, no expansion into AFL-dominated states, not enough players to fill teams, and fewer registrations of juniors were just some of the many signs that the game was not as healthy as proclaimed from the head office. For many years, the data had included the enhancement of other functions associated with the sport such as Oz tag, touch football and the introduction of the women's format from a low base, to hide the flat to declining growth of the men's game.

Full-on contact rugby league is not for every person, and the other options such as Oz tag and touch football are great alternatives to play and to be involved with the rugby league family. These alternative options should be utilised to grow the sport but not used to inflate real data and hide issues within the game.

The decline in playing numbers is a reflection of a lot of the other issues that have impacted the game. Some of the issues we have touched on already in this book, such as leadership, NRL governance, country rugby league decline, integrity, strong code of conduct, financial models, operational execution, and having the right people involved who represent the code well.

All of these inputs are playing a part in hurting the playing numbers involved in the game. It is not a case of simply one problem holding the code back.

The NRL and the game need to reflect on the old adage: *The whole is greater than the sum of the parts.*

The whole game is intricately tied together, which is a fundamental lesson the game key stakeholders and leaders have never grasped, with egos and selfish agendas often coming first. If you have fewer players, you have fewer teams, so you then have weaker competitions. If you have weaker comps, you then have fewer fans following the sport; if you have fewer players, clubs, and teams, and weaker competitions and fans, you have a weaker NRL and code with less revenue and interest coming into the game.

They all need each other to survive! It's a giant circle!

Dr Hunter Fujak in his excellent book *Code Wars* stated that it is critical for any sporting organisation to have strong playing numbers, especially in the youth markets, as this often then translates to kids who are more likely to participate in the sport and be a fan for life, often introducing their own family into the sport. Fujak stated that when the AFL recruited a child between 0-12 to play Auskick, this set off a chain of events many years downstream including consuming far more content and games. Fujak went on to say the AFL could pay parents $100 per child to play a season of AFL and the sport would see a significant return on investment in terms of lifetime value returned from that child as an AFL consumer.

Fujak states that rugby league's potential erosion of participation into the future could lead to a generational timebomb. He believed that the development of touch football and Oz tag were a wise strategic move to counter potential decline in participation and to keep players involved with the code.

The women's game has seen good early growth, though it lags a fair way behind the numbers of the AFLW. Nonetheless, the game has started the NRLW with six teams to compete in the 2021 season and has been expanded to ten teams to compete in 2023, after initially four teams in its early foundation. The women's State of Origin has been a huge success, with the game being shown on free-to-air prime time, the television figures holding their own with many NRL matches. Many fans have enjoyed the game, with fans believing the game was how the NRL used to be played before the professionalism era reigned. The women's game has also expanded well across the country, with junior to senior girls now playing the game for their respective clubs. Numbers for the women's game should continue to increase, but the game cannot take this for granted and will have to work hard against heavy competition in a growing market.

Oz tag and touch footy are key instruments for keeping folks involved in rugby league. Both options have a large player base, with touch football believed to have 600k playing the game nationally. The NRL would be crazy not to leverage off those numbers and interest. These two sports under the umbrella are great alternatives to keep fans playing and involved in the game.

The NRL implemented an NRL touch comp that was aired on Foxtel, with seven NRL teams entering men's and women's teams in the competition in the first year, but it was later stopped.

Touch and Oz tag are great alternatives to push rugby league in AFL-dominated markets, and, with both genders and mixed playing options, it provides a great environment to introduce new players to the sport. Both these sports have many other benefits for the game such as a far wider age demographic, quicker games, more relaxed social interaction, a large female playing base, midweek games rather than weekends, and a family friendly environment.

The quartet of men's, women's, touch and Oz tag plus disability provides the NRL with many options to introduce both men and women into rugby league. The game's leaders need to have the five bodies working cohesively together, providing all demographics with the opportunity to be involved with the game and promoting rugby league fans for life. These bodies could and should be working far closer together. In particular, touch football's female base provides the NRL with great potential opportunities to further the sport.

It is much easier to get a current fan to spend money than to try and attract new clients or customers. Any business knows this to be true.

The red flag of concern is the playing numbers within the men's game in both juniors to seniors. Some of the earlier mentioned matters are affecting these numbers, but the game also has other issues, such as the costs of playing the game, insurance costs, the size of Polynesian players, white players' flight, parents' behaviour, code of conduct and behaviour, poor reputation and having well-run local leagues nationally that enhance the code's reputation and integrity as a great and enjoyable sport to play.

Playing numbers are central to a thriving sport and its long-term health. The rugby league family has five options to grow the game for both the women's and men's game and should leverage each option to promote the game at all levels and ages.

POLITICS

Fans want sport not politics.

Do you want to be a sporting organisation or a political organisation?!

SINCE 2016 UNDER then CEO Todd Greenberg, the NRL has taken a sharp turn to become far more involved in political matters than in previous eras or past administrations of the game.

These social and political matters include the support for such social issues as Black Lives Matter, domestic violence, women's rights, LGBTQ, Harmony Week, climate change, mandatory vaccinations, the Voice Referendum and other social causes. This follows a global trend of major sporting bodies becoming far more involved in social matters, led by America's leading sports such as NFL, NBA, and MLB, to European soccer leagues such as the EPL all becoming far more political on and off the pitch.

For many rugby league fans, this has caused much outrage and disgust – fans who just want to watch and support rugby league as a sport, which was their one outlet to get away from the pressures of life and the politics played out daily in the media. Sport was to be enjoyed for sport! It was a pure enjoyment for its own sake!

Other groups and individuals, many who don't necessarily support the code, or love or follow the game closely, have loved and praised the NRL's high-profile stance in supporting more political activism such as those mentioned above, as well as the band Macklemore supporting gays at the NRL Grand Final entertainment show, indigenous social rights, the national anthem removal, the Voice Referendum and the vaccination rollout getting support from the new mob in today's society.

The new mob was baying for blood when it was announced in 2021 that Israel Folau would like to return to the NRL after a stint with French rugby league team Catalan Dragons.

The NRL's own media department has put out a large amount of content on its own website in support of these matters; many others in the mainstream press have also supported the push for more political activism in the sport.

When the 2020 NRL season was launched, utilising the most famous song associated with the game – Simply The Best by Tina Turner – the ad was filled with political activism that had absolutely nothing to do with rugby league. South Sydney player and Indigenous Star Latrell Mitchell was draped in an Aboriginal flag by the beach, with South Sydney coach Wayne Bennett commenting that he was furious at the NRL for arranging Mitchell to appear in the ad when he had no idea how he would later be portrayed by the NRL. Two women kissing each other from the women's State of Origin was also included. There was also the support for LGBTQ with a song for gay support (Macklemore performing during the 2017 grand final). If its intention was to unite the game's fan base, it had the opposite effect, with only division between fans and commentators over the ad. Much of the focus on the footy and the intended upcoming NRL season had been overshadowed with backlash against the politics and social matters in the advertisement.

The ad set off a chain reaction and got fans offside, with many hating the amount of non-related rugby league content and all the political left agenda that has become the norm under Todd Greenberg's tenure and now continues with Andrew Abdo and Peter V'landys' leadership.

FOX Sports also ran the same song, Simply the Best, as an advertisement for the upcoming 2020 NRL season preview, but with Jimmy Barnes singing, which stayed strictly with rugby league content and images. Loyal fans were very supportive of the ad and content, the majority saying it was far better than the original content delivered by the NRL.

In April 2019, ex-NRL player Israel Folau and then current Rugby Australia test representative quoted a Bible verse on his Instagram page. The quote was from Galatians Chapter 5, v19-21.

Folau had been very vocal about his religious belief and stance towards gay marriage, both online and through his church. After his Instagram posting, a media firestorm played out in the public and press, with both sides of the argument having strong views on the matter. After internal investigation and high-level talks, Rugby Australia did not allow Folau to play in the 2019 Rugby World Cup in Japan. Folau was later terminated from his employment and then sought legal proceedings, which were later settled for an undisclosed figure.

When discussions occurred about Israel Folau potentially rejoining rugby league in early 2020, both Peter V'landys and Todd Greenberg were very critical of Folau's stance and made it clear that he would not be allowed or registered to play the code.

In 2021, Folau attempted to again rejoin the NRL after a stint with the Catalan Dragons in the English Super League, but was again declined. Folau had backing and support from ex-parliamentarian and billionaire Clive Palmer. He ended up playing with Southport Tigers in the local Gold Coast League. Palmer and Folau had a number of press meetings, which again drew widespread attention, with both supporters and detractors. Palmer had stated he would potentially seek legal proceedings to allow

Folau an opportunity to return to the NRL. Folau ended up signing a contract to play rugby union in Japan for 2022.

Many fans were very critical of the NRL's stance in blocking Folau from returning to rugby league, as the game has had a long and checkered history of poor culture after many years of off-field misdemeanours. These have included such incidents as violence towards women, public nuisance, drunken behaviour, drugs, players gambling on the game, two Bulldog players getting involved with Port Macquarie high school students whilst on a school visit, to list just a few off-field incidents that have tarnished the game's reputation and image.

It was hypocritical for the game's two senior leaders to be playing out the moral guideline over Folau's potential return when in its own backyard was a list of serious misdemeanours from numerous players over many years, far more serious than anything Israel Folau ever did or said. Numerous polls showed most of the public was in favour of Folau being allowed to return and play rugby league again. Folau ended up joining the Catalan Dragons for the 2020 season, a Perpignan-based French rugby league team playing in the UK Super League.

The 2020 State of Origin series saw the game again caught in a media storm when the NRL announced it would not be playing the national anthem before the game. This had followed the past year's series when NSW indigenous players got swept into a media storm about not wanting to sing or support the Australian national anthem.

The announcement of the NRL removing the anthem was met with a strong backlash from its own fans as well as the greater community. The NRL quickly realised that this was a poor decision and announced that the anthem would be played before Origin.

Andrew Abdo fumbled his way through media conferences with poor excuses after the retraction, but it was clear the removal of the national anthem had come from the top tier of the game, the ARLC, with V'landys and Abdo's full backing.

Many fans and commentators had been critical of Greenberg's move to involve the code in more political and social matters and not focus on rugby league matters. As mentioned in previous chapters, there are many major issues and challenges that the game must resolve, yet more focus during the Greenberg era and now under V'landys and Abdo was given to these social matters at the expense of core rugby league issues, which was hard to comprehend.

This turn to the left has divided the game's fanbase. Many long-time fans have stopped supporting the code since its involvement in more political/social causes, and it seems to be intensifying each year, with many political issues across the globe now looking at using sport to leverage public attention and support.

For any sport or organisation getting involved in social and political matters, it can be very risky, and many organisations, both from sporting and business, are learning the hard way. The NFL had its kneeling incident with the national anthem when Colin Kaepernick from the San Francisco 49ers and other players started kneeling during the anthem, which divided the sport, losing many fans and costing the NFL millions. We saw in 2023 the huge backlash when Bud Light supported LGBTQ in a media and public relations nightmare which cost the company tens of millions and has now seen the company lose its number one ranking as America's most popular beer.

TV ratings have declined sharply for major American leagues such as the NBA, NFL and MLB when those leagues have chosen to support Black Lives Matter and kneel during the national anthem. The backlash from long-time and core fans to those leagues has been swift: walking away, not supporting or watching leagues, and not spending a cent on the sport.

One sport to buck the trend of getting involved in politics has been the UFC. Under the aggressive and strong leadership of Dana White, the sport has made things clear about its focus and priorities and has no time for political correctness. The UFC numbers and ratings, in the face of Covid, support their strategy and beliefs!

Current CEO Andrew Abdo, when speaking on question time on ABC, made it clear that sport and rugby league have a role to play in social issues. This comment drew the disgust of many long-time fans who want the sport to not mix the game with politics and keep to its core focus of rugby league.

With this philosophy and agenda driven from the top, it is clear the game now walks a tight line without offsiding loyal and long-time fans.

2022 saw more controversy over the rainbow Manly Sea Eagles jumpers that were designed to support LGBTQ, with six players unwilling to wear the jumpers, which then became a huge media issue that divided public opinion. The issue destroyed Manly's season and again caused many fans to be upset with woke politics involved with sport.

In 2023, we have seen the NRL throw its full support behind the upcoming Voice Referendum, despite no consultation with fans, many who do not support the referendum. There can be no doubt that this support is coming from current ARLC Commissioners and senior management at the NRL. Current ARLC Commissioner Megan Davis is one of the architects of the Voice Referendum and yet this huge conflict of interest has received no media coverage or debate when high-profile board members are pushing forward an agenda that the NRL is supporting.

In summary, starting under Greenberg and now Abdo and V'landys and the ARLC, the NRL has become far more involved in political activism/social matters at the expense of the running of the game at all levels.

The game has more than enough problems on its hands than to be involved and advocating for political and social issues, which outrages many of its core fan base, who do not support these agendas. The game should be spending far more time on looking after its own backyard and improving rugby league rather than trying to be a moral guideline for society.

Fans enjoy coming to the game and getting away from the politics and stresses of life, and sport can be a great outlet to relax and enjoy the code they love with family and friends.

The game's continual trend towards activism in political and social issues will backfire, just like we are seeing with declining revenues and ratings in major league American sports. Many core fans are sick to death of the politically correct left agenda encroaching in all areas of their lives, and now the NRL as well.

The game is going down a dangerous path and will lose money, fans, sponsors, and players, if it continues to mix politics with sport.

Don't mix politics with sport.

I will say that again: Don't mix politics with sport!

INTEGRITY

The time is always right to do what is right – Martin Luther King

Without trust you have nothing in any relationship, be it business, selling services or personal relationships.

Stand on the concrete of truth.

OVER THE LAST decade, many supporters and critics have raised concerns with the NRL over perceived integrity issues across the game that are starting to erode the faith, confidence and trust among fans and the general public. A worrying number of issues have rocked the game in recent seasons, and the NRL's response to these many incidents has not created much faith or confidence in the head office as a source of confidence, competence and trust.

I'm not usually one for social media, but if you randomly hop on Twitter or Facebook feeds, the fans definitely have strong views and believe the NRL has lost integrity and trust on many matters inside the game, and are blind, deaf or just incompetent with regard to what has been happening on and off the pitch.

Some of these issues are:

- Salary cap breaches (Melbourne Storm, Cronulla Sharks, Canterbury Bulldogs)
- Drug issues – Cronulla
- Third-party payments – unfair competition
- Betting (gambling) – influence on the game
- Judiciary – inconsistency
- Perceived favouritism for some clubs from NRL head office
- Refereeing – nepotism, inconsistency and performance
- TV schedule – Bronco's Friday Night Football monopoly and perceived special treatment of certain clubs
- Employee and commissioner appointments to the code
- ARLC governance
- Media television rights negotiations
- Conflicts of interest – Peter V'landys, Phil Gould, Braith Anasta, Nine and Foxtel Staff, QLD Labor party member appointments to NRL and other key stakeholders
- Hypocrisy of the media when leading journalist Paul Kent was charged with domestic violence
- Lack of transparency and accountability
- NRL leaving out recent television deals financials in annual reports
- Mismanagement of NRL finances with no accountability or honest expenditure audit outcomes
- New rules such as six-again – total inconsistency of application of rule in game fixtures

Without integrity and trust in the sport, you're left with nothing. Integrity and other values are the foundation for any organisation, and it is paramount to the code's survival and long-term future that they are fiercely protected. Once trust is lost from stakeholders, be it any stakeholder, such as players, fans, media, sponsors or the public, it is very difficult to win it back. Numerous scandals over the last decade have rocked the code, and each time this occurs, it puts a dent in the code's trust with all stakeholders. The NRL has not helped themselves with the position they find themselves in, with poor governance of the game and poor decisions on key matters that have created only more and more problems.

So much scrutiny from the media and wider public is now put on the code that it must defend itself at all costs. The rugby league media is probably the most aggressive in all of Australian sport and seems to thrive off the sensational headlines to gain attention and news clicks. News media today feed off the negative and love to create sensation over the slightest matters.

Integrity issues are costing the code more than just weakening trust and confidence from the public. It is also having huge financial ramifications including loss of fans, sponsors not wanting to be involved with the sport, influencing parents' decisions on what sport their kids should watch and play, and this damages the game's brand, which is critical for the respect and trust of the code.

The actual cost to the NRL would be staggering in numbers if there was a true figure available on the impact of lost trust after years of contentious and controversial matters that have inflamed the game.

Whilst the game's past and current leadership has tried to address some matters such as player behaviour, betting within the game, perceived nepotism among referees and other matters, the game still has a very long way to go to clear the deck and build strong confidence and trust within the code.

For too long, the NRL, under the direction of the ARLC, has been indecisive and not dealt with matters that need to be closed off, and applied many band aid solutions. The game needs strong and decisive leadership in addressing issues so the NRL, clubs, and players are clear about what the ramifications are if they break rules.

Rules and policies are one thing in an organisation, but culture is a completely different animal!

The NRL and ARLC have never understood this important statement!

Whilst the code has had numerous incidents over the last decade, generally, the NRL response will be for a head office spokesperson to talk to the media and outline how an investigation will occur, and that this will be held by some internal panel or discussions with senior leadership of the NRL or ARLC to determine an outcome. This is all treating the effect, not the actual cause!

The cause is where the real problems lie, and the cause is that the NRL has a culture problem from top to bottom in the game! The poor culture of the game can go as far back as 1998 when the NRL era commenced.

Your culture is nothing more than your values, leadership, beliefs, attitudes, behaviours and interactions on a daily basis. You are what you do, not what you say! Or as George Washington famously said: *Deeds not words*!

Gambling deals, third-party payments off the books, off-field incidents, greed, lies, direct appointments, excessive spending, lack of transparency and accountability is rugby league's culture!

Do you build your house on sand or rock?

Without a proper foundation, you can never maintain success!

Isn't it interesting that despite all the money that has passed through the code in the last 2 decades, the game has very little money left? As a sport, it has never had the character, integrity or maturity to handle and keep the money that has passed through the game. You never hear this point discussed by the media or rugby league fans.

The game can be seen as similar to a drunken sailor who wins the lottery and then has no money left within a short time after the lottery win. The person had never developed the right characteristics to keep the money and just blew it all. The NRL's story is of a similar nature.

The game had strategic goals and plans for more revenue from various sources, but had nothing in terms of integrity or culture across the game to hold it together. The game got the money but never had the character to be able to keep it.

NRL leaders must put the code on a strong footing and solid ground and not allow anything to be involved in the game that is not built on trust and integrity or that may damage the game's integrity and reputation. For too long, the NRL has been lukewarm in protecting the game's reputation and trust.

The code needs to protect the game's reputation at all costs. It must stand strong to defend integrity and keep trust and confidence with all our stakeholders. From the top to the bottom, the NRL must act with integrity and stand on the concrete of truth.

The game needs to change its culture across the whole sport, and, yes, you do become what you do in deeds!

The NRL must rebuild total trust and faith in its conduct and the greater game. The consequences will be significant if not dealt with.

RULES AND REGULATIONS

A body in motion stays in motion.
A body at rest stays at rest. – Isaac Newton

You're not in the sporting business;
you're in the entertainment business.

If you mix red and blue together,
you don't get red or blue, you get purple.

IF YOU MIX red and blue together you don't get red or blue, you get purple instead! Rugby league in its own search for perfection has messed around with the game's DNA so often via modern technology, second and third referee jurisdiction, wrestling and many terrible new rules introduced such as the six-again rule in 2020, captain's challenge, and high tackle blitz, all which has completely changed the face and structure of the game, and sadly, for the worse.

This ongoing tampering and tinkering of the game and rules made the 2021 season nearly unwatchable for most fans, with lopsided games and boring play, causing many fans to turn off.

The game today now resembles nothing of its glory days!

The 2021/22/23 product is more like a fast-paced touch or tag game; the balance of defence vs attack has swung far too far to the attacking team. The physical battle between the forwards for middle dominance has evaporated, with the six-again rule completely changing the flow and aesthetics of games. The modern game is all about speed, with fast play of the ball, sideways ball movement and more of the ref's six-again calls. It's not the rugby league we used to know, no matter how the NRL and media portray it!

Old warhorse player types such as Shane Webcke, Petero Civoniceva, Glenn Lazarus or Paul Harrigan would struggle in today's game and are slowly being removed from the game for the modern athletic speed players such as Cameron Murray, Isaah Yeo, Patrick Carrigan and Jake Trbojevic.

The shape and size of players has also changed greatly in the last 10 years. Size, leanness and power are the new criteria, with today's player body shapes all quite similar, compared to past eras of the game. Barely any NRL player today is under 95kg-100kg.

Whilst the game's players today are the wealthiest, strongest, biggest, fittest and fastest to ever play the game, the actual entertainment of the game has declined since the professional era began. Bigger, stronger and faster does not equate to a better game to watch or more entertainment and excitement, and, for some reason, this bit of wisdom has been lost or misunderstood by those in charge.

The game, in its search for perfection, has lost its way and seems at a loss about how to get back to a game product that is great to watch, entertaining, balances attack with defence and has a rhythm to the play that suits many shapes and sizes.

Random rule introductions without any trial and error process or testing before implementation is a recipe for failure, and that is exactly what the NRL leadership has done over the last decade.

Every rule they have introduced has been a failure and they now have no idea how to get out of this mess, with leaders such as V'landys denying or defending from critics any new rules introduced. The NRL is a billion-dollar sport and yet the code is a laughing stock regarding how it operates in such a shambolic unprofessional manner, which really is an embarrassment to the code.

The six-again rule introduced by, of all people, NRL chairman Peter V'landys, would possibly be the worst new rule ever in the game's history and certainly in the modern era. The six-again rule is very inconsistent, with different interpretations of the rules and very difficult to understand. Six-again penalties are providing enormous momentum, dramatically swinging game momentum, and have made the game feel more like touch football. Referees have not been held accountable in managing this new rule, with no backlash from the NRL, but this is what happens when you mix red and blue together.

How one person such as Chairman V'landys can make and change rules as he wishes is an embarrassment to the game's governance. One has to question how much V'landys really knows about the game and how he got to wield so much power at all levels of the game.

Aesthetically, many historians of the game would argue that around 1994 was when the game was at its peak. Defence, attack, kicking, unpredictability, a middle forward battle, all led to great rugby league viewing and action.

The advent of the professional game changed the game totally for both coaches and players. There have still been great games since the mid-'90s and great teams since this period, but as a trend, the game is on the wrong path for viewing that is engaging and enjoyable, and the decline in ratings supports this.

Today's fans complain about the style of the current game being played, which at times seems like groundhog day, with consistent repetition, every team playing the exact or similar style, it seems, similar shaped runners in attacking movements, sweeping backline plays full of second man and decoy runners, bombs on the last tackle, to corners for tall wingers to leap, slowing down of the ruck area, wrestling to dominate the ruck with new jujitsu/wrestling maneuvers trying to turn ball runners on their back rather than their belly to slow the play the down, enabling a team to dominate a side with fast-line defence. All of this has led to a product that is not as enjoyable or unpredictable as in past eras and one that needs addressing quickly to bring some flavour and sparks back to the game.

The Melbourne Storm under coach Craig Bellamy, which has been the most successful team of the modern NRL era, has been accused of not playing the code in the right spirit by many critics, with the Storm's intense desire to win at all costs pushing all boundaries. The Storm introduced wrestling and many other new defensive artforms, many from mixed martial arts like jujitsu, wrestling and sambo to slow the opposition down, which has outraged many involved in the game, including opposition clubs, media and the fans. Melbourne Storm tactics have been followed by all the clubs today, but one cannot place all the blame on the Storm, as the NRL leadership has allowed this to continue on to this day. However, the Storm were key instigators in the modern game we see today.

Modern wrestling and jujitsu moves would be one of the worst sins ever allowed to enter rugby league in its entire history!

Rugby league needs to remember it is in the entertainment business not the sporting business. Fans want to spend their money and time on entertainment, and the current game product has been in fast decline over the last decade, losing appeal for viewing enjoyment. The drop in television ratings and crowd attendances supports this view.

The game's leaders over the last 20 years have become addicted to looking for perfection within the game, with the philosophy that if everything is ruled and measured correctly, the game will be run perfectly. This philosophy could not be further from the truth.

The NRL has tried to implement and follow many of the NFL's game management ideas and rules. But rugby league and NFL are completely different sports. NFL is a stop/start sport built on power and explosion, whereas rugby league operates so much better when in motion and bringing fatigue, stress and unpredictability into the game. The minute the game is stop-starting, the entertainment quality declines sharply for players and viewers.

The game introduced the video referee to support the on-field referee in 1997 during the Super League season, but the introduction of this technology has made the game a much weaker entertainment and viewing product.

Originally, the video ref was designed to look at any try reviews, but in the last 2 decades, along with the second referee, its role has expanded, to the detriment of the product. Non-stop interruptions during play are a common theme in every game now, with multiple stoppages to look at minor matters. Free-flowing play has been lost due to the video ref and new rules. The interchange rule has become irrelevant, as there are now so many stoppages in play with video ref interruption.

The biggest problem the video ref brings to the game is it causes the game to lose its rhythm. Great rugby league has a back and forward rhythm to it like other sports such as tennis, squash, cricket and boxing. When the rhythm is paused, the momentum and flow departs the game. It's like hitting non-stop red traffic lights when driving – it gets very frustrating.

The one referee was brought back in again after Covid, replacing the two-referee system, due to financial issues with head office. The second referee had created more inconsistency between each referee and added more stoppages to the game.

Rugby league is meant to be played in a free-flowing spirit, and its unpredictably separates the game from rugby union, which is known for regular stoppages and penalties. Many of the great teams in history, such as the France national team of the '50s, Parramatta Eels in the '80s, Canberra Raiders in the late '80s and early '90s, Brisbane Broncos in the early '90s and the West Tigers team of 2005 were so admired because of their unpredictability and free-flowing offence that was a pleasure to watch for all fans.

Each time rugby league makes a new rule and then adds another and another, it is fundamentally changing the game from its original form. It's become like a system in financial terms that grows more and more complex with every new rule or change.

New rule introductions are like government tax hikes. They say they are temporary, but history shows they rarely, if ever, go back to their original form. And just as rugby league has introduced the video referee, the bunker, multiple referees, head-high crackdowns, captain's challenge and the six-again rule, they have never gone back, no matter how bad these rules have been for the game.

There are a number of changes needed to reform the game and improve viewing and coverage:

- Get rhythm back into the game – it promotes real fatigue and unpredictability.
- Eliminate the video referee.
- Get the bunker out of the game.
- Lessen the referee's impact on a game, like in other sports.
- Remove wrestling and MMA from the game.
- Remove the six-again rule.
- Remove captain's challenge.
- Remove golden point.
- Trial new rules in proper testing before any implementation.
- Have rules committee not run by NRL coaches or staff with conflicts of interest.
- Have a game that promotes all shapes, sizes and styles of play: small, large, athletic, endurance, strong, etc.

Rugby league must go back and remember it is in the entertainment business and people want to watch entertaining sports. The product we saw from 2020 to 2023 is not of the highest quality. With each new rule change, the game is on a trajectory of getting further and further away from its foundation as a code and moving to a more and more complex system.

The search for perfection is flawed. Let the game flow with its man-made refereeing mistakes and unpredictability, which then makes players rely more on courage, discipline and commitment, and brings more real fatigue into the game, and allows more body shapes and sizes to succeed in the game rather than the modern-day prototype of power-shaped athletic players we see today.

Wrestling, bunker, video referee, captain's challenge, golden point, and six-again are just some of the many new rules that are cancers in the game, and if the NRL doesn't treat them, the game will continue to suffer more moving forward!

EXPANSION

You're either growing or dying.

The promise of the future is an awesome force.

Why would people in non-heartland rugby league areas not love rugby league?

IN 2018, AFL premiers West Coast Eagles reported the largest profit of any sporting team in Australia. They reported a total operating revenue of $82 million for the 2018 financial year. Western Reds were once an expansion team under the ARL banner, entering the league in 1995, but were one of the casualties of the Super League civil war at the end of the 1997 season. Whilst the West Coast Eagles have soared with record profits, huge membership numbers, a new stadium (Optus Stadium that has a capacity of 60k) and the 2018 premiership, rugby league, the second biggest sport in Australia, was not even in the Western Australia market, a market they once had a professional club in and a market in which they could and should have had much success: a market that has 2.2 million people in Perth alone, a sound domestic infrastructure already in place led by the WARL, quality stadiums, many expats now living across the state working in the mining and resource sector, big sponsorship and state government grant opportunities that would have provided the game with a greater national presence and a great time zone for east coast television viewers.

Even after the removal of the Western Reds from the NRL, Perth continues to show its appetite for rugby league in recent years:

Perth – Rugby League Games

2017 Test – 21k – Sold out

2018 NRL – 40k – Season opener

2019 SOO – 60k – Sold out

2022 SOO – 60k – Sold out

Many NRL club games – Strong crowds

The story was the same for the South QLD Crushers, permitted entry into the competition in 1995 to provide Brisbane's heartland with a second team within the huge Brisbane rugby league market and provide the Brisbane Broncos with a rival, which had, until then, complete monopoly on the Brisbane and south east QLD market. They entered the competition, and, after a solid first season with five wins and a very respectable average, with crowds of over 21,000 per game, the match against the Broncos attracted nearly 50,000 fans for the first local derby.

But they too were one of the first casualties of the Super League war, run out of town by the Broncos at the end of the 1997 season and the politics of a restructured 1998 NRL season.

In February of 2020, expansion in Brisbane was again on the table, as discussed by new chairman Peter V'landys, who stated the game must have a 17th team based in Brisbane to ensure rugby league continues to dominate the QLD market and provide media outlets with their preference for another Brisbane and Queensland team in the NRL. One could have wondered what might have been with the Crushers if they had not been kicked out of the league and what huge opportunities the game has missed removing them from the competition. The Crushers were not failures, as many commentators believe, but more victims of circumstances, with a civil war destroying the game and dirty politics in the aftermath, as part of the reunification of the two leagues.

Whilst rugby league had internal division and no clear definition of purpose for the sport since Super League, the AFL machine since the 1990's governance restructure has been aggressive in building a national footprint, with expansion into Perth, Adelaide, and Brisbane, and recent new teams in Greater Western Sydney and Gold Coast Suns, and is currently completing a large due diligence process on the sustainability of a team from Tasmania entering the AFL with confirmation that a Tasmanian team will enter the 2028 AFL season as the 19th team. In 2017, the AFL even tried to grow their game internationally, taking games to China and New Zealand, both countries that have no history or infrastructure with the sport. Their boldness and audacity left rugby league for dead.

Recent Expansion Teams:

AFL

Sydney Swans

Brisbane Lions

West Coast Eagles

Adelaide Crows

Fremantle Dockers

Port Adelaide Football Club

Gold Coast Suns

Greater Western Sydney

Tasmania – Hawthorn/North Melbourne – play home games in Tasmania

Tasmania – State's own team and brand now going through due diligence and business case but were confirmed this year as the 19th AFL team, expected to enter the league in 2028.

Teams Removed:

Fitzroy Lions – 1996 – Merged with Brisbane Lions

Rugby League

Newcastle Knights – 1988

Brisbane Broncos – 1988

NZ Warriors – 1995

North QLD Cowboys – 1995

Melbourne Storm – 1998

Gold Coast Titans – 2007

The Dolphins (Redcliffe) – 2023

A number of mergers has also been seen between Wests and Balmain (Wests Tigers – 2000) and St George and Illawarra (St George Illawarra – 1999).

Teams Removed Since 1995:

Western Reds – '95-'97

South Queensland Crushers – 1995 -'97

Adelaide Rams – '97-'98

Hunter Mariners – '97

Gold Coast Chargers – 1998

North Sydney Bears – 1999

South Sydney Rabbitohs – 1999 – returned in 2002

Northern Eagles – Central Coast – 2002

The AFL implemented its strategic vision for the game, with teams spread across Australia providing huge leverage to become the nation's number one sport, with a truly national sport geographically that has provided more media opportunities, more exposure, bigger sponsorships and bigger TV audiences, with far more reach, whilst after the Super League war, rugby league's footing and national presence became smaller and smaller, and many opportunities were missed, which still hurts the code today.

The rationalisation process of the league to create the NRL in 1998, may be one of the code's greatest strategic blunders, with teams from Perth, Adelaide, Brisbane, and North Sydney all removed from the game, which still haunts the code today.

Rugby league cannot challenge AFL as the nation's number one winter code unless it expands. You cannot be the nation's leading sport without having a place in major markets such as Perth and Adelaide, which have a combined population of four million people.

The law of scale and magnitude currently favours the AFL, who can reach more customers and potential fans with a larger habitat base across the nation. The total pool of customers and fans greatly favours the AFL in the current market, with the AFL playing games regularly in six states, compared to the three states in Australia plus Auckland for the NRL.

The AFL now has a large lead on the NRL on the five-city metro TV ratings, and the gap continues to get larger each season without any NRL presence in non-heartland cities. The AFL expansion strategy is now also starting to see good signs for growth in the Sydney and Brisbane markets, after many years of heavy investment.

The question is: will the commision lead the NRL to expand or will we see self-serving stakeholders such as NRL clubs, players, media partners and state bodies stop any further expansion for selfish reasons and agendas?

The game must think bigger and expand. We have a great game that should be spread to all parts of Australia and New Zealand, not limited by small thinking and self serving stakeholders.

The past expansion teams discussed were never provided the chance to succeed. The game was in a civil war during the Super League, and no sport or club was going to thrive during this period in the code's history.

The AFL's commitment to support expansion teams provides a clear difference in the philosophy between the codes and its leaders. Once the AFL makes the decision to expand, they pour in all resources available to make the new teams succeed. Both Greater Western Sydney and Gold Coast Suns have received enormous funding over the last decade.

The AFL has key television contract clauses that provide free-to-air coverage into each home state for all home state teams including Sydney Swans and Brisbane Lions, which helps the game provide greater exposure.

Basically, the AFL has a far better media strategy to grow and expand the game into all areas, but especially into newer markets such as Brisbane, Sydney and the Gold Coast. The opposite occurs in the NRL: if the Melbourne Storm are playing and the game is only shown on FOX Sports, Melbourne viewers cannot watch the game on free-to-air for some games if not covered by Nine: a key contractual agreement difference for growing the game that the NRL has missed.

Whilst the AFL has expanded with national professional teams, as mentioned, it has also built a sound infrastructure underneath at the amateur and domestic level. Across every state in the country, there are competitions for men and women in nearly every region in the land, a true achievement when you consider how big Australia is and that the game was once a predominantly Melbourne-based league with historic strong presences and ties in Adelaide and Perth.

In comparison, the NRL has built basically no new structures or strengthened the domestic game in AFL heartlands outside the top-tier NRL heartland zones.

The AFL has a dedicated website for each state and its own state bodies, and is growing the game rapidly through development officers, regional managers and keen volunteers. It has made large inroads into traditional rugby league heartland areas, especially in the grassroots markets of NSW and QLD.

In comparison, rugby league has had no vision, belief, appetite or sincere drive to grow the game in new areas outside of its heartland fan base. The

NRL believes taking a one-off State of Origin game each year to Perth, Adelaide or Melbourne, a pre-season 9s tournament or an odd club game interstate is building sound infrastructure in new markets. These are merely exhibition games catering to some expats and curious interstate fans, for which games are generally funded by interstate state government's desire to drive tourism, but there is no sound infrastructure or programs underneath being built and there is very little foundation for the long-term future.

Local state league affiliates such as the Western Australia Rugby League (NRL WA) have done an honourable job with little funding, limited resources or support from the NRL to grow the game in the west in a market dominated by the AFL.

The game has a reasonably strong local regional competition in the Perth market and has expanded across the state, with leagues in the southern region of the state, which includes teams south of Perth such as Bussleton, Albany and Bunbury, and a league all the way up north in the Pilbara and the Kimberley, with teams such as Broome, Port Hedland and Karratha being just a few of the teams. The Western Australia Rugby League has used the 9s and shorter tournaments to attract players and fans.

Over the last 20 years, millions and millions of dollars have been wasted within the game, yet there is no growth or domestic expansion in many new markets, let alone NRL teams. Areas such as Tasmania, South Australia, Regional Victoria, the Northern Territory and southern NSW/VIC border areas or known as part of the famous Barassi Line have been forgotten, and in 20 years, have seen very little infrastructure or investment to show, or rugby league is totally absent in these markets.

Peter V'landys stated early into his tenure as chairman that he did not see any benefit in rugby league expanding into AFL stronghold markets such as Perth or Adelaide, stating, "They can keep their boring jumping game." This was an extremely ignorant and arrogant comment coming from the highest-ranking official in the game, and did not provide much optimism to fans for expansion into the future.

V'landy's did agree to expansion, with the Redcliffe Dolphins to enter the 2023 NRL season after strong support from media partners and other stakeholders. There is no doubt that Brisbane deserves another team, but the whole process was questionable, with no true tender process for both Australian and NZ teams, media partners dictating where the next franchise should come from, and the lack of true independence in the decision-making process.

The AFL's expansion both with professional teams and domestic leagues is on a completely different level to the NRL. The AFL are a far more professional organisation, with clear goals, stronger middle management and many development officers employed, and clear objectives to expand the game. The NRL, on the other hand, is still quite amateurish, with no vision, weak plans and no appetite to expand, and not having the right management or resourcing capable of growing the game in traditional AFL heartland markets and across Australia and NZ/Pacific.

Across Australia, there is a battle going on between the sports. Rugby league has lost huge ground since Super League, and AFL and is now the clear leader in Australian sport. Its growth will soon become exponential, with a sound development and expansion plan being implemented. If rugby league wants to be the sport's biggest and best code, it needs to start taking an interest and become far more professional in building interstate domestic leagues, or it faces the long-term prospect of always being behind AFL and potentially losing even more ground to its great rival.

The game has already lost nearly 25 years! With 25 years of hard work and investment, the game could have had more successful expansion teams like the Melbourne Storm, North QLD Cowboys or Newcastle Knights. We could have done a Sydney Swans or Brisbane Lions on the AFL.

Early into Peter Beattie's short tenure as chairman before Covid, he was clear about wanting expansion into new markets, stating the game must expand or die. Only a few months later, he backtracked on his statements and was now talking down all expansion. Again, the NRL had no leadership and was embarrassing itself in front of the public. The code was found again to be indecisive and drifting along aimlessly as regards expansion and planning.

Travelling extensively throughout Australia and New Zealand and spending much time in AFL heartland the last 2 decades, it has always surprised me how little of an understanding the NRL has about its own product in newer non-heartland markets. There is interest in the game in these markets. It may not be number one or even number two, three or four, but there is interest and further potential, something recent leaders have not seen or grasped.

Hobart, Warrnambool, Perth, Karratha, Port Hedland, Bussleton, Broken Hill, Mount Gambier, Geelong, Christchurch, Wellington, Dunedin, Queenstown, Palmerston North, Darwin, Echuca, Albury, Bunbury, Bendigo, Ballarat, Launceston – I have visited these places many times and there is a niche interest of many people in rugby league!

I have seen it through the big screen in pubs, good numbers at State of Origin games in clubs and pubs on weeknights, chatting with locals, and merchandise worn on the streets. Peter V'landys and co would have you believe that no one knows rugby league outside of NSW and QLD – this is complete rubbish!

Many cities today that have very little top-level rugby league presence such as Perth, Adelaide, Hobart, Wellington, Geelong, Dunedin and Christchurch all have markets where rugby league could build a much stronger presence from top to bottom.

American sports such as the NFL, NBA, MLB, and NHL knew how important expansion was to their long-term future and the financial benefit many years ago, and the AFL and many other domestic sports are now following suit.

There is no standing still; you're either growing or dying!

INTERNATIONAL

Test football is the highest honour and it always will be.

TRAVELLING THROUGH THE UK and Europe many times in the cold months of January and February, you quickly find out how huge an event the Six Nations Championship is between England, Ireland, Scotland, Wales, France and Italy. Fans pound the streets and pavements as they wait around the pubs in great anticipation for every game. The Six Nations, which began in 1910, has become an absolute powerhouse event in terms of money and the attention it brings to rugby union in the northern hemisphere, with extensive media and print coverage, camaraderie and banter between the home nations, and the large sponsorship and vast awareness it brings to the sport, which makes you ponder just how much rugby league has lost by now only having a very limited international program/calendar and the lackadaisical attitude the NRL have in promoting and supporting the international game.

Never was this more apparent for the whole world to see when the NRL announced in July 2021 that both the Australian Rugby League and New Zealand Rugby League would not be attending the 2021 Rugby League

World Cup to be held in England in November of 2021, due to safety concerns around Covid for all players.

This decision, with the full support of all NRL clubs, was a sledgehammer to the World Cup organisers, after many years of hard work in preparation to host the event, which included large commercial deals, government grants, stadiums, sponsorship, television agreements and large-scale promotion to the whole of the United Kingdom, left the event in total disarray.

World Cup and UK Rugby League representatives such as Simon Johnson, Jon Dutton and Troy Grant were outraged at the NRL's decision at such short notice after much hard work and preparation from organisers. Such was the outrage, that the BBC website had never had so many comments for rugby league about the Australian Rugby League's decision to cancel attending the World Cup. The comments were scathing on the reluctance of Australia and New Zealand to travel to England for the World Cup.

The NRL media machine went to work after strong criticism, stating that the players were not keen on attending the event, but this was untrue, as the players were not even consulted on the decision. Rugby League Players Association leader Clint Newtown confirmed players had not been consulted on the matter. In fact, 85% of NRL players surveyed by various media sources wanted to attend the World Cup.

After crisis meetings with key stakeholders, World Cup CEO Jon Dutton announced in August 2021 that the event would be cancelled and would be delayed until 2022.

The NRL were hiding behind Covid as their reason to not attend the cup. This made V'landys and the NRL look amateurish, with Wimbledon Tennis being held and England also hosting the European Cup for soccer. The Olympics would go ahead in Japan, and Rugby Australia and cricket teams were having or were about to have international tours. Basically, the Australian and New Zealand rugby league teams were the only international teams that would not travel internationally for any sport during this period.

The real truth for the no show was the NRL clubs did not want to release players to attend the event due to potential injuries and work overload, and the NRL under Peter V'landys' tenure has a disinterested and lackadaisical attitude towards the international game. Self interest ahead of the greater game was yet again seen in rugby league, a theme so common in the NRL modern era.

V'landys arrogantly stated at the backlash from RLWC organisers: *"I was surprised. I think they thought we were convicts in our prisoner outfits."*

That remark may go down as one of the most ignorant, arrogant and egotistical comments from any leader in the history of the game. Event organisers had poured years of time, effort and money into organising the event. Players from other countries, many not professional, had sacrificed much in preparation for the event, and yet that did little to stop V'landys having a swipe at his critics. It only exposed his arrogance and lack of understanding and historical knowledge of the international game, and the selfish attitude of the NRL and clubs.

The international game was once seen as the highest honour within the sport, but gradually, over time, has fallen away. Since the birth of State of Origin in 1980, it has become the pinnacle for many in the game in Australia, as Australia has dominated the international scene since the late 1970s, only losing the 2008 World Cup final in Brisbane to New Zealand and the Four Nations twice in the modern era.

What is even sadder is that rugby league was the author of the original World Cup concept. The first Rugby League World Cup was conceived in 1954 and held in France, played between Great Britain, Australia, New Zealand and France.

Rugby union now has a monopoly on the international game, with its World Cup held every 4 years becoming one of world sports' biggest events, at the top of its heavy international calendar.

The 2019 Rugby Union World Cup was held in Japan to huge crowds and audiences and earned the code vast sums of money. The World Cup has been hosted by numerous countries including Australia, New Zealand, France, the UK and South Africa, such is the game's popularity around the globe. The development of Japan to compete with existing rugby union powerhouses and then host a successful World Cup was quite an achievement for expansion and growth, one of the greatest expansion stories of any sport in modern history.

Rugby union in Australia has an extensive international calendar, with the Wallabies playing in the Tri Nations against New Zealand, Argentina and South Africa, and also playing the Bledisloe Cup against the All Blacks alongside the Tri Nations. They often play international games against opponents before the Tri Nations/Bledisloe Cup series and often complete a northern hemisphere European tour in November/December each year.

Today, a new generation of rugby league fans brought up in the NRL era are not aware some of rugby league's finest moments in its history are from the international game. The Kangaroos are not well known and many fans have no emotional connection with the national team.

Australia and old rivals Great Britain have had a long intense rivalry in the sport, with many famous matches. The Invincibles tours of '82 and '86 won widespread fame for the flamboyant style, with the Kangaroos thrilling UK crowds with players such as Sterling, Kenny, Meninga, Miles and Lewis. The 1990 second test at Old Trafford between Australia and Great Britain is seen by many as the greatest international game ever and one the code's all-time greatest games, with Australia scoring a thrilling victory with incredible tries from Cliff Lyons after some brilliant ad lib play and Mal Mening's incredible try at the end of time after Ricky Sturt burst through the defence in the dying stages to secure a famous victory and keep Australia's hopes of holding the 1990 Ashes Series, which they eventually won 2-1.

Some of Great Britain's famous wins include the 1992 upset at Melbourne, with over 10,000 touring Brits supporting them to a 33-10 victory, and

Game 1 of both the 1990 and 1994 Ashes Series at Wembley. The '94 series was famous for Welshman Johnathan Davies' dashing solo try in the 12-man Great Britain win after Shain Edwards had been sent off early in the match.

One of Great Britain's last famous victories was the 2006 Tri Nations game in Sydney, where Great Britain upset Australia 23-12 in an exciting game that had erupted early in the game with Wilie Mason knocking out Stuart Fielden, leading to an all-in brawl.

Incredibly, Australia has not played England or Great Britain since the 2017 Rugby League World Cup Final, where Australia won 6-0 against England in a classic contest in Brisbane.

The French Rugby League tour to Australia in the 1950s will live long in the game's folklore. The tour captivated the Australian sporting public's imagination, with huge crowds at all test matches, when the unknown French team's first visit to Australia with its unstructured and expansive playing style stunned the Kangaroos, winning both the 1951 and 1955 series. The 1951 series pitted rugby league legend Clive Churchill and French legend Puig Albert against each other.

Powerhouse forwards Ellie Brusseand and Edouard Ponsinet, who both terrorised the Aussie packs, and star fullback Puig Aubert, are just three of the legendary figures of the French game from the 1950s.

The 2008 World Cup victory by New Zealand in Brisbane was one of the biggest boilovers, with the Kiwis completing a stunning second half comeback to secure a famous 34-20 victory over hot favourite Australia. Billy Slater's blind pass mistake that led to a Kiwi try from Benji Marshall will live long in the memory of many fans and in rugby league folklore.

One has to ponder why the international game lost its shine, when once it was the brightest shining light and highest honour in the game.

There are many reasons: Australia's recent dominance over other nations for an extended period, the Super League war, the professional era from 1995, English Rugby League switching from a winter to a summer calendar, rugby union turning professional in 1995, Australia's lack of interest in being a leader and developing and growing the game, no structured plan or itinerary from IRL, lack of quality playing-depth internationally, the 2000 World Cup disaster which lost millions, both NRL and UK Super League clubs not allowing the international game to grow and prosper, the NRL and UK seasons being far too long and not allowing a proper international calendar, professional clubs not willing to release players, the international game's poor governance and leadership, and many other reasons have all halted the international game reaching its potential.

In more recent years, some stakeholders, from newer nations to experienced rugby league folks, have made an effort to grow the international game, as many now see the vital importance of the international game. There is an international governing body (IRL) that coordinates the international game, but this is still made up of members from the NRL such as Andrew Abdo and Peter V'landys and other international representatives. The last four World Cups hosted in 2008 (Aus), 2013 (UK) and 2017 (Aus and NZ) have been well received, with the 2013 UK-hosted event being the best event since the 1995 event in England and Wales. The 2022 event was held across England.

The Pacific nations have made great strides in growing the game, with many utilising the grandparent rule to have players of higher calibre represent countries. The quality of recent internationals that included teams such as Tonga, PNG, Fiji, and Samoa has increased tremendously, and many teams would have surpassed most of the European competitors in playing capabilities.

Tonga, Fiji, Samoa and PNG have had one-off victories over heavyweights of the international game, Australia, New Zealand and Great Britain, in recent years, and look to have a great future if an international program is consistent.

The international game is a great way for rugby league to show the code to casual visitors, many who do not support an NRL club, and the NRL are more likely to take a casual interest if Australia is playing. Rugby union, soccer and cricket have leveraged the national team profile to grow their respective codes, and rugby league must regrow the Kangaroos brand to compete with other codes. The Kangaroos have nearly become obsolete in recent years, playing very few games, whilst other sports realise how important the national team is for their profile and branding. The Kangaroos were once one of the nation's most recognisable teams and have now vacated the market for other national sports and lie dormant - anchored down by the game's new breed of leaders and selfish NRL clubs.

The NRL and premiership clubs have been some of the biggest blockers of the international game re-emerging and expanding. The NRL season is far too long, playing games from February to October, which includes around 24-26 rounds plus a final series, and it seems NRL HQ has no interest or is indifferent to having a proper international series either mid-year or at the end of the year.

Clubs are unwilling or indifferent about supporting the international game, stating they are afraid they may get star players injured who will then be unavailable for the clubs, or that clubs could potentially lose revenue from less regular season matches.

This is such short-term thinking, which actually does the game far more harm than good, not just in Australia but around the world. The international game is such an important layer of the game, in its ability to drive the code's popularity and revenue, introducing new fans, bringing back some of the great rivalries in the sport's history, providing an international flavour to the code, a layer which AFL does not have (no international game), and creating opportunities for players and fans to watch their country play the sport they love.

Both Australia and England representatives have a duty to grow the game - for the southern hemisphere, Australia must grow the Pacific and NZ, and England must grow the home nations, and Europe. A vibrant international scene for the game opens up all sorts of possibilities and opportunities that the game cannot afford to forget or lose.

One only has to look not just at the international calendar for rugby union but the event factor these games have. World Cups, Bledisloe Cups and British and Irish tours – these are real events that bring so much more excitement to the game, and fans look forward with great anticipation to the big series and events many years in advance.

The international game is not a rival to the NRL, clubs and Super League; it is one of the game's great allies and can help the code grow and prosper. But it needs to work with it, not against it. Unfortunately, it has been left to rust for too long. Let it shine! It's one of the code's greatest ornaments!

It is the highest honour in the game!

WORLD CLUB CHALLENGE

The best against the best

THE WORLD CLUB Challenge was first played in 1976, had a hiatus until 1987, and has been played every year until the year 2000, up until the Covid outbreak. The World Club Challenge is an annual event which pits the NRL champions against the UK Super League champions in a game to be crowned the best club team in world rugby league.

The WCC has produced some memorable moments in its history, such as the 1994 WCC with the Wigan Warriors' stunning upset against the Brisbane Broncos at Brisbane's ANZ stadium, winning 20-14 in front of over 54,000 fans; Widnes' famous win in 1989 against Canberra in front of over 30,000 fans; St Helens in 2001 coming from behind with victory against the Brisbane Broncos to win 20-18; and the powerful Bradford Bulls side dominating the Andrew Johns-led Newcastle Knights, winning 41-26 in 2001 and again in 2006 against the Wests Tigers.

The Wigan Warriors were the last UK winners at home, beating the Cronulla Sharks 22-6 at the DW Stadium in 2018 in front of over 21,000 fans, until St Helens shocked Penrith in Australia with a famous golden point victory in 2023.

NRL champs have had many fine moments in its history, including the Sydney Roosters' back-to- back wins in 2019 and 2020 in the UK, winning in high-quality games against the Wigan Warriors and St Helens, and dominant impressive wins by Melbourne, South Sydney, North Queensland and Manly in more recent times. The Brisbane Broncos' win over Wigan in 1992 in the battle of the glamour teams was another highlight in its history.

The Sydney Roosters and the Wigan Warriors have been the most successful teams from each league in the World Club Challenge history. Up until 2020, the event has been played 28 times, with NRL teams winning 15 times against the Super League's 13 times. Since 2009, the game has been dominated by the NRL premiers, with NRL champions winning nine times, compared to three wins for Super League teams.

International soccer realised a long time ago the value of an international club challenge competition. The UEFA Champions League has now become the biggest club competition outside of the Soccer World Cup. The UEFA Champions League is an annual event which pits the best of European soccer clubs against each other, including famous teams such as Liverpool, Manchester United, Chelsea, Juevntis, Barcelona, Real Madrid, and Bayern Munich, and has now become the most wanted and prestigious trophy in club soccer.

The Champions League has brought huge money, television ratings, sponsorship, glamour, crowds and excitement to the club game, and has surpassed local leagues by far with its glamour, high status and ability to match the best against the best and find out which really is the best team amongst the powerful European football clubs.

Whilst rugby league will never reach the popularity, size, money and glamour of the UEFA Champions League, the World Club Challenge is an important instrument in rugby league's arsenal to grow the game.

In more recent times, the UK clubs and leaders have been far more supportive in the continuity of the World Club Challenge. In a country where soccer, cricket and rugby union dominate the headlines, the World Club

Challenge gives the UK game some glamour, with the one-off game providing much needed media attention and awareness about the game in the UK. Since 2000, the UK has hosted the event for all but three exceptions, with games being played in Sydney in 2014, Melbourne in 2018 and Penrith in 2023. Those games attracted good crowds, with the 2014 event bringing over 31,000 in attendance in Sydney, the Melbourne game over 19,000, and 14,000 in wet conditions at Penrith in 2023.

But in general, the NRL and many Australian commentators are lukewarm about supporting the concept, though current Sydney Roosters coach Trent Robinson is a vocal advocate and big supporter of the concept.

Why Australia and the NRL are not as supportive of the event is a mystery, though, to be fair, in recent years, the NRL champions have dominated the event, and some clubs think it impacts NRL season preparations when they have to travel to the north of England in January or February for each new season.

Nevertheless, rugby league needs to keep this event and become far more aware of its strategic significance and importance. Super League leaders and NRL management should work together, with the aim to make the game the biggest it can be, with key metrics such as crowd, media attention, sponsorship and TV ratings.

One key thing that needs to be determined for the success of the World Club Challenge is when the match should be played. To date, it has been played in January or February of the following year after the respective grand finals which are held in both hemispheres in October. In the event's early years, the game was played around 2 weeks after each respective grand final.

There are pros and cons for having the game in the same year after the grand final or in January or February of the new season. Having the game a few weeks after the grand final allows both clubs' winners to field the same team that won the premiership. Often players change teams or retire after the GF, and the team that won the competition does not field the same team in the WCC in the new season.

Some believe it should be the opening game in the UK season, which is worthy of consideration. Others believe the World Club Challenge should be extended to four to six teams and have a mini competition.

During the Super League competition in 1997, the game ran an international Super League WCC competition mid-year, with Australian teams dominating the English clubs, often by large scores.

The game has been a solid draw for fans and media for over 20 years of its existence, and any future decision must be to put more importance on the game regarding when it is played and located, and how it will be marketed.

This game has the potential to be a far bigger drawcard for the game, and NRL and Super League officials should work together to build the event. Anything that has an international flavour is a positive for rugby league and the fans. The UEFA Soccer League is a great example of what could be.

NEW ZEALAND

WHILE THIS BOOK is predominantly about the future of Australian Rugby League, the game should strongly consider its strategic partnership with our colleagues across the ditch in New Zealand.

The Auckland Warriors (now the New Zealand Warriors) joined the old ARL competition in 1995 with a blaze of fanfare and noise, but over the last 20 years, most pundits would say the club have been huge under-achievers, both on and off the field, with a few shorts burst of success in that period, including two grand final appearances in 2002 and 2011, losing both grand finals.

NZ has a population of around five million people and rugby union is by far the biggest sport in the country, much like how AFL dominates in Victoria. Rugby in NZ is like a religion, with the national team the All Blacks one of the most recognisable brands and teams in all of world sport. The famous All Black jersey can be seen everywhere you go when travelling around NZ.

The All Blacks run of success in the last decade, which has included two World Cup wins in 2011 and 2015 and domination of every trophy including the Tri series, Bledisloe Cup and European and British Lions tours, has been the stuff of legends, a golden era that may never be equaled again. Some rugby experts say that the run of success for the All Blacks ranks as one of the greatest teams or eras to ever play rugby union or any sport.

Rugby league in New Zealand, on the other hand, has struggled to extend its footprint, with the game supported and played mainly by people in the North Island, mostly in and around Auckland, where the code has its strongest region geographically. The Warriors seem to be every Kiwi's second team and many fans jump on the bandwagon when they start winning, which has been all too infrequent in the club's history.

Outside of the Auckland region, many areas across New Zealand are struggling for a higher profile, places such as Dunedin, Nelson, Napier, Invercargill, Rotorua, Palmerston North, Wellington, and Christchurch, just to name a few.

Rugby league may never challenge rugby union in NZ as the number one sport, but there is plenty of room for substantial improvement, greater market share and potential growth to build a far larger foundation and fan base across New Zealand.

I have visited and travelled the country many times, and many locals involved with the game have mentioned to me that the game needs a big kick of momentum and massive changes to turn things around, if it is ever to reach its potential after so much promise for many years, and now many regions where the game was once strong are now in permanent decline for a variety of reasons.

Some would say that the responsibility for the running of NZRL should be left to the NZ folks, but, much like Australia under the NRL, with similar issues already identified in this book, it seems NZ is having difficulties in growing the game, with domestic and grassroots leagues struggling. Many say the games does well when the NZ Warriors are winning, but the game needs far better strategies and operational practices to build a solid foundation in NZ for grassroots and domestic levels, and bring more quality and professionalism off the field.

Much like how the AFL has been dominating the sporting market in Australia since the Super League war against the NRL, the NZ Rugby Union is a far more professional organisation compared to its NZRL counterpart and has left rugby league in New Zealand miles behind. The professionalism, audacity, belief, finances, resources and investment between the codes is like comparing a Porsche to a Corolla.

Whilst New Zealand has the Warriors to compete in the NRL competition, which provides good coverage and attention to the club and game nationally, the game has significant issues in grassroots and domestic leagues in both the North and the South Islands and needs a regular international program to revitalise the game. The game's aim needs to be strength, not just with the Warriors but at all levels, from grassroots to domestic to international!

The game in New Zealand needs massive reform to make this happen. Like with the NRL, as described in earlier chapters, the game has similar issues holding the code back. The game in NZ is lacking strong leadership, strong governance, adequate finance and middle management capacity to build the game with really good foundations. Without these fundamentals being executed, the game will continue to struggle, and the gap with its rugby union counterparts will continue to get bigger.

The game needs much more funding, focus and investment to relaunch grassroots rugby league across the country. It needs to be aiming to have local domestic leagues in every region of the country, with strong playing numbers and adequate teams. This has been one area that has slowly declined and needs massive focus and attention to revitalise the game. Once strong hotbeds for the game like in old mining areas in the west coast towns such as Westport and Greymouth have seen drastic decline, for a variety of reasons. Larger metropolitan areas such as Wellington and Christchurch, which both have a long history with the code, need a renaissance to revitalise the game in these posts.

Before the Warriors joined the ARL, NZ rugby league had strong semi-professional-like teams in cities such as Auckland, Wellington, Christchurch and Napier. These teams often used to play trial games against professional

ARL teams and this was one of the reasons for the ARL expansion with the Auckland Warriors, after strong crowds and interest in these trial games for many years.

A higher national level league sitting under the Warriors is a must for the code. NZRL should consider modelling how the Big Bash cricket was able to rebrand and restructure itself from the old state bodies' cricket to the Big Bash concept, with a national presence that has captured the public's attention in a very short timeframe. A national league sitting under the NRL in NZ has potential for television coverage and would also support playing quality and pathways that can only support the game in New Zealand and for the Warriors.

A six to eight team comp with teams from both islands, including Auckland, Wellington, Christchurch, Napier, and Dunedin, would be massive for the game and could provide a presence and challenge to the Super Rugby and Mitre Ten format rugby union has in place in NZRU.

Many people in rugby league greatly underestimated the strategic importance of New Zealand to not only the NRL but their importance and vitality for international rugby league. New Zealand has a long proud history with rugby league and has produced some marvellous players in that time. Alongside the Warriors' entry into the ARL and two grand final appearances of the national team, the Kiwis have had many famous victories, including the Four Nations final in Leeds, England, ending Australia's long dominance and the 2008 stunning World Cup upset in Brisbane.

NZRL have really let their national team slip in terms of brand and presence the last few years compared to other national sport teams, with their inactivity hurting the national team profile and presence. Their decision to not attend the World Cup in October of 2021 was another huge blunder, with NZ cricket winning the world test series against India in England, cricket gaining much recognition, on top of the All Blacks' desire and appetite for international tours and high-profile games.

The leaders in NZRL have to leverage the national team profile to grow the game. The national team is the quickest way to gain media spotlight and get casual viewers interested. A world-class team which has the potential to beat the Kangaroos provides unlimited opportunities both commercially and financially for the code. Nothing else can bring that exposure, unless the Warriors are in major end-of-season fixtures in the NRL.

Their aim should be to be the best team in the world and have regular meaningful tests and tours against international teams. The Bledisloe Cup is huge for rugby union and is eagerly anticipated each year. NZRL has to be aiming for Australia and New Zealand playing its own version each year and not just a one-off game scheduled deep in cricket season.

With the improvement of the Pacific nations, many possibilities are available for the international game in NZ for potential tours, competitions and matches.

New Zealand Rugby League with its already solid fan base nationally brings its own media deals to the game through Sky NZ, on top of other commercial arrangements for the NRL.

Sky NZ has extended its deal with the NRL until the end of 2027, which also had rival media outlets bidding for the rights. Sky's investment shows the game has much untapped potential. After winning the rights from the NRL, Sky NZ stated there were one million people who follow rugby league in NZ.

The leaders of the NRL should be working closely with our NZRL and NZ Warrior colleagues. They are not our enemy but important partners to the NRL and its long-term future. Both bodies should be working together and sharing information to grow the game. It's a win-win for both the NRL and NZRL.

Money, knowledge, systems, awareness, technical skills, marketing, content, and structure designs are all things the game could support our NZ counterparts with.

NZ is one of the few markets where rugby league holds a strong advantage over AFL. Many opportunities have been missed in the past but we still have the power to mould the game in NZ, and the NRL should be doing all it can to strengthen the game nationally in New Zealand at all levels and we owe it to our Kiwi neighbors after the Warriors spent 2 years on the road to keep the NRL going during Covid.

NZ Warriors CEO Cameron George slammed the NRL in 2023 for the treatment of the club after what the club had sacrificed during Covid!

I have a strong belief the game has plenty of upside all over New Zealand. There is genuine interest and a strong core fan base, and quite often the fans cross over to support both codes.

Rugby league in New Zealand has long been the sleeping giant waiting to be awakened from its slumber. The gold is waiting to be found, but do the leaders representing the game have the ability to mine it?

PACIFIC ISLAND DEVELOPMENT

ON THE BACK of tremendous support from the people of Tonga, along with some strong performances in recent years and leveraging the grandparent rule to their benefit to field a very strong team that led to victories in recent years over the big three of international rugby league – Australia, New Zealand and Great Britain – Tonga has provided rugby league and the Pacific game with a big boost of momentum.

Sadly, this momentum had all but stopped with Covid, the cancellation of the World Cup for 2021 and the non-participation of Pacific nations in meaningful international games and tournaments and lack of long-term investment in these nations.

The 2022 RLWC would again see the Pacific nations perform strongly, with Samoa reaching the cup final.

The Pacific nations include representatives from Papua New Guinea, Fiji, Tonga, Samoa and the Cook Islands. Today's NRL demographics of player backgrounds has changed significantly from 20 years ago. Today's game has a much higher representation of Pacific Islanders in the NRL. With their physique and size and strength, the sport is a natural fit for Polynesian and Pacific Islanders to play and succeed in rugby league.

Some of the best players in the NRL are from the Pacific Island nations, including players such as Villaume Kikau from Canterbury Bulldogs, who is from Fiji, and Justin Olam from Melbourne, who is from PNG, and many more Pacific stars in the NRL.

Whilst many players in the NRL are now from Pacific Island nations, the NRL is still not doing enough to strengthen and grow the Pacific nations in their own countries.

PNG is probably the best developed of the Pacific nations, with the PNG Hunters playing in the top-tier QLD Cup against QLD's best state teams. The decision by the QRL to expand to PNG should be applauded. The Hunters have brought a lot of excitement and flavour to the QLD Cup, including winning the league in 2017. PNG is madly passionate about rugby league and the code is the country's most popular sport, with fans idolising the players in the NRL.

PNG's last proper home international prior to the 2022 World Cup was victory over the touring Great Britain in Port Moresby in 2019, but they have not played at home since this victory. Based on this performance and with the Hunters competing in the QLD Cup, we are seeing a much higher standard of play with the PNG boys, and this new pathway is providing great opportunities for players to further their career.

Fiji Silktails have been permitted entry into the NSW Ron Massey Cup after many years of demanding inclusion for their own team in Australian leagues, but have not played due to the Covid outbreak. (They started in 2023.) Fiji is another team which will win many fans over with their flash attractive style of rugby league when they do get their chance on the pitch in 2023. Fiji played some exciting football in the 2019 international series in Australia and New Zealand, and was a semi-finalist in the 2017 World Cup, losing to eventual winners Australia.

The strategy and plan to grow and strengthen the Pacific nations is quite unclear, as much good work has now all but been halted or lost with the inactivity of no games since 2019 until the 2022 Rugby League World Cup. There is much potential and opportunity to strengthen these nations, but without an active plan and regular schedule, no momentum can be mounted or sustained. The stop-start calendar is killing any real progress.

Whilst these Pacific nations had good results up until Covid, many of these results were supported by the use of the grandparent rule policy, especially by Tonga, Fiji and Samoa. To many, this eligibility guideline makes a mockery of the rules when you have players playing State of Origin in Australia and then potentially playing for multiple countries. There are many examples of players swapping countries to play.

Rugby league's biggest issue in Pacific countries is there is no infrastructure or foundation. The NRL is working on a random top-down approach, allowing players to utilise the grandparent rule to strengthen Pacific nations and add to the international scene, but this does nothing for long-term growth and investment. Nothing gains respect for international sport more than true homegrown players!

The NRL and the International Rugby League really need to be investing in grassroots local leagues and pathways for players, and having regular international competitions for the game to grow and blossom in these nations.

The 2017 World Cup semi-final between England and Tonga was played before a full house of 30,000 in Auckland, which was one of rugby league's best ever international games, with Tonga roaring back from a 20-point deficit to nearly pull off an impossible victory over England. The Tongan fans again turned out in great numbers for international games in 2018 and 2019.

Despite this enormous support for Tonga and other Pacific nations, very little has been done to capitalise on this potential in the Pacific Islands.

Whilst rugby league has basically sat back and done nothing, rugby union has pounced, with two new teams from the Pacific entering the 2022 Super Rugby season – Moana Pasifika and Fiji Drua. After many years of debate, rugby union in NZ has decided to invest heavily in the Pacific, after years of criticism for no investment in the Pacific game outside of

New Zealand. A huge opportunity has again been missed by rugby league, much like how the removal of Perth and a second Brisbane team has hurt the game long term and allowed other sports to capitalise on the code's poor decisions, when the market and opportunity were right in front of the game.

The NRL never had a better opportunity to drive momentum and awareness of rugby league in these nations, which have long been historically rugby union-dominated. There was a real opportunity to make rugby league the number one sport in all of the Pacific, with the right investment and strategies.

While the game has missed recent opportunities and allowed rugby union to get the early start in the Pacific, the code now has to get back to work and believe in the game, when so often our leaders do not.

The only way the game can grow and prosper in the Pacific is from strong leadership and funding from the NRL and the International Rugby League. The Pacific nations do not have the finances, leadership and resources to implement long-term structures and investment programs, and the responsibility has to fall back to the NRL and the International Rugby League. So often, selfish agendas come before the game itself, and now the NRL must look out and support our Pacific neighbours.

The top-down approach of random international games leveraging the grandparent rule is no strategy for any long-term growth and investment. Real investment means setting up grassroots leagues, funding and training staff to manage the game, setting up infrastructure, having local leagues and having a meaningful and active international calendar.

The Pacific nations are also key strategic international trade partners for the Australian Government due to their commodity resources and the potential threat from heavy Chinese investment in the Pacific and their key geographic locations in the southern Pacific.

The NRL should be working closely with our government and Pacific leaders to utilise rugby league to build and partner with the Pacific nations. The game could get government funding to work with and support these nations. Former Australian Prime Minister Scott Morrison used rugby league in 2019 to meet with Fiji leaders whilst the Kangaroos played Fiji in Suva.

Many fans are not aware of the sensitive political climate of the southern Pacific, with China's aggressive expansion for commodities, trade and dominance in the region. China has moved aggressively into the southern Pacific region, and many governments and geopolitical analysts are concerned with their aggression and behaviour and how they have forged financial contracts with the poorer Pacific nations as part of the belt and road initiative.

Rugby league is a great way and common bond for the NRL to work with our government and the Pacific nations' leaders to build friendship and trust within the region.

A thriving Pacific game provides endless possibilities for the NRL and the international game. The NRL has missed recent opportunities but must take charge and be custodians of the game and pour some heavy investment into the Pacific that will last for generations to come.

The fruit will be worth it!

MEDIA

Who controls the media, controls the mind – Jim Morrison

The media's the most powerful entity on earth. They have the power to make the innocent guilty and to make the guilty innocent, and that's power. Because they control the minds of the masses – Malcolm X

RUGBY LEAGUE IS one of Australia's highest-rating programs, and with that comes much attention from the media through both written, television and radio/podcast formats.

While the game is played on the field, it attracts enormous coverage off the field, for many of the wrong reasons. The game and players are to blame for a lot of problems that attract negatives with the media, but the media are also relentless in their attacks and agendas on the game and its players.

No Australian sport receives intense media coverage like rugby league. The Sydney-centric gossip newspapers operate very similarly to the English tabloids, and not even other major national sports like AFL or cricket get anywhere close to the negative press that rugby league receives.

Click bait news items seem to be the thing of the day and rugby league is easy fodder.

Rugby league is no clean skin and has committed many sins and must take responsibility for many misdemeanours. The players and clubs every year seem to be dragged into some off-field incident, no matter how much training and education they receive from the clubs and the NRL. These incidents have included drunken behaviour, assault, fighting, disorderly behaviour in public places, attacks on women, rape accusations, chasing school kids on school visits, Mad Monday parades gone wrong and many other incidents.

I am definitely not defending the behaviour of the players and they deserve the punishment for many of these incidents, as discussed, when they have been warned and educated so many times and for some reason it still does not get through to many players about their responsibilities. The overwhelming majority of players, though, are well behaved and good representatives of the game, but there continues to be a minority whose behaviour tarnishes the greater game and other players.

Whilst player misbehaviour is real and has caused the game great damage, the game is also fighting media outlets who are looking for any opportunity to attack the game and grab attention, often in a negative manner.

Some of the worst offenders of this are the code's supposed media partners – the Nine network and Foxtel/News Corp. Both organisations have trashed the game relentlessly in years gone by, a game that has given both networks so much attention, coverage, ratings, money and the honour to be involved with rugby league. Certain journalists from these organisations seem to take great delight in attacking the game with negative coverage. Some may say negative coverage sells, but it also does great damage to the reputation and image of the code.

The hypocrisy was never more apparent than when News Corp's leading rugby league writer Paul Kent was charged with domestic violence, and both News Corp and Foxtel staff and writers were silent about the incident. Kent has been taken off air in 2023 until the court matter is resolved. Kent had been one of the leading writers attacking players for off-field incidents and now the roles had been reversed and the media were silent. Kent deserves his day in court, and is innocent until proven guilty, but the incident showed the lack of truth, independence and integrity, and the utter hypocrisy of the rugby league media.

The lack of media independence was never more apparent than during the 2023 State of Origin series, with Nine media staff involved in both the commentary and game, with Johnathan Thurston, Cameron Smith and Billy Slater for QLD and Brad Fittler and Andrew Johns for NSW, all members of their respective Origin teams.

Slowly but surely, the tide has started to turn in the information digital age, with many fans now calling out journalists and media representatives directly for their blatant attacks on rugby league via social media networks such as Facebook and Twitter.

These journalists include Phil Rothfield, James Hooper, Paul Kent, Brent Read, Matthew Johns, Gordon Tallis, David Riccio, Paul Crawley, Danny Weidler, Phil Gould, Brad Walter, Andrew Webster and Michael Chammas, plus many more.

The AFL, which also receives huge coverage from newspapers and television in Melbourne and around Australia, does not get anywhere near the negative criticism and attacks that rugby league receives.

One could argue that both the NRL and AFL have similar cultures and misdemeanour history with player behaviour, but you could also argue that the AFL has had far more serious off-field issues than rugby league, including major drugs issues with star players and ex-coaches, including Ben Cousins' drug problems, the West Coast Eagles' culture from the early 2000s, the Essendon Football Club drug scandal, clubs tanking for higher trades, racism, and many other similar off-field incidents as rugby league, but it does not get attacked or attract the negative press that rugby league does from the northern media landscape. The Sydney media is very English tabloid-like and now takes great delight in attacking rugby league with click bait articles all aimed at getting clicks.

Author Michael Warner details the AFL's ugly culture in his excellent book *The Boys Club,* which laments how the AFL has achieved unparalleled success in Australian sport in recent years, but has also an ugly side to the success. Warner dissects the culture developed under current and ex-CEOs Andrew Demetriou and Gill McLachlan, and former chairman Mike Fitzpatrick, who seized control of the game with unparalleled power and developed a win at all cost mentality, paid themselves enormous salaries, and walked over anyone in their way. Their tenure has been rife with conflicts of interest and they developed a boys club culture that gave preferential treatment to their mates and only those who abided by the boys club rules, a culture that did not care who was in its way and had no regard for integrity or being good honest custodians of the game.

The AFL is believed to have an informal agreement between the code and its media partners that they will uphold the image and reputation of the game and stay away from dirty off-field media attacks and portray the game in a positive light via newspapers and television networks with partners. The AFL has even taken a dictator-like stance in removing journalists and media representatives who do not abide by informal expectations and rules or who do not show the sport in a favourable light or who investigate matters they do want exposed or brought to light.

Michael Warner was one of the journalists barred from entry to the AFL for articles written in The Melbourne Age that the AFL did not like or approve. In 2020, an AFL journalist was disciplined for reporting on a Richmond Tigers player's wife's Covid breach whilst in a quarantine hub in Brisbane.

The media coverage of rugby league goes far deeper than just attacks on the code for repeated player behaviour. Today's media is relentless, with stealth-like hidden corporate agendas in its coverage that will do anything at any cost to get what the company wants, including trashing rugby league and having total disregard for the truth.

Much like a lot of today's corporate world, it's a dog eat dog culture, willing to do anything to accomplish its often selfish agenda.

Today's coverage of the game is at an all-time low for truth and integrity, despite fans being able to find content everywhere from multiple sites and writers that the sport has never seen before as well as many excellent independent sites.

One of the ugly sides of the professional game we are seeing today is when sports meets the corporate world and then meets politics. Major media networks and rugby league media partners leverage staff writers and high-profile personalities to trash the game or push hidden corporate agendas that only suit themselves and deprive many fans of honest and truthful reporting.

The often negative and biased influence can be seen everywhere in today's media in recent years, from television deals, general discussions, new teams, expenditure, rules and regulations, State of Origin, international rugby league, enterprise agreements, player disputes, and NRL scheduling.

Peter V'landy's appointment to the NRL Chairman role is a prime example. Foxtel and its newspaper publications such as The Daily Telegraph and The Courier Mail are huge supporters of V'landys and have remained strong supporters, no matter the actions and poor decisions from the chairman. It was clear early in V'landys' tenure that News Corp wanted him in the role and that he was their guy and they wanted to negotiate any media deal with him. 2021 and 2022 were a disaster for V'landys and his poor leadership of the league, yet the media outlets turned a blind eye. High-profile representatives from News Corp such as Paul Kent, Phil Rothfield, Brent Read, Paul Crawley, Matthew Johns, and James Hooper praised and defended the NRL Chairman on basically any issue and turned a blind eye to many of the chairman's poor decisions and outcomes for the game and gave no truthful scrutiny.

One only has to look back and compare the media coverage of recent NRL leaders such as Greenberg, Smith, Beattie and V'landys and see if the coverage was consistent, honest and transparent. It was very clear for all to see that V'landys received far more favourable treatment in print and television compared to some of his peers.

Why were the media so supportive of V'landys? Obviously, this is related to money, power and corporate benefits. Foxtel got a cheaper deal on the TV rights when extending existing rights negotiations with V'landys and had key influence on expansion discussions, rules and scheduling.

V'landys also held his role with NSW Racing, which included a possible News Corp takeover of Tabcorp at one time, which was a clear conflict of interest within the game.

In 2020, Channel Nine was all over V'landys; the man could do no wrong. The network and its major stars and writers such as Gould, Chammas and Weidler praised him through various outlets, especially after the return of footy following the initial Covid outbreak.

Channel Nine got a reduced deal with television rights, as mentioned in earlier chapters, and had a major influence on rules and expansion decisions. Much similar to News Corp coverage of rugby league, Channel Nine coverage turned a blind eye to V'landys disastrous leadership in the 2021 and 2022 seasons. Backroom media deals and cheaper media extensions were possibly repaid with positive coverage of V'landys performance, when, in reality, 2021 had been one of the worst years in the game's long history, with 2022 not setting the world on fire either.

What is astounding in some of the coverage is that high-profile media representatives such as Phil Rothfield, Phil Gould, Paul Kent, James Hooper, Matthew Johns, and Danny Weidler and many more have made an absolute fortune from the game. The game has provided these men with a salary and lifestyle only few could imagine – a game that has given so much to each, and yet they take and take, and, in some ways, rape it for personal and corporate agendas.

The game's so-called media partners have not been partners at all. The continual attacks on the game from its supposed media partners are causing the game great damage and hurting its reputation, image, value, sponsorship potential, enticing kids to want to play the game, and its long-term future.

Hidden corporate agendas misinform the public, along with high-profile media personalities and selfish egotistical agendas played out in the mainstream, deceiving the public and hurting all parties involved, where some of the media personalities actually want to be the stars of the game and have a bigger profile than the players.

Once the game used to just cover the actual games; now it has moved to a dangerous place where corporations are leveraging their resources for set agendas that are willing to sacrifice all truth and integrity for winning at all costs! Many fans are now starting to wake up to the usual tactics and set agendas from many leading media journalists.

Never was the agenda-driven and biased media more apparent than the 2023 coverage of the NRL and RLPA dispute and the unfair and rude treatment of RLPA President Clint Newton. Both Foxtel/News Corp and the Nine network ran a smear campaign against Newton in the media, with appalling behaviour from Gordon Tallis, James Hooper and Karl Stefanovic, who all behaved unprofessionally when interviewing Newton, with childish antics. Both media outlets did not want to listen to Newton's side of the story and were not interested in the facts or truth of the dispute, and were supporting the NRL in the matter, which supported both networks' position. The lack of truth and independence was apparent for all to see, no matter which side you supported in the dispute.

This new media landscape we see today is one of the greatest threats to the game and its future!

PART 3

COVID AND RUGBY LEAGUE

"How did you go bankrupt?"

"Two ways. Gradually, then suddenly."
– Ernest Hemingway *(The Sun Also Rises)*

IN LATE 2019, news came out about a mystery virus in China, later to be named the coronavirus (Covid). No one knew at the time of the destruction and chaos it would soon bring to the entire world.

Whilst travelling overseas in February of 2020 around Europe, many reports were still coming out about the mystery virus in China, but it wasn't until I returned to Australia that the rumoured seriousness of the virus had been confirmed and countries across the globe were in a panic. Starting in Wuhan, China, followed by Italy, South Korea and Iran, these countries were locked down first. Tourist cities such as Venice and Rome in Italy and Madrid and Barcelona in Spain, normally flooded with tourists, were deserted. The virus soon rapidly spread across the entire globe and stopped all countries and economies in their tracks. Many were locked down and told to stay at home, with only essential services permitted to be performed.

Flights were stopped, restaurants, gyms and shops were closed, schools were shut, and the whole world and economy were basically shut down. The Western world had not seen a pandemic like this since the Spanish Flu in 1918-1920, the Asian Flu in 1957-1958, the Hong Kong Flu in 1968-1969, or further back to the Black Death in 1346-1353. By April 2020, 109,000 people worldwide reportedly had died of the virus and nearly two million people around the globe had contracted the virus, figures which may or may not be true, with so much unverified information prevalent.

Then Australian Prime Minister Scott Morrison placed Australia in lockdown, with only essential services open. Some state borders were blocked around the country and the economy was in lockdown, with no idea when things would change or revert back to normal.

Following the initial Covid outbreak and lockdown in March of 2020, Australia has seen one of its darkest chapters in its history, or at least since the Japanese attack on Australian soil in 1942. State premiers broke rank when constitutional loopholes allowed states to control borders, and Australia was basically operating on a state-by-state level nationally. The country had never been literally so divided.

Scott Morrison was seen as weak and impotent, with state premiers such as Dan Andrews, Gladys Berejiklian, Annastacia Palaszczuk and Mark McGowan walking all over the PM, despite the fact the federal government were funding most state departments, who were already in record levels of debt and having informal agreements in national COAG cabinet meetings to reunite Australia and its borders.

With the prime minister showing no strong leadership, premiers soon filled the leadership void and started acting more like dictators in all states, unchecked. With enormous egos and power out of control, businesses and sectors have since been destroyed, yet some sectors such as government employees remained on full pay, working at home. Mental health issues skyrocketed, schools closed, putting enormous stress on families, debt levels rose out of control, inflation soared, record levels of suicide and loneliness were seen, travel, hospitality and service industries destroyed, communities torn apart in an Australia that had never been more divided or so frail and weak.

What was more concerning was the police enforcement of new Covid rules in major states like NSW, Victoria and QLD. The police became more like SS officers from Nazi Germany. Many incidents were filmed of police brutality towards Australian citizens, often not shown in the Australian mainstream media but mocked in the international press, how our police had gone rogue and were mistreating many innocent citizens. Police were captured on film punching, kicking, choking, wrestling, harassing, shooting and tear gassing a mix of citizens across the country.

The mainstream media, like within the rugby league journalistic circle, were running hidden agendas, often promoting a fear agenda over the real truth with Covid, as bad news is often good for ratings and clicks. Stories were flooding the web over apocalypse scenarios. It was hard to know what the actual truth was, with large conglomerates controlling much of the Australian media landscape today and unelected state health bureaucrats now deciding the country's fate

The fight soon turned to vaccinated vs unvaccinated against each other, which is still playing out across the media and public today. The underlying theme with the Covid response is individual liberty and freedom vs state rule and power, a theme that has been played out throughout history.

State and federal governments threatened that all Australians must get vaccinated, whilst many in the nation did not support this policy, believing in freedom of choice. Many Australians were in the opposite corner, advocating for vaccinations to move the nation forward. Potential threats and consequences for the unvaccinated included loss of job, no international travel, no entry to sporting events, bars, restaurants and clubs. It seemed the unvaccinated would be shut off from society totally. Civil unrest soon followed, and great anger and division within the country.

The Melbourne riots of September 2021 were early signs of great anger and division within the community. Canberra saw possibly Australia's largest ever freedom protests in February 2022.

The forced lockdown by elected representatives and unelected health bureaucrats is now looking worse than the actual virus and may be the worst policy blunder since Gallipoli in 1915. The consequences of this will be felt for many decades to come as the national economy struggles in a post-Covid world, with over $7 billion spent by the government during Covid, resulting in surging inflation that is now wiping the lower and middle classes out.

What is most concerning is the trend towards communism in Australia in such a short period of time. Many eastern European and former USSR expats have commented on how we are now moving rapidly towards a communist country, hard to disagree with after so much upheaval since early 2020.

Covid also exposed fascist-like relationships between mega corporations and governments. Similar relationships had been seen under Hitler before and during World War Two.

Unfortunately, many in society from all age demographics don't have any awareness and understanding of historical events, but as Mark Twain said eloquently, "History never repeats itself, but it does often rhyme," or as Winston Churchill said, "The farther back you can look, the farther forward you are likely to see."

Rugby league, like everything else in the world, was enormously impacted by the Covid outbreak. The NRL started round one of the 2020 season with crowds in attendance, but the growing fear of Covid was in the back of everyone's mind. Crowds were low for the opening weekend, as people were becoming more and more fearful of the virus, and many were not sure how long the competition would continue, until being stopped, potentially by the government.

Round two of the season went ahead but the government soon blocked any crowds from attending, and social distancing rules were applied to the general Australian public. It was a strange feeling watching the games with no crowds in attendance, but the NRL under V'landys had strong resolve to push on.

It soon became apparent that the virus was expanding around the globe and Australia would take strict action to stop it spreading. This left rugby league with a serious problem on its hands. No matches would mean no money from media outlets Foxtel or Nine, and other forms of money from crowds, merchandise and sponsorship would all be put on hold. The blood flow of the game – cash flow – was about to be stopped and the game was about to face one of the biggest challenges in the code's history, certainly the biggest since the Super League war!

Peter V'landys took the lead and clearly outlined that he would do whatever it would take to keep the competition going ahead. Many options were looked at and discussed during the early stages of the pandemic to keep the game going. These options included moving the players to a remote island, relocating clubs to Sydney, Townsville, Central QLD, or a resort to keep the competition proceeding, and implementing strict health guidelines that players must adhere to keep playing. The code was put under extra pressure when the New Zealand Government made a decision that would not allow the Kiwi club players to leave NZ if they returned home, so they were quickly based in the Gold Coast and Tamworth temporarily until the situation had been resolved. (They returned to NZ and got clearance to return to Tamworth later.) But as the pandemic became worse around the globe, state borders were soon closed, making it very difficult for the competition to continue, with teams in the NRL coming from NSW, VIC, QLD plus NZ. The game was still looking at air charters and resort hosts to keep the players, until Peter V'landys announced that the competition would be suspended after ongoing health concerns, with leading medical specialists recommending the game be put on hold, as player safety could not be guaranteed.

All play was suspended until a later date to be confirmed. On the 8th of April 2020, V'landys announced the competition would recommence on the 29th of May 2020, with more details to be confirmed.

Whilst the game was put on hold, it was soon clear the code was in deep financial trouble. Early in the virus outbreak, V'landys was adamant rugby league must continue on, stating to the media it was un-Australian without rugby league being played. He also stated that the NRL and clubs may need government support, should the competition be put on hold or stopped for a long duration. This caused backlash from the general public about sporting bodies getting government funding preference.

Without the lifeblood of television money from Channel Nine and Foxtel, the game had no cash coming in and was left with an emergency crisis, or, as we discussed in Part 1, was thrown into Stage 4 Grasping for Salvation.

Emergency meetings were held with key stakeholders, and intense pressure from the media and fans gripped the game. Without the payments from media outlets, the game had limited money and assets to handle any long period of no play, and many of the concerns outlined in this book were becoming true before our eyes in the most unlikely manner.

The code had reportedly built around a $50-$150 million fund in reserves (the number changes depending on who you speak with) and this fund would only allow the game limited time with its huge expenses to run the sport plus continue paying clubs, players and NRL employees.

Once play was halted, the cuts were quick and brutal. Many employed in the game were stood down with no pay, which included most football departments, clubs, and state bodies. Leagues clubs were closed, and players were soon left with the realisation they may need to take drastic cuts in pay for the game to survive. They eventually came to an agreement after RLPA president Clint Newton and the NRL players would take a pay cut for the game to survive.

Former CEO Todd Greenberg came under huge media scrutiny for his perceived mismanagement of funds of the game and the huge running costs of NRL HQ, and many called for Greenberg to be removed from the game immediately.

The game's past mismanagement of resources had come back to bite the game hard. It had limited cash reserves in the bank and huge operational costs that could not be contained, with no income flowing into the game. The game had moved from Stage 3 to Stage 4 in a blink of an eye and was now at potential risk of moving to Stage 5 if play was stopped for an extended period.

Rugby league responded as only rugby league can, by putting on a brave face and stating everyone was in this together, but this was not the truth, with disagreement and division evident for all to see between key stakeholders such as clubs, media partners, player unions, state bodies and the NRL.

Both media companies used Covid to attack the other media partner, and both attacked and leveraged their own media outlets over the NRL's fiscal mismanagement, but this media storm was about reduced payments for the next television rights. Phil Gould and Phil Rothfield got into an online spat over Nine's attack on the NRL and Nine not being involved more in the game's decisions moving forward, after comments from then Nine CEO Hugh Marks criticising Todd Greenberg and the NRL.

Former Channel Nine CEO Hugh Marks criticised the NRL for its mismanagement of the game and funds and for not being consulted by the NRL on proposals to move forward. Marks' criticism was followed by stinging rebuttal from Phil Gould in his Sydney Morning Herald column, and other Nine network employees also attacked the NRL and Greenberg. Some could understand Nine's actions, others were calling it a strategy to bring down the value of future TV rights. NRL player reps were soon in heated arguments with Todd Greenberg and NRL HQ, with concerns around no payment of superannuation for players, the mismanagement of game resources and the potential for player payment cuts. Manly half Daly Cherry-Evans was reported to be very angry and abrupt during a players union meeting when asking Greenberg about the game's mismanagement of funds and future payments, and was reportedly advised not to attend another meeting with NRL representatives.

Questions were now being asked: could all 16 NRL clubs survive the crisis? Clubs have had a long history of needing extra funding to survive. Was the salary cap unsustainable moving forward and how would clubs survive if finances were much tighter for all parties?

Shane Richardson (former South Sydney CEO) appeared on NRL 360 and stated that there was far too much greed in the game and that the game's spending had been reckless and unsustainable for far too long, going way back to the 2015 funding issue with former chairman Grant and the NRL clubs, and that current and past management would not take the hard position to resolve the issue. Richardson, who had also done a past strategic project in NRL HQ was adamant the clubs' and players' current funding expenditure could not continue into the future.

Numerous media outlets and outsiders criticised the NRL HQ for having too many staff and wasting millions. The Daily Telegraph did a report showing the NRL Headquarters employed more people than the English premier league soccer. The game's digital business unit was also discussed, as not returning the investment that had been poured into it, and to many, it is not clear or understood what the role of the digital arm was and what its long-term strategy was for rugby league and the NRL. Media partners were very concerned about the NRL's inhouse digital arm's ability to impact Nine and Foxtel's operations and the potential ability for the game to bypass media partners and sell content direct to consumers, as more and more entertainment and sporting services are moving to streaming models, potentially making the NRL's digital arm competitors with the code's existing media partners.

As usual, media partners had vested interests, with the threat against the NRL digital arm, and were leveraging their media outlets and staff to protect their own turf and vested interests.

With the game stopped and only limited cash reserves to cover a few months' expenditure for players and some of the game's employees, the NRL needed to get the game restarted asap with crowds or not to get television money and have some cash coming into the game.

Finally, after the suspension of the competition in March of 2020, the game started again on May 29, with Brisbane facing Parramatta in Brisbane. The competition was to be played over a shortened 20 rounds, finishing with the grand final on October 4, with the State of Origin series to be played after the season in November, the first time in its history the Origin series has not been played mid-year.

NRL CEO Todd Greenberg would be one of the first big casualties of Covid, removed from his role in April of 2020.

There had been some alternatives discussed for the restart, including a new conference system model, and State of Origin to restart the competition when back up, but the game's leaders finally agreed on a structure. Many of the options were still with a money-first game mindset, such was the necessity of the NRL for cash to ease the financial pressures.

Many would argue that Covid was a once in a century event, and to some extent that would be true. All sporting codes and businesses were affected by the virus, but there were also multiple signs flashing well before Covid that showed the game had big internal problems that would eventually come to light. There was always going to be a snowflake that would lead to an avalanche and Covid was the snowflake for the NRL.

The 2020 season finished with the Melbourne Storm defeating minor premiers Penrith Panthers before a half-sized Olympic Stadium, and QLD under coach Wayne Bennett would upset the Blues to win the State of Origin series 2-1.

2021 was a fresh start for the competition, but Covid was still lingering nationally. Victoria was still in and out of lockdowns under premier Dan Andrews, but the northern states had been able to go on with day-to-day life in a reasonably normal manner. The season started with capped crowds in attendance and the game was slowly getting back to some normality, though the NZ Warriors had to be based in Australia again and the Melbourne Storm were in and out of Melbourne and QLD with each new lockdown.

Once again, the 2021 season was thrown into chaos, with the virus moving north to Sydney and Covid numbers increasing rapidly in Sydney and NSW mid-2021.

In July of 2021, a decision was made to move 12 NRL teams to the south east of QLD and continue the league up north where the weather was much warmer and Covid was not as rampant. Queensland Premier Annastacia Palaszczuk allowed the NRL to continue the season in QLD despite strong criticism and backlash across the country after border closures, with many citizens declined entry into QLD. But footballers were seen as being given preference over everyday Queenslanders and other Australians. The Tweed and Coolangatta border region closure caused high emotion and sensitivity in the community.

Quarantine guidelines would again be implemented like in the 2020 season, to keep the 2021 season alive, and all games would now be spread across QLD but mainly played in the south east of QLD in Brisbane, Redcliffe, the Gold Coast and the Sunshine Coast. Other games were played in Mackay, Rockhampton, and Toowoomba, with the Cowboys continuing as per normal in Townsville.

This again was a huge financial hit to the NRL and its clubs, even after such a tough 2020 season. Crowds and gate takings were down again significantly for all games in QLD. Revenue, merchandise and other other sources were also hit extremely hard. Most big leagues clubs in NSW had never experienced such tough times, with trading halted in most parts of the state for an extended period of time. Many NRL clubs have long needed the financial support of leagues clubs to operate.

The 2021 season finished with the grand final between Penrith Panthers and the South Sydney Rabbitohs, with Penrith winning a nailbiter 14-12 in a great game of football played at Suncorp Stadium for the first time, with just under 40k attending the match.

The Covid period has added another intriguing and chaotic chapter to the code's long and turbulent history.

Covid had changed rugby league in ways no one could have expected, and its shock will probably have a long-lasting effect for the sport and country.

PART 4

HOW DOES RUGBY LEAGUE RESPOND?

THROUGHOUT THIS BOOK so far, we have discussed a range of topics that identify declining trends for the game of rugby league in Australia and we have also looked at a number of alarming issues that are holding the game back.

We discussed in our intro to this book, based on Jim Collins' model of analysing many organisations, signs to ward off decline. Before the Covid outbreak, rugby league was sitting probably at around Stage 3, with some parts of the game in Stage 4 in the lower non-professional functions, but, being generous, we would say Stage 3 overall is the health of the game.

Once the Covid pandemic struck and the game was suspended, the game went to Stage 4 literally overnight, grasping for salvation and in serious discussions with Nine, Foxtel and potentially government officials to ease financial pressures and future risks.

The game has now countered this crisis with rushed extensions to media deals to raise capital for far less money before longer-term media deals in 2020 and 2021 with both media partners and removing large operational expenses from the game, including a reported 25% cut from NRL Headquarters.

This does not at all mean rugby league is out of the woods yet, in fact, far from it!

Were the signs real? Could we see the declining trends across the game? Was it a signal or just mere noise? Can we now see the prior warning signs more clearly after Covid?

Looking back, it is often much easier to see the stages of decline from a distance rather than being in close and in the heat of battle.

Can we not see the hubris (Stage 1) of key stakeholders within the game? Just before Covid, NRL clubs had complained about CEO Todd Greenberg being in meetings with the clubs and not giving attendees his attention or focus and being immersed on his phone.

John Grant's tenure as ARLC Chairman was one of ego and selfishness, and his big money farewell was one of his legacies of being at the helm. He also gave the clubs and players more funding (130% of cap) after the payment dispute in 2015, which was reckless, to save his own skin rather than what was best for the future of the code.

Clubs and players continue to put themselves before the game and squeeze every last penny they can get rather than invest long term and produce long-term fruit at all levels.

Media stakeholders and high-profile media personalities continually overemphasise their importance and push set agendas, and, when not getting their way, make attacks to stir up discontent with the greater public and don't care what damage is done to rugby league, despite the tremendous returns the game has given many public figures and media outlets.

Commissioners continue to make no real progress, but seem more interested in appointment to a high-profile sports board to further their

CV and grow their own personal brand rather than to make rugby league stronger for future generations.

Peter V'landys in his time as chairman and CEO has basically become the sole ruler of the NRL, controlling all decisions and power within the game like nobody ever before, with his media buddies glorifying his ego in return for favorable treatment. He arrogantly ridiculed organisers of the Rugby League World Cup despite cup organisers' years of hard work and preparations that then had to be cancelled. His ego is out of control, he is unchallenged for poor decisions in 2021 and 2022, and not questioned or called out by his media friends, results that will impact the game for many years to come.

In Stage 2 (Undisciplined Pursuit of More), we now see consequences of reckless spending where billion-dollar television deals had passed through the game and yet the game had limited funding to survive post-Covid, with no assets to fall back on. The AFL, who were also heavily affected by Covid, at least had some assets to support the game, which could enable funding from financial institutions, with its ownership of Marvel Stadium, allowing leverage with banks. The NRL had no banks which could or would provide a loan; the only possibility was British hedge funds.

Covid really exposed the lack of discipline, which no one in the game could defend. Peter V'landys was clear that the game's expenditure had to be reduced drastically and the game must become far more sustainable to survive, as also stated by Shane Richardson. Huge blow-out costs from NRL Headquarters, expanded football departments, excessive player and club payments were never going to be sustainable or affordable long term and have now all been exposed during Covid.

There was clear evidence about the lack of discipline in the financial management of the game but it had also been shown in country rugby league, playing numbers, declining television media deals, flat crowd growth, television ratings and zero expansion of the game.

This leads directly to Stage 3 (Denial). Continually over the last decade or more, leaders from David Gallop to David Smith to Todd Greenberg and now Andrew Abdo and Peter V'landy's have defended the game's fragile position, whilst defending the game with numbers and storylines that don't tell the whole story, despite warning signs apparent for all to see on many metrics and trends.

It is now clear for all to see: up until very recently, the NRL had had very little money in reserves, has virtually no assets, poor leadership across the game, an ARLC that governs poorly, which is causing even bigger long-term issues, a contracting supporter base nationally from past years, division that still occurs between stakeholders with no common trust among them, no real strategy to grow the game, and deep structural issues within grassroots and country rugby league.

Even after a terrible 2021 NRL season – some would say the worst in the game's modern history or at least since the outbreak of the Super League war in 1995 – leaders such as V'landys and Abdo put out statements that still tell the tales of a code that is vibrant, strong and healthy. This denial continues post-Covid, despite the mounting issues plaguing the game.

The game in parts has now entered Stage 4 after Covid (Grasping for Salvation) and it is still teetering on the edge, despite the still many positives in the game that don't tell the full story.

Many major sporting codes have been plunged into crisis in the last 10 years, such as Rugby Australia, A League soccer and cricket, and rugby league is now quickly following those professional sports.

It has always been the actual game that has saved the code in past years, not the administrators and leaders, media personalities, media outlets or players, all who have come and gone. The code was in dark days in 1997 during the Super League war, but the ARL grand final between the Newcastle Knights and Manly Sea Eagles provided a much needed boost when the code was at its lowest point, with many people doubting the future of the game. That game will forever live in the code's analogues, but it was not just the result, it was the feelings that reinvigorated the fans with faith in rugby league again when it really needed a boost after years of a bitter civil war.

The 2021 season was no different. During a season of boring fixtures and lopsided games, you were again reminded of why rugby league always finds a way to bounce back from despair, with two cracking finals games between Penrith and Parramatta, and a week later when Penrith faced the Storm that had fans on the edge of their seats to the end and an enthralling grand final between Penrith and South Sydney in Brisbane. When played at its best, very few sports can match rugby league as a spectacle.

2022 saw a classic Game 3 of the State of Origin series, where QLD would outmuscle the Blues in a pulsating contest, and the 2022 preliminary final between the Cowboys and Parramatta was the game of the season, with Parrmatta holding on for a thrilling victory.

The game has tremendous amounts of resilience, but too often its stakeholders do everything imaginable to test this character trait, unfortunately.

Strategic Inflection Point

Andrew Grove, former leader of technology giant Intel, was a 20th century business icon admired by many leaders around the globe. In his famous book *Only the Paranoid Survive*, Grove stated that every organisation will eventually face a strategic inflection point that will have a major impact on its business. Grove stated how you and your organisation respond will determine your future and destiny!

Grove was facing his own strategic inflection point when Intel, which was in the tech memory business at the time, was facing huge challenges with its function and product line due to an initial fault with the product and then further challenges from Japan and international competitors in a global price war, who were selling their products much cheaper compared to Intel. Grove and Chairman Gordon Moore had an epiphany one day and asked: If we got kicked off the board and brought in a new CEO, what do you think that person would do? They both replied the new CEO would get Intel out of the memory business and enter the semiconductor microprocessor business, and this is exactly what Intel did under Grove and Moore's leadership in facing their own strategic inflection point. Intel exited their core profit-making business function and purpose and put all their focus into the semiconductor business.

Moore famously said later after this decision to change business operations to Grove, "We need to hire people who can work in the semiconductor business and not from the past memory chip business."

Intel stands today as one of the world's biggest and most admired companies, and Andrew Grove has been a major influence for many famous business leaders such as Steve Jobs, John Doerr, Ben Horowitz and many other entrepreneurs in the technology industry.

The question now stands: What will rugby league do in facing its own strategic inflection point?

Rugby league is in an unusual position in 2023 and beyond. It is not just facing one strategic inflection point that threatens the code's future, but potentially multiple inflection points.

Covid is without question one strategic inflection point for the game and the sporting landscape and market in Australia. Its impact on rugby league since the initial outbreak in March of 2020 cannot be questioned. The outbreak has forever changed the game. Operational revenue has been reduced, already causing major restructures within the game, including 25% cuts to head office, players' wages temporarily reduced, club staffing cuts, rushed media deals renegotiated through the NRL's own fault for far less revenue, and the commercial impact of no crowds and other match day revenue.

The NRL clubs' other major partners and income sources such as leagues clubs are also really doing it tough after Covid. The clubs, along with the NRL television money, have been the main two income sources for most NRL clubs, but the league's clubs have been smashed during Covid, with long extended periods of closures and revenues falling off a cliff from pre-Covid numbers.

Covid's biggest change to the game has been its hit on the game financially. The 2020 and 2021 seasons were both down on total revenue from 2019 highs, when taking into account inflation and 2020 Origin accounting. In September of 2021, the NRL had to hand out another $7 million to be distributed to the NRL clubs due to the effects of Covid. Media revenue, game day revenue, league clubs' revenue, commercial revenue, and sponsorship revenue have all been hit hard during the outbreak.

The whole Australian economy is currently in contraction, with roaring inflation, record levels of debt at private, corporate, state and federal levels, huge government deficits, rising interest rates, and declining revenues for many corporate entities. These economic challenges will likely continue on for the next decade or more, as often the world moves in cycles, as identified in the great book *The Fourth Turning* by Strauss and Howe, which talks about historical cycles in 20-year cyclical blocks.

The easy money of former years is now a thing of the past, and the game will have to work far harder and smarter to hold a strong position within the Australian and international sporting market.

The second strategic inflection point is the gorilla in the room. In Australian sport, that gorilla is the AFL. We have spoken about and made comparisons with the AFL often throughout this book; they are the game's biggest rival and threat. For many years, rugby league fans used to hate rugby union and think it was their greatest rival. For over a century, the two rugby codes' fan bases have had great disregard and sometimes deep hatred for each other, from the game's early breakaway beginnings of working class vs the rich and social elite, to the French Vichy Government banning rugby league during World War Two, to the beginning of the professional sport era in 1995 and the ongoing player signing battles between both codes. But while all eyes were on rugby union up until the early 2000s, the old VFL league that had a meager $3 million in assets in the mid '90s and many clubs teetering upon financial collapse now sits as Australia's strongest sport, a sport that dominates five states, a code that earns more money than the three other major football codes' combined yearly earnings from rugby league, rugby union and soccer in Australia, and now wants a far greater market share in rugby league's heartland, New South Wales and Queensland.

In World War Two, famous war general Douglas MacArthur was evacuated from the Philippines Island Corregidor, which was under direct attack from the Japanese. MacArthur led a bold and daring escape with his family and a few aides after being ordered by President Roosevelt to evacuate immediately or face capture from the Japanese. MacArthur escaped on a small PT boat through dangerous sea paths full of large Japanese ships, to eventually land in Australia to command and lead the Pacific theatre of war for the allied forces.

Before MacArthur's arrival, Australia had been thrust into the war on home soil, with Japan bombing Darwin, and there was a great deal of concern and fear that there would be more attacks on Australian soil, including the much larger cities on the east coast where most of the population resided.

MacArthur met with Australian and allied wartime leaders on arrival, who told the great general that our strategy to win the war was a plan called the Brisbane Line Defence Plan that would work on defending the major cities of Australia, from Brisbane down to Sydney and Melbourne. Australia would basically fight a defensive war and give up large parts of this massive country to the north and be open to invasion, as they believed the country's sheer mass and size was too much to defend.

When MacArthur assumed charge of the Pacific theatre, the whole direction and strategic plan of the war changed immediately. MacArthur condemned the Brisbane Line strategy to Australian war leaders, calling it too timid and defensive, and said that Australia and the allies could never win a war against Japan fighting such a defensive strategy.

MacArthur's plan was to take the fight to the Japanese and meet the Japanese empire head-on in battle and be far more offensive than the proposed defensive strategy. The allied forces would move resources and troops to the far north of Australia and then engage in an island-hopping offensive war that would go through Papua New Guinea, the Dutch East Indies (Indonesia), Singapore, and the Philippines, that would eventually lead to Japan being pushed back by the allied offensive. America would eventually detonate atomic bombs at the end of the war on Japanese cities Hiroshima and Nagasaki to end the war, with the Japanese Emperor surrendering to MacArthur aboard USS Missouri in Tokyo Bay in 1945.

Today, rugby league is facing a similar scenario to that which MacArthur faced when arriving in Australia during World War Two, in a sporting and business context against the AFL. Rugby league has its own Brisbane Line strategic plan to defend the heartland states of New South Wales and Queensland.

Peter V'landys has made it perfectly clear the game will fight the AFL by defending the heartland states at all costs, with the options of any expansion into new markets ruled out completely and no real appetite to grow the international game. The 17th NRL license will come from Redcliffe, QLD. The game's strategy to defeat the AFL is to own NSW and QLD. The left hand will be New South Wales, the right hand, Queensland.

Fighting the AFL with a Brisbane Line-like defensive strategy is extremely risky and is an unwinnable long-term strategy against an opponent that is far better resourced and can fight an all-out offensive war against the NRL and already is making large inroads into the grassroots markets in the northern states.

Clear metrics are now showing AFL is the number one code in Australia and that it could be about to reach a critical phase or what Groves called a strategic inflection point after many years of heavy investment in the northern markets.

The AFL strategy has been a long-term investment process, now around a generation in years since their first strong attempt to attack the Brisbane and Sydney markets. Considering their heavy investment of funds and resources, one would actually think they would have made more progress in the northern markets. Seeds, though, are now starting to show signs of growth in the northern states across all levels of the sport. The game is well embedded in NSW and QLD. Grassroots numbers are very strong in both Brisbane and Sydney, with a growing presence in the regional markets of both states.

Television numbers are slowly increasing on free-to-air, with a good following, now consistently around 20k-50k for most free-to-air games, with higher audiences when local teams such as the Lions, Suns, Giants and Swans are playing. Marquee games such as grand finals and big finals games involving home state teams have rated very strongly in the last three seasons. When the 2020 AFL season relocated to QLD, viewing and playing numbers saw good increases across QLD and they looked to have continued into 2021/2022. The Brisbane numbers look quite solid, with the Lions recent on-field success helping strengthen their share of the market. The Sydney Swans are now one of Australia's strongest brands and clubs, and have a strong footing in the sporting landscape in NSW. The AFL has furthered its extension and expansion into the Western Sydney market with the GWS Sydney and has poured in enormous resources, with slow and small signs of traction now starting to appear in the fast-growing corridor in Australia of Western Sydney.

The battle for the hearts and minds of the youth is where the real fight for future customers and fans lies. This is a battle where the AFL in both state markets looks to have a strong chance to increase its share in the market in future years. The process of a grassroots player becoming a lifelong fan is a key battle to win a supporter for a person's lifetime and then move generationally through that first seed of new fan. The AFL has a clear advantage in this market today against the NRL.

Comparing some of the numbers between the codes provides a good indication of where things are, with the gap between the codes getting bigger on many metrics. The last time the NRL outrated the AFL in a grand final was 2015 and 2014. Since 2015, the AFL has dominated.

2019 total revenue:
AFL – 793m
NRL – 528m

2020 total revenue:
AFL – 674.8m
NRL – 417.2m

2021 total revenue:
AFL – 738m
NRL – 575.1m

2022 total revenue:
AFL – 870m
NRL – 593.8m

Total supporters nationally (Roy Morgan Research) 2019:
AFL – 7.870m
NRL – 5.593m

National interest: (Roy Morgan Research) 2019:
AFL – 41%
NRL – 31%

Crowds average 2019:
AFL – 35,122
NRL – 15,804

2022:
AFL – 30,842
NRL – 16,248

Comparative Google search 2004-2023 (August): NRL/AFL/A League/ Super Rugby:

NSW:	NRL – 69%, AFL – 25%, A League – 5%, Super Rugby – 1%
QLD:	NRL – 62%, AFL – 33%, A League – 3%, Super Rugby – 2%
ACT:	NRL – 51%, AFL – 43%, A League – 3%, Super Rugby – 3%

TAS: AFL – 89%, NRL – 9%, A League – 2%, Super Rugby – 0% (less than 1%)
SA: AFL – 88%, NRL – 8%, A League – 4%, Super Rugby – 0% (less than 1%)
VIC: AFL – 88%, NRL – 9%, A League – 3%, Super Rugby – 0% (less than 1%)
WA: AFL – 87%, NRL – 10%, A League – 2%, Super Rugby – 1%
NT: AFL – 68%, NRL – 30%, A League – 1%, Super Rugby – 1%

Comparative Google search 2004-2023 (August): NRL vs AFL (Australian states)

NSW: NRL – 75%, AFL – 25%
QLD: NRL – 66%, AFL – 34%
ACT: NRL – 52%, AFL – 48%
TAS: NRL – 9%, AFL – 91%
SA: NRL – 8%, AFL – 92%
VIC: NRL – 9%, AFL – 91%
WA: NRL – 10%, AFL – 90%
NT: NRL – 30%, AFL – 70%

Grand final ratings 2019:
AFL – 2.939m
NRL – 2.640m

2020:
AFL – 3.812m
NRL – 2.966m

2021:
AFL – 4.11m
NRL – 3.596m

2022:
AFL – 3.06m
NRL – 2.76m

Outside of NSW and QLD in Australia, the NRL has only the presence of the Melbourne Storm in AFL-dominated markets. The game is called the National Rugby League, but the Trans-Tasman League may be more applicable to the NRL.

The Storm, after enormous success on the field, have definitely found a niche market in the AFL-dominated Melbourne and greater Victorian market. The Storm have a good member base of around 30k, solid crowds and excellent TV numbers. The Storm are loved by Foxtel and are the highest-rating team on Foxtel, probably the highest-rated team in the whole game in recent years, with the lack of on-field success for the game's powerhouse team, the Brisbane Broncos in more recent times (up until 2023). The Storm's free-to-air numbers are okay in Melbourne without strong support from Nine to gain more viewers, but the code does not have the same commercial free-to-air arrangement that interstate AFL teams have in each state, with live free-to-air games being shown every week on their main channels. The 2006 NRL Grand Final ratings in Melbourne featuring the Storm were higher than both Brisbane and Sydney, with 875k viewers in Melbourne alone, compared to a Sydney audience of 817k and Brisbane of 806k. The 2020 grand final featuring the Storm saw 608k watch in Melbourne, while other recent Storm grand finals also rated well, with 2018 - 551k, and 2017 - 644k viewers.

The Storm have undoubtedly been a great expansion and addition to the game of rugby league in a new major market, but despite that success, the current administration has made it clear the focus will be on dominating and owning the heartland markets of NSW and QLD, which is in some ways an odd and backward decision for the code, or the politics of rugby league is at play again, with existing clubs and stakeholders happy to look after their own interests first.

With the NRL having little share or presence in the AFL southern and western markets (WA, SA, Tas), the AFL has not had to worry about its own backyard and counterattack threats from other codes. There has never been a Brisbane Line mindset with the AFL; they have always been far more audacious about spreading the game nationally, and that mindset goes back many years, even well before the professional era.

The AFL can be far more offensive-oriented in northern markets when they don't have anything threatening their own markets. With the AFL putting more and more pressure for market share in the northern states, the NRL has to spend far more money and allocate much more time and resources to defend their heartland markets.

The opposite is true in the five states dominated by the AFL. It's more of a maintenance program, with its culture so embedded in each state, than an environment of intense market rivalry and competition.

Slowly but surely, the AFL continues to chip away at the northern markets. The free-to-air ratings and media exposure may not quite show this progress yet, but there are warning signs for the NRL if you look deeper into the trends and demographics of the supporter base. AFL television figures in northern markets are increasing slowly, with QLD figures looking very promising the last 2 to 4 years, and they are getting a small increase in market share each year. The grassroots game continues to gain a larger share of the market, which generally transfers to lifelong supporters of the game

AFL commercial arrangements in the northern states are very strong, with one-city teams in a national competition always attracting extra attention from potential sponsors for greater branding awareness, as the Brisbane Broncos, Melbourne Storm and North Queensland Cowboys do for the NRL. The Swans and Lions have very good commercial deals and excellent media deals to reach both free-to-air and pay television audiences every game.

With the intention from the NRL to fight a defensive strategy against further AFL invasion, the question is: will this succeed for the NRL? Can the NRL hold or increase its market share in ratings, crowd attendances, grassroots numbers and commercial deals?

Another QLD team based in the south east will be great for another local derby with the Broncos, such as the former rivalry in early games between the Broncos and Crushers, and another QLD team will attract attention for other QLD teams. The extra QLD team from Redcliffe (Dolphins)

will also help support the code for more media saturation, dominate commercial deals and help the code across the whole south east and strengthen QLD's State of Origin success with a larger player pool.

The real question is: What percentage of rugby league heartland markets will the AFL get in key metrics? In the current climate, I cannot see the AFL losing more market share in grassroots. The trend definitely looks up, and, if anything, it's likely they will increase market share in the grassroots in future years.

If you gain a greater market share of the grassroots, it usually equates to future lifetime fans, and if the AFL gets more market share in the grassroots, it is also likely to translate to more television consumers and more people interested and attending games in NSW and QLD for the AFL. This patient process sometimes takes a long time for the seeds to show its fruit, but eventually it does happen.

The NRL will also continue to hold a strong market share in the heartland markets, but the question is: What will that be?

The NRL may continue to be the number one sport in these states, but it can also continue losing a small percentage of the market each year. It is hard to see how the NRL can gain more share of the market and dominate, like V'landys believes it will.

Total fans had declined for the NRL between 1994 to 2023 and it is hard to see, with the current direction by existing NRL administration, how this will be reversed without entering new markets or changing media strategies.

The game's dependence on television revenue is another fact that will make it hard to win a long-term war against the AFL. 61% of the total revenue for the NRL in 2019 came from media broadcasters, down from highs of 64% in 2018 and 67% in 2013. The AFL broadcast rights accounted for 50% of total revenue in 2019.

The game may continue to be quite strong in the heartlands, but as a whole, sport nationally could be contracting in supporters and getting smaller. The current Brisbane Line strategy from the NRL does not give it much opportunity to grow. The Brisbane Line defensive strategy utilised by the NRL will end up working against the game. No battle in war, business or sport can be won fighting from a totally defensive position and mindset. The AFL has the upper hand in this battle: a home base not needing to be defended, large cash and resources to attack with, and continual growth in grassroots markets which are slowly starting to show fruit. It's impossible to see how the AFL would not get bigger and the NRL get smaller as sports nationally.

PART 5

In the final part of the book, we examine further some of the key issues impacting the game and look deeper into some of the key solutions to help the game move forward.

SOLUTIONS

Leadership
Governance – Australian Rugby League Commission (ARLC)
Vision
Building a culture
Finance
Television
Media
Country rugby league and grassroots
Touch football
Middle management
NRL product
NRL schedule
International
World Cup Challenge
Expansion

LEADERSHIP

FOR RUGBY LEAGUE to rise again and meet the challenges of a post-Covid world and steer the game towards greener pastures, the leadership needs to rise across the whole game to a whole new level. Everything falls and rises on leadership!

For nearly 2 decades, the game has had the wrong people leading it. Recruitment has been poor for the top role of NRL CEO and other senior roles within the game, with a long history of a mismatched set of skills and characteristics required for leadership roles in the game, including philosophy, love and passion for the game, true independence, decisiveness, and strong honest character that was badly needed and missed in past appointments for senior roles, due to a lack of proper due diligence in any recruitment process.

The NRL CEO role requires a diverse leadership skill set to successfully perform the role and lead the whole game. Leading the NRL means overseeing the whole game, not just the top tier of the NRL but the whole game from top to bottom across the nation, and this requires skills including strong leadership, knowledge, operations experience, being a visionary, having a cool temperament and a service attitude, as well as courage and deep passion for the game.

As mentioned earlier, since 1998, four CEOs of the NRL have all come from outside as external candidates. Todd Greenberg could also be considered an external applicant, although he did have a role as Head of Football at the NRL before being appointed CEO, but this was a very quick transition to the CEO role, and most of his apprenticeship and management experience was in a senior role with the Bulldogs.

Andrew Abdo broke the mould in winning the role after performing a number of senior roles at the NRL Headquarters before being announced CEO in September 2020, with strong support from current ARLC Chairman Peter V'landys, though Abdo is not a rugby league man, as he only become involved with the sport when starting employment at the NRL in a corporate appointment.

NRL era CEOs 1998-present:
Neil Whittaker
David Moffett
David Gallop
David Smith
Todd Greenberg
Andrew Abdo

The recent appointments to the top role at the NRL have been very questionable, and, in my opinion, not enough due diligence was carried out and the past leaders were not the right people to be leading rugby league in this country. None of the past appointments had the right blending of intelligence, vision, acute rugby league knowledge, team and culture building capabilities, courage, independence, integrity, financial IQ and a servant attitude towards the whole game. Some may say this is harsh, but as the Bible says, *By their fruit you shall know them.*

Many of the past and current appointments have had part of the technical skills required to excel in the role, but I don't believe in the NRL era the game has had an executive leader with all those attributes at the top steering the game.

If you compare the last three CEOs of the NRL to the AFL's leadership in the same period and the results under Arthurson and Quayle before the NRL era, there is a clear differentiation in output, impact, reputation, results and legacy, or, as the Bible says, the fruit!

Everything is always a matter of opinion but results are real! Results are always your best judge and metric.

The question then is: What does rugby league need to take the game forward? We can easily just say 'leadership,' but there are many types and styles of leaders from history who have done sterling jobs in leading a diverse range of causes: Winston Churchill's courageous stand to rally the British people to fight against Nazi Germany in WW2; Steve Jobs' relentless pursuit of perfection in technology, with innovative new products that would put a dent in the universe, as he stated to his staff; Andy Grove's amazing leadership to lead Intel back after the move to the semi conductors market and his incredible ability to set and achieve a grand vision and teach and inspire people within his organisation; Ronald Reagan's Peace through Strength policy in dealing with the Soviet Union to tear down the Berlin Wall and let freedom ring across eastern Europe; John Wooden's incredible humility after extended success with the UCLA basketball team; Abraham Lincoln's resolve to keep the union together in the face of a civil war where 600,000 lives were lost, and to abolish slavery; Robert E Lee's magnanimous attitude to unite the country after defeat in the civil war; Genral's Douglas MacArthur and General George Patton's offensive mindset when leading in the European and Pacific theatre during WW2; George Washington's burden and strength to fight for freedom, no matter how bleak it seemed, and win independence for the American people from British rule; Alexander Hamilton's intellectual brilliance to construct an economy that would allow America to become a world superpower; famed boxing trainer Emmanual Steward from the Kronk Gym, who trained many champions and revived many champion boxers' careers and his unique ability to analyse fights as a commentator and see what others could not see when commentating; Ancient Greek

Pericles' role in building the Greek Empire that would inspire civilisations for thousands of years to come; Augustas during the Roman Empire; and Jesus Christ teaching the world the Christian way that would start with just 12 disciples and inspire billions of followers to this day and still survive through fires, famines, floods, diseases and wars.

Each leader has got to be true to himself, and that list shows the many different qualities and styles of leadership.

Let's look at some qualities that are needed in the senior leadership at NRL HQ.

Servant Attitude

There have been many famous quotes on service. Here are some great ones:

> *Ask not what your country can do for you – ask what you can do for your country* – John Kennedy

> *Find a way to serve the many, for service to many leads to greatness* – Jim Rohn

> *You can have everything in life you want, if you will just help other people get what they want* – Zig Ziglar

In the modern internet age when everyone has the latest technology and accessories, new powerful phones and social media to interact with the world at their fingertips, the idea of serving your fellow man and stakeholders has been forgotten and has slowly gone out of fashion.

The idea of being a servant leader is foreign to many now, in times where everyone is becoming a self-publicist on social media in pursuit of selfish attention and fame, which has now also become all too common, with many leaders today across various industries with their egos impacting their ability to lead an organisation.

But this is what rugby league needs badly from its leaders in order to meet the challenges of the day and build a legacy that will survive for many generations to come and allow the game to thrive and prosper.

For far too long, the game has been held to ransom by greed and power from many stakeholders, including players wanting bigger paychecks, clubs wanting more money and control, NRL commissioners not doing the professional job that comes with the responsibilities, media companies and personalities only ever thinking about money and their profiles, and past leaders looking out for only a select few stakeholders.

All stakeholders at one time or another during the NRL era have been selfish for only selfish gain, where the loser in all of this has been the game itself.

The game needs a totally new culture and philosophy, and this starts with the CEO at the NRL for rugby league, who shows through deeds not words.

With a change in attitude and philosophy to serve the game, the sport can do incredible things.

Instead of asking what's in it for me, why not start by asking: How can I serve my stakeholders in the game?

How can I make the game better?

How can I make it more affordable to attend games?

How can we make the game a better family experience?

Can we make the game a better spectacle?

How do we grow the game internationally?

How can we grow the game in non-traditional states?

How can we grow the game in general?

How do we get more people playing the game?

How do we get more females involved in the game?

How can we support country rugby league more?

Can't we see how much better the game would be, looking at serving the stakeholders of the game first rather than a profit-first mentality that has left the code in a near dire financial position in recent years?

It's a funny thing that often occurs in business and life, that the more you chase money first, the less you have of it. In Australian sport today, the NRL, A League and Rugby Australia could all vouch for this, with their money-first philosophy from leaders and yet little funds in the bank.

A servant leadership model needs to come from the CEO/chairman and be pushed all the way down through the game's culture.

Behaviour plus attitudes equals culture, and these are the changes the game needs badly from the top.

Service leads to greatness, not the money-first attitude that continues to plague the code.

Visionary

Where there is no vision, the people perish – Bible, Proverbs

Think Big – Donald Trump

We become what we think about – Earl Nightingale

The promise of the future is an awesome force – Jim Rohn

Rugby league badly needs leadership that can set and achieve a bold vision for the game. For far too long, rugby league has played it safe to keep existing stakeholders happy and not dared for greatness, but for the game to grow and challenge AFL and reach its full potential, we need far more boldness. The past leadership's limited and small thinking has set the game back greatly and allowed the AFL a much easier time in implementing its long-term strategic vision of a national league across Australia. (Full credit to the AFL for bringing in new teams strategically over the last 30 years to provide a national footprint.)

Rugby league has had the embarrassing problem of being indecisive and not knowing what the code wants and being unable to communicate this to the rugby league base. Leaders and senior management have come and gone over the last 2 decades, but the game's major goals and direction have been unclear to supporters and stakeholders, both internal and external. Continual off-field distractions, mixed with selfish pursuits from internal stakeholders, and the game has wasted time, drive and energy on things that have achieved limited return.

A strong bold vision allows the game to direct its resources and energy to what matters and eliminate time-wasting activities that achieve nothing. Goals and vision provide energy and bring light to where the game is and where it needs to go. It gives hope to those who may be struggling within the game or those who feel forgotten.

The game needs bold leadership that will set a clear vision and direction for the code. Leaders must forget about the past and set a bold new course for the code. As the Bible says, *Let the dead bury the dead*. The things that seem impossible can be achieved if the game has some faith, courage and persistence to make the game better. We have a great product that people will love if we give them the opportunity, but we need faith and courage to attempt this.

Our game is full of excitement and entertainment when played the right way, and even the harshest critic would acknowledge this. You only have to see the comments about the 2021 grand final between the Rabbitohs and Panthers or the decider of the 2022 Origin series, both pulsating games that can hold their own with any major sport in the world when played at its best.

Rugby league can and should be doing much better, but it takes vision to see and believe this. American Author Earl Nightingale famously said, "We become what we think about," and that statement is very true and worth thinking about for the whole game. Our vision and goals of the past have been small and limited, with more focus on internal bickering over greedy pursuits and petty arguments, which have never led the game to greater levels of success. The game's leaders cannot see an NRL team in

Perth, Adelaide, or Wellington, they cannot see new domestic leagues across the nation, they can't see international rugby league overtaking State of Origin as the game's pinnacle. They can't see a renaissance of the international game and tours both at home and abroad.

How could we ever make this a reality when the leaders don't believe it could happen? We really do become what we think about! The NRL thinks it can't go to Perth and yet the AFL believes it can succeed in the northern states. Thoughts do have a funny way of becoming things. If you can see your vision in your mind, you can hold it in your hand!

Rugby league in Australia needs a new grand vision and boldness for the game that will last for generations to come, and, yes, we do become what we think about! So let's think grand thoughts and back them with strong discipline and persistence with our time and resources, and dare greatly.

Rugby league is a great game and our leaders must believe that the game can go to a whole new level. As Teddy Rooselvelt, said, *"The credit belongs to the man ... who, at the best, knows, in the end, the triumph of high achievement, and who, at the worst, if he fails, at least he fails while daring greatly, so that his place shall never be with those cold and timid souls who knew neither victory nor defeat."*

Let's dare boldly!

Courage

Courage is rightly esteemed the first of human qualities - Winston Churchill

You will never do anything in this world without courage - Aristotle

With so many stakeholders involved in the game with many different agendas and mixed needs and wants and a politically correct culture both in the media and society that pushes for conformity to the modern mob's ideas and beliefs, the game needs a strong leader with backbone and strength that will go against the push and pull of the day and stand for what is right, ethical and not necessarily popular, doing what is best for the game against vicious opposition.

Past leaders in the game have lacked the internal resolve and strength against strong criticism, instead, bowing to media rights owners, players' and clubs' demands and a politically correct culture in society, and, in the end, have kneeled to the pressures of a ruthless culture when dealing with stakeholders.

When leading an organisation with so many stakeholders who have opposing views, there will be times when the leader will need to go against many key associates and do what is right for the game before vested interests, to stand for what is right and honourable.

Rugby league is now in an era when there are many sensitivities and delicate matters that will require great courage from the game's leaders.

You have serious financial issues that will invoke high emotion with clubs, players, state bodies, and media companies, to balance the budget and provide financial assistance and support for all of the game's stakeholders. Some stakeholders cannot get what they want, to the detriment of the whole game, and this will require courage and balance to keep working relationships healthy whilst not always giving stakeholders what they want.

Television and other corporate deals will continue to be negotiated moving forward. The role of HQ and its operational function, along with the two state bodies, will need to be worked out. Grassroots and country rugby league have major challenges from internal and external threats. These are just some of the many challenges that lie ahead.

The next leader needs high-level resilience and courage to lead the game through these challenging times and deal with the many difficult stakeholders. The greater game needs courage to do what is right for the game against selfish and greedy pursuits from internal and external stakeholders, and must think about the whole game's mission and purpose, not just a few select elite representatives.

The game's future depends on this.

Brains

Intelligence will be required to steer the game through these difficult times ahead. With Covid causing economic chaos across all sections of the economy, the recovery will be a long, slow, and difficult process for most Australians. Many will be out of work for extended periods, or on reduced hours, and business will do it tough for the next decade plus, with record debts and deficits nationally as well as surging inflation.

The media landscape is changing rapidly and old business models that were once successful are now being made obsolete by new digital players and models such as streaming services like YouTube, Disney, Amazon, Netflix and many other independent and new players. Rugby league legacy media outlets such as Nine and Foxtel are in an environment of rapid change and testing times, and will face ongoing challenges within their own companies in order to survive and prosper into the future.

The leadership needs to be aware of the changing times after the pandemic and have the creativity and flexibility to move the game forward, not based on past decisions.

Outside-the-box thinking will be required to rejuvenate the game with future commercial deals and how the game sells itself to domestic and international stakeholders.

The new digital world we live in today can obliterate sectors and competitors in a blink of an eye. The past model of red ocean epic competition where it is brand against brand fighting for its share of the market has been reshaped by blue ocean innovators who are creating completely new markets, offering more value at less cost. The blue ocean leaders can be seen everywhere in the business and sporting landscape: Cirque du Soleil, a new innovation of the traditional circus; Airbnb shaking up the old motel business; Uber shaking up the taxi industry; Apple products shaking up multiple industries with innovations like the iPod, iPad, and Mac leaving competitors in its wake; and UFC reshaping the fight game. These are just a few examples of the innovation and creativity that is required to get on top and stay on top, one where innovators are now making the old models obsolete by creating completely new markets in an ocean of blue with little or no competition, rather than the old dog eat dog culture of red ocean competition.

High intelligence, strategic thinking, emotional Intelligence (EQ), reflection and outside-the-box thinking will be required to deal with a diverse range of stakeholders, from media companies, players, clubs, government officials, sponsors and the fans.

For intelligence without courage is as static as courage without intelligence is rash!

Operations Experience

Solid operations experience is desperately needed to lead, support and oversee the running of a billion-dollar business on a day-to-basis with key functions such as:

Finances

Operations

HR and Safety

Sales, Marketing and IT

Digital Business

Legal

Community Development

NRL Partners – NSWRL, QRL, Touch Football

The CEO and senior leaders will be required on a daily basis to work with existing staff and set high standards whilst also reporting up and down to the stakeholders of the game.

The headquarters of the NRL has come under much scrutiny in recent years for bloated staff numbers and huge overheads, which had already seen senior leadership make cuts to the business in late 2020 after

Covid, and now they will need to raise the bar and deliver higher quality services and content.

Grassroots, school, domestic and country leagues have stern challenges ahead, and the game must bring a far more professional operation business model to support these functions. For far too long, AFL middle management and their operations teams across the nation, led from Melbourne and other states, have been putting rugby league to shame. On the ground at both the professional and community level, the AFL is a highly professional operating team, well led, well financed, with strong middle management capabilities compared with rugby league's more amateurish unorganised coordination of its leagues that we have seen since the beginning of the NRL era.

Operations experience is essential for successfully running the game and getting the right people in those seats and driving high standards across a diverse range of business units and functions. Our leaders need to know how to drive both high output and a strong culture within these functions of the business off the field.

Execution is critical, and for far too long, the NRL have blown money away with programs and strategic plans that have provided no fruit. Ideas and plans are worthless without sound execution.

As Jack Gibson said, "Winning starts in the front office."

Team Builder

As mentioned earlier under Leadership, the game's leadership needs to develop and build a strong culture and team that emphasises the game. Fans must come first, along with a foundation of integrity, high standards of professionalism and performance that promote a culture of responsibility and accountability.

The culture should not be dependent on one charismatic leader, but one that can sustain the game for generations to come and prepare leaders to take over from current leaders when the right time comes along for succession.

Over the 2 decades, the culture at the NRL has continually changed with every new CEO and senior role appointment and further changes on the commission, but none of these leaders have made a lasting impression on building a great team and culture that endures. This must change if rugby league is to ever reach its full potential and operate more cohesively and drive more output, quality and innovation.

The business world is not sport against sport but rather each management team vs the competitor's management team, and rugby league needs to build a strong team that can bring more horsepower to the sport.

More Leadership = More Horsepower
Your culture = behaviour + virtues repeated

As any good leader will tell you, the right people in the right seats and removing the wrong people from your business is essential to any organisation's success.

It is critical that rugby league has the best people involved in the game in a host of various roles, from its executive leadership team, to operational roles, to middle management functions on the ground, to key financial functions, to HR, to accounts, to grassroots officers, to country footy, and on and on. The whole is certainly greater than the sum of its parts.

The right people in the right seats sounds easy to do, but it is very difficult to build and execute a strong team for any business. Rugby league faces big challenges from AFL and other sports and entertainment. The economic headwind and competition from other sports and entertainment will require the best people within tightened resources for the game to prosper and fight off future threats.

The ability for leaders to work with a wide range of professionals is key to developing existing talent, which promotes a cohesive environment.

The leaders of the game must build a strong team across the sport and cultivate a culture that will endure past one leader, with statesman-like qualities the game has not seen for over a generation.

Peace and War-time Leadership

Every business goes through the seasons and changes of life and each season requires a different type/style of leadership to manage the conditions.

Not many people speak about the different seasons requiring different types of leaders. I call them peace and war-time leaders, and both are needed in their respective seasons in business and in life.

Peace-time leaders often have an environment where they are the dominant players and their industry often has no outside challenges, profits are easy and things are running well, there are limited internal or outside challenges, and things just seem to go along smoothly.

War-time leaders are the complete opposite. They face circumstances when an organisation is at risk, it has no cash or is facing a life-threatening matter to survive, a bankruptcy or new competitor is killing their business, or an outside emergency threatens the future and life of the business.

Famous war-time leaders have included Winston Churchill, Douglas MacArthur, George Patton, Steve Jobs, Andrew Grove, George Washington, and Abraham Lincoln, who each faced stern challenges of the day to survive and lead their teams to victory despite serious adversity and challenges.

Very few leaders succeed in both environments, and one is often great in one and poor in the other. It's not impossible to do well in both, but generally leaders only perform at high levels in one.

Rugby league is in a season of stern challenge for the future of the game. The game after Covid now faces many obstacles and challenges to rise again. The game's revenue has been reduced with no play in early 2020.

Media partners are also in a difficult financial position but fighting back with new digital alternatives. Supporters, sponsors and governments will also likely have less money available moving forward than before the Covid crisis.

A war-time leader and mindset will be required to drive the game forward. Peter V'landys has taken the lead in running the game since Todd Greenberg's departure and seems to have taken ownership on all big matters, with a war-time-like can-do attitude, especially during Covid in early 2020, but after that period, has performed miserably on other issues within the game.

War-time leaders don't get caught up in political correctness matters; they do what must be done in the face of stiff criticism. They do what's best for the game and the people involved. They tell the truth and face the truth, no matter how brutal it all may be. The end result is all that matters, no matter how they get there.

Humility

That emotions rule the world is an unknown universal law, and this principle has been both positive and negative in the history of mankind. Faith, love, loyalty, and passion are all very powerful emotions when directed for a common good and purpose and have achieved incredible things in history. But on the opposite side of the coin, fear, greed, ego, anger, envy, jealousy, doubt and worry can be just as destructive, and history is full of stories where negative emotions have led to destroyed lives and businesses, wars, friendships ruined, marriages destroyed and countries which have collapsed.

Rugby league has a long history, from the Super League era of negative emotions impacting the game, such as greed and fear from key stakeholders, causing much destruction to the code, and this still continues to plague the code today.

Big egos seem to be synonymous with rugby league, with many past stakeholders often having very strong views on what should happen with the game and how it should be led. It often seems to be a "my way or the highway" attitude and "I don't care who is in my way as long as I get what is best for me!"

Some genuine humility would bring a real freshness to the game in a time where everyone believes they need to have all the answers, speak the loudest, get major newspaper write-ups, want attention, and show everything off to impress others on Facebook, Instagram, Twitter and the internet.

Humility that knows its limits, does not have all the answers, recognises that I need and am dependent on others' help and support to achieve the game's objectives, that everyone is important, and I am just a temporary servant to the game: this is not weakness but real strength, and the game needs much more of this.

Humility is a virtue and one the game needs much more of from its leaders.

In Plato's Republic, Socrates commented that the reluctant ruler is the only one who should lead the polis. Often, those who want power want it for the wrong reasons.

Passion and Love for Rugby League

Lastly, the right leader must have a genuine love and passion for the sport. He or she does not need to have played at the highest level but must have had some involvement with the code and have a burning desire to see the sport succeed and prosper for generations to come.

Closing Thoughts about Leadership

Everything falls and rises on leadership, and the NRL's future will greatly depend on the quality of the code's leadership.

The game is begging for the right kind of leadership at the NRL. Statesmen are needed urgently.

GOVERNANCE - AUSTRALIAN RUGBY LEAGUE COMMISSION (ARLC)

GOVERNANCE IS THE biggest issue facing rugby league. If rugby league is ever to reach its full potential in Australia, it needs to get the governance model right once and for all. If it cannot get the governance right, the game will continue to lag behind and see more infighting between stakeholders, and conflicts of interest will continue to cause a loss of faith and trust with the public. More discontentment among key stakeholders outside the game's current power base has been the ongoing story of the NRL era.

Since the formation of the ARLC in 2012, the game continues to be dragged down by internal politics, internal fighting between stakeholders, media power, lack of real independence, and power plays between NRL Headquarters, media companies, clubs and players. There was an original desire for an independent commission that has proved to be anything but independent. Today, we see again more than ever the fingerprints of media and networks and select stakeholders such as clubs and players leading the game's decisions for self-interested purposes. Independent is the one thing the ARLC has not been during its short existence.

The game now has its third chairman with Peter V'landys, after previous stints by Peter Beattie and John Grant.

Covid exposed the ARLC's poor fiscal management of the game and irresponsible financial position throughout the last decade. Former CEO Todd Greenberg was criticised heavily and was the fall guy for the game's limited financial reserves, but he was not the only person who should have taken some blame. Since its inception in 2012, the whole ARLC board and past members have been found absent in not making sure the game was in a better financial position.

After Covid, Peter V'landys took the role of leading the game out of the crisis and has well and truly crossed the demarcation line between chairman and CEO, seeming to do both roles rather than just the traditional chairman function. There was no doubt to anyone he was now the boss and calling the shots for rugby league. V'landys was the key negotiator with players, clubs and media partners during and after the crisis, and then led the charge to restart the game after the initial freeze as a result of the virus. V'landys negotiated with the government representatives about a return for rugby league and also negotiated with media partners for the renewal of television rights during and after Covid in 2020/2021.

Too much power has been given to V'landys during his current tenure and not enough questions have been pressed from the media and other stakeholders. There is no doubt that V'landys is a News Corp man. Every decision he has made during his tenure has greatly benefitted the media giant.

Such V'landys decisions include:
- Reduced television rights for Foxtel that were absent in official ARLC reports
- Long-term extension to Fox's NRL deal at discounted rates
- The Dolphins as the NRL's 17th team
- Doing deals without going to any tender process, favouring News Corp needs and wants
- No tender process outside of QLD for NRL's new team

- Bringing in another QLD team so more Bronco and Dolphins games would be on Foxtel and Kayo
- Driving Kayo subscription through Broncos, Dolphins and Storm
- Pulling out of the 2021 World Cup – Foxtel did not have the rights until the cup was rescheduled for 2022

The commission's role is to represent and grow the code across Australia. Their statement on the NRL website says:

"Formed in 2012, the ARLC is the governing body for Rugby League in Australia. It sets the overall strategic direction for the game and works to ensure that the administration across all levels of Rugby League can meet the demands of being a modern, professional and well governed sport. It has responsibility for funding the game at all levels and helping the game to grow and foster both in Australia and internationally.

"Roles and responsibilities

The role of the ARLC is to be the single controlling body and administrator of Rugby League in Australia. It has responsibilities for fostering, developing and funding the game from the junior to the elite levels.

"The ARLC also organises the NRL competition, the State of Origin and Australian representative matches and works with the International Rugby League and other Rugby League bodies to foster Rugby League throughout the world.

"Recognising the significance and profile of Rugby League in communities all across Australia, the ARLC also has a commitment to promote the welfare of young people, the Rugby League community and their interests."

So what does rugby league need to make the governance better which will result in better outcomes for the whole sport? Looking at their statement from their website, it is clear that the ARLC is not fulfilling its mission or role across the game in Australia.

Many sports around the world have different governance models. Let's look at some of Australia's major sports.

Cricket Australia

CA has elected representatives from each state member, plus three independent seats.

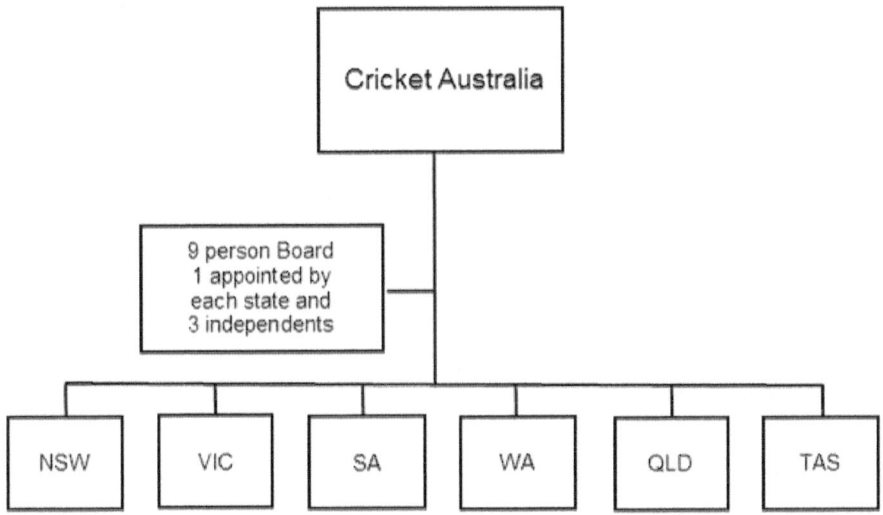

Australian Rules

The AFL has an elected commission which does not include clubs or state affiliates and is a more of a federal governance model directing the game.

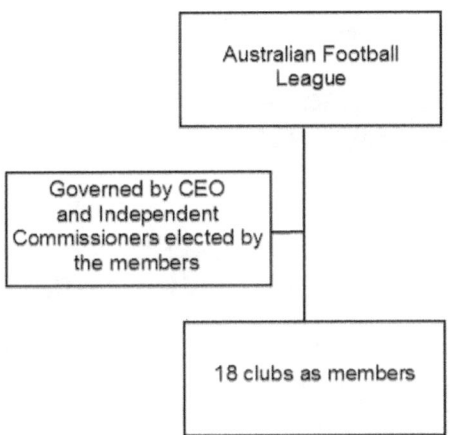

Rugby Australia

Rugby Australia has a board of directors composed of a president and chairman presiding over eight independent non-executive directors. The states, players or franchises are not members of the governing board.

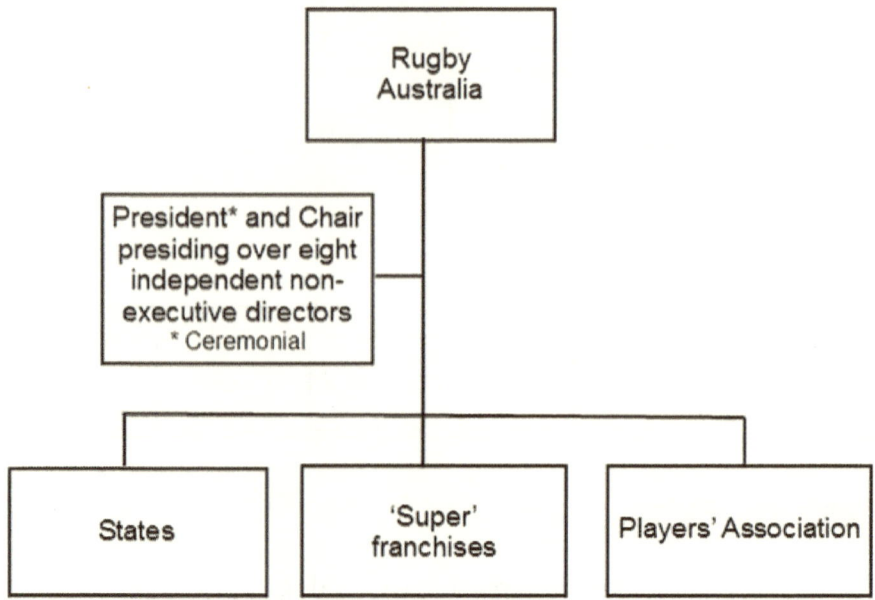

Soccer

Football Australia is changing its model in 2024.

Much debate has surrounded the clubs, players and state body affiliates' power and whether they should have more or limited power in the running of the game.

This decision is one of the biggest for the code's long-term success and the legacy of Peter V'landys and the ARLC.

Some believe the clubs and the RLPA should have more power and have representation on the ARLC and for any decision that impacts the game. The clubs and players are key stakeholders who drive the major revenue for the NRL through media deals but also have strong bias in doing what is best for themselves and not other stakeholders, who may have a much more limited voice and not support the best interests for the long-term sustainability of the code.

The previous salary cap deal agreement was far more than probably the game could afford, but after much disagreement with NRL clubs and past chairman John Grant, the ARLC agreed to this, and now lower levels of the game are feeling the consequences.

Many fans and commentators have a different view of the current players' and clubs' power and believe there should be much more balance of power within the commission, with more power to grassroots, country rugby league, state bodies, interstate bodies, and international affiliates.

Greed, self interest and conflicts of interest have been a thorn in the game for far too long and this has been magnified in the professional era.

Everything falls and rises on leadership, and the game needs far better governance and quality from the commission, working in a cohesive alignment to make the game grow and prosper and represent all stakeholders across the game at all levels.

So what can we do to make the commission better for the greater game of rugby league in Australia?

- **Select the right people on the board who possess a diverse knowledge and deep passion for the game.**

The game needs the people on the commission who have the right mix of experience and knowledge to best serve the greater game. It needs deep rugby league experience and historical understanding of the game, it needs knowledge of country rugby league, knowledge of the state bodies, international game exposure, it needs grassroots experience, it needs sound business, investing and financial acumen, legal, human resources, operational and marketing experience.

The sum again is greater than the individual.

The game's current ARLC chairman and board members:
Peter V'landys – horse racing
Peter Beattie – ex-premier, politician
Wayne Pearce – rugby league
Gary Weiss – business
Alan Sullivan – legal
Megan Davis – academic
Tony McGrath – business
Kate Jones – politician

Only one current board member comes from a background of rugby league, this being Wayne Pearce, with the rest of the members from a mix of business, politics, legal, and academic backgrounds.

Since the inception of the commission, the code has had a very strong presence of ex-business and political members on the board. Many believed that the inclusion of ex-business executives and political representatives would be the best thing for the commission and the game in 2012, but this has proven to not be true, and the poor results of the commission support this view. A lack of rugby league historical knowledge and awareness and an understanding of the game in country regions and grassroots and the challenges from the AFL and other sports has hurt the game during the commission era.

The appointment of ex-political members has been a huge failure. The fact that two former senior Labor figures from Queensland have been appointed to senior roles on the ARLC is worth questioning and how this has all come about when there's no voting process. The commission has moved away from being a rugby league board serving the game nationally to an elite aristocracy that elects or appoints individuals directly.

So what skills and knowledge are needed on the ARLC?

As stated, the commission has lacked strong rugby league operational experience mixed with historical whole-of-game awareness and understanding, but it is still very important to have some independent business and professional experience on the board to deal with running a billion-dollar sport.

- **Deep passion and love for rugby league**

The first criterion for any person to be appointed on the commission is a deep passion and love for rugby league. The world is full of executives and career climbers wanting to be on boards only to further their own professional careers and feed their ambition and egos. It's very hard to have great governance when your elected board members don't really care about the organisation they are a member of and are only interested in the money, perks and attention of being on a high-profile board.

Many boards around the world can be <u>described as having absentee ownership!</u>

I question why, since 2012, so many ex-business executives and politicians have wanted to be on the board of the commission. I am not saying they are bad people, not intelligent or who have had bad intentions, but I do question their authenticity and passion for the game when we badly need commissioners who have the right kind of ambition and reasons, who are not there for selfish and egotistical gain but to add real value and serve the greater game. Do they really care about the game in country towns such as Leeton, Tamworth, Young, Toowoomba, Bundaberg and Cooma? Do they care about the progress of grassroots in Logan, Roma, Cairns, Wagga Wagga and Western Sydney? Do they care about growing the game in non-heartland states such as Tasmania, Western Australia, Northern Territory and South Australia? Do they want to see the international game grow and compete with rugby union globally?

In future, board appointments must meet clear criteria to be successful in becoming an appointed commissioner.

Future criteria/checklist:

Reason for wanting to join the commission?

What has been your involvement with rugby league?

What do you want to do to improve rugby league?

Background check: rugby league historical knowledge?

Biggest issue confronting the game?

Biggest opportunity?

How can you serve the game as a commissioner?

What are the three things the commission needs to do now?

Are you a member of other boards?

These are just a few examples of questions that could be included in the process during future recruitment.

- **Knowledge and skills**

A governing body that provides excellent governance and leadership requires a diverse set of skills from representative members. When running a billion-dollar business that has a diverse set of stakeholders, multi-skilled members are needed to oversee HQ's running of the game, whilst also setting the strategic direction for the game.

Any entry into the commission must also be merited and approved, with strong skills and knowledge from applicants.

The game needs a diverse skill set with sound rugby league experience at the top level, the running of the game operationally, country rugby league experience, and grassroots understanding. Some of the business skills that non-rugby league independent representatives can bring, such as leadership, finances, investments, legal, accounting, risk management, human resources, good governance, sales and marketing, operational, digital and media and strategic thinking are just some of the mix of skills the game needs from independent commission members.

We need board members who can question the running of the game at HQ, who can see the challenges and opportunities ahead and can steer the whole of the game into better waters.

- **Courage, honour and duty**

Some of the qualities that have stood the test of time are courage, honour and duty.

Winston Chuchill said courage was the finest of all virtues.

Douglas McArthur said duty, honour and country were three hallowed words that say what you ought to be and what you will be.

George Patton said duty was the essence of manhood.

These three words are not merely words but virtues that have led men and women to tremendous success and overcome some of the most adverse conditions.

Our commissioners need integrity and honour because without trust there is nothing to fall back on. Trust is one of the qualities the game badly needs at the top, to stand on the concrete of truth!

What is needed is the duty to do what needs to be done, no matter the consequences, the duty to make the game financially strong, the duty to fix and improve grassroots footy and the country game and the many other challenges that the game faces, the duty to make the NRL and the game of rugby league the best it can be.

Courage is needed to go against the crowd in a politically correct age and say what needs to be said no matter what the consequences. For far too long, the game's senior leaders have not seized problems by the nose and sorted things out.

These virtues are needed to provide an example for the rest of the game's leaders and stakeholders.

- **Recruitment, not direct appointment**

All board members must go through an open recruitment process <u>that is not direct appointment!</u> One of the big changes that needs to occur with the commission is the removal of the direct appointment process for commissioners. There must be a transparent recruitment process open to all people interested in rugby league from all levels of the game. A direct appointment process has created a culture where we now only see a select elite aristocracy that can get appointed to the board. It's become more about who you know than what you know. We have seen in recent times that ex-Labor politicians are getting fast-tracked to the board without any prior rugby league background or experience. Many potential and qualified commissioners from grassroots, country rugby league, state bodies, interstate and international are not given any opportunity to apply for commissioner roles, and this needs to be changed immediately. An open process with an independent recruitment panel must be implemented asap.

- **Limited timeframes for board members**

Board members should be given timeframes in order to keep the commission fresh and innovative. Too many boards become stale and lazy, with many members staying years overdue.

The founding fathers of America led by George Washington's fine example believed in a maximum of two terms. They believed absolute power corrupts, and history has proven this to be true. There always needs to be a restraint of power because of the ugly side of human nature.

- **Which members on board**

Currently, eight members sit on the board, and, as stated, seven are from a non-rugby league background, with Wayne Pearce being the only exception. How can the game get the right blend and mix of business, operational, financial, investment and rugby league knowledge across all levels of the code to drive growth and help it reach its potential?

We stated the qualities we look for in our executive leaders on the commission and now we need to identify the right membership model that can best represent the code and make sound decisions.

The Bradley Report from 1992 recommended an ARL board comprised of:
- Two members representing NSWRL
- Two members representing QRL
- One representing the other states
- One representing ARL clubs
- Two independent directors who were not paid employees or office bearers for any club, with one residing in NSW and the other in QLD. Should not be elected for more than four terms, as this would reduce ability to bring in new perspectives to board.
- General manager

The Kerridge Report after the ARL/Super League schism recommended an ARL/NRL board comprised of:
- Two members representing NSWRL
- Two members representing QRL
- One representing the other states
- Two representing ARL/NRL clubs
- One representing ARL/NRL players
- Two to three independent directors (with three being the ideal number)

Both sides have their pros and cons, but the governance structure for the game must be what is best for the greater game and not just a select group at the elite level of the NRL. The whole is greater than the sum of the parts. As stated, the game needs the right blend of rugby league and outside independent experience to help govern the game.

Let's look at some draft models the ARLC could consider with designated seats.

ARLC current model:
Eight members - Independents

No designated criteria or background. Directly appointed through commission.

Model One:
Three – Non RL/Independents
One – NRL
One – NSWRL
One – QLDRL
One – Interstate members WA/SA/VIC/TA/NT
One – International

Model Two:
Three – Non RL/Independents
One – NRL clubs
One – NSWRL
One – QRL
One – Grassroots
One – Country rugby league
One – International

Model Three:
Four – Non RL/Independents
Four – RL nominated

Model Four:
Four – Non RL/Independents
One – NRL clubs
One – Grassroots
One – Country rugby league
One – International

Model Five:
One – NRL clubs
One – Grassroots
One – Country rugby league
One – NSWRL
One – QLDRL
One – Interstate WA/SA/VIC/TA/NT
One – RLPA
One – International
Two – Non-Rl/Independents

One – Chairman

Model Six:
One – NRL
One – NSWRL
One – QLDRL
One – RLPA
One – NRL clubs
One – International
One – Grassroots
One – Country rugby league
One – Interstate – WA/SA/TAS/VIC/NT
Three – Non-RL/Independents

Model Seven:
One – NRL
One – NSWRL
One – QLDRL
One – RLPA
One – NRL clubs
One – International
One – Interstate – WA/SA/TAS/VIC/NT
Three – Non-RL/Independents

There we have shown a number of different models and ideas to get people thinking about what may work best for rugby league. Nothing will ever be perfect but we should aim for excellence in governance, with the right skills, knowledge, and genuine authenticity and love of the game.

The model that I believe would serve the game best is one that has representation from the entire game, from bottom to top, which includes members from grassroots, state bodies, country rugby league, interstate reps, international and professional NRL players, and external independent business/financial reps. Since Super League, the majority of power, money and influence has lain with three groups: the NRL HQ, players and clubs, whilst other important stakeholders such as grassroots, country rugby league, state bodies, interstate, international and others have been forgotten in the strategic long-term operational decisions.

- **Constitutional amendments**

The membership, once agreed upon, that represents the whole game and provides a voice for all stakeholders, would then need to be amended in the constitutional framework of the commission so it is written into the framework and is legally binding.

Amending the constitution of the commission for the lower leagues may also be necessary, to ensure their voice and future for funding, voter membership, and other matters associated with the sport.

Constitutional amendments may also be necessary to legally ensure the game survives and is not held to ransom, as seen during Super League when clubs were able to join the breakaway league when there were legal loopholes with club licensing agreements.

A restraint on power in the constitution is necessary to **protect rugby league from rugby league.**

- **Independent information flowing to ARLC**

The lack of honest and transparent advice received by the ARLC is questionable after such a poor record, with many poor decisions coming from the board in the short existence of the commission. As mentioned in Part 2, there are questions about where they are getting their information from to make executive decisions. One would assume data, information and reports are coming directly from the NRL head office, led by both Chairman Peter V'Landys and CEO Andrew Abdo. As discussed, senior management inside many organisations can often hide or not disclose key information to board members for fear that their role, organisation or performance may come under more scrutiny from Board members.

The commission must hire key independent representatives not employed by the NRL, but engaged directly to the ARLC to provide independent and truthful advice for a number of functions of the game. These could include grassroots, state league's, country rugby league, interstate, finances, New Zealand and the Pacific, media relations and television agreements, international and anything the board and commission need key information and knowledge on to make sound strategic decisions for the sport.

This extra layer of advice will provide much more security, awareness, auditing and independence and support better decisions being made by the commission and improve governing standards.

Knowledge and power must work together for optimal outcomes and this can only occur when there is a sharing of key information between stakeholders with real facts and not the hidden agendas we see too often in the corporate world today.

- **Right power**

*Nearly all men can stand adversity, but if you want to test a man's character, give him **power*** - attributed to Abraham Lincoln

You gotta be able to see the trees and the forest

Napoleon Hill once said that emotions rule the world. He was the grandfather of personal development and former advisor to President Franklin Roosevelt during the Great Depression. He also gave the famous quote to Roosevelt: *The only thing we have to fear is fear itself.* Negative emotions such as fear, greed and ego have been an anchor to rugby league's ship of progress for decades now, with continual infighting between stakeholders since Super League, which has stalled many opportunities and growth for the code.

The former NRL (1998- 2012) governance model of shared ownership between media outlet News Limited and the NRL, to the current ARLC (2012-present) format has allowed many issues to linger for an extended duration with no solution.

The four main stakeholders involved have been the NRL HQ, NRL clubs, media companies and players. Many of the recent and current disagreements with rugby league have been monetary issues related to salary cap, club spending, Club licenses, player payments, player behaviour, fines,

NRL spending, NRL leadership, industrial agreements, structure of football, under-spending on other areas of rugby league, and other matters.

Peter V'landys walked into an environment where NRL Headquarters, under former leader Todd Greenberg, thinks the clubs and players are greedy and are not prudent with their spending habits, whilst players and clubs think the opposite: that the NRL does the same thing and has no control over expenditure at head office.

When John Grant was chairman of the commission, he was involved in a dispute with clubs and players over payment allocation in 2015. The game had already spent too much but Grant had promised the clubs and players an allocation of around $13.6 million per club, a figure the game clearly could not afford, as supported by former Rabbitohs Chairman Shane Richardson, who said the game was overspending whilst doing a project role in NRL Headquarters. During this dispute, there were strong fears the game could potentially have another Super League war on their hands, but an agreement was eventually reached. However, the high expenditure is hurting the code now with limited cash reserves to defend the game against the virus or another potential black swan event.

Clubs and players, with the support of the RLPA, want to share ownership of the game. Current rugby league industrial collective agreements are reported to have a percentage of income off the game's total revenue earned.

Some high-profile media representatives believe the players and clubs should have much more inclusion and power in key decisions for the code and become full members of ARLC or have a stronger membership representation. There can be no doubt that the clubs and players draw large amounts of capital and cash flow into the game and are very important stakeholders now and into the future.

Historically, some clubs in modern times have mismanaged resources, including finances, and have needed the NRL to step in and provide extra support in an era which has never had or seen as much money from television deals. Very few clubs actually make a profit, with the exemption of one-city teams like the Brisbane Broncos and a few others who have made modest profits in recent years such as North QLD Cowboys, South Sydney Rabbitohs, Canberra Raiders and Melbourne Storm, but many other clubs have had financial difficulties in recent years, including Manly, Newcastle and St George.

The clubs and players in both 2020 and 2023 wanted more power and say in the direction of the game, but at the same time, many NRL clubs have mismanaged past finances along with the NRL. This has even caused discontent between the wealthier clubs and poorer clubs, with the poorer clubs complaining that the game and media outlets favour big-name teams such as Brisbane and Melbourne, compared to Manly and other poorer clubs who did not get a fair allocation of salary cap (with third-party payments) and prime-time media attention from media networks.

The risks with giving the clubs and players more power in the commission is they will be selfish and focus on looking after themselves first and forget the rest of the game. This was proven correct when in 2015, former chairman Grant agreed with both the clubs and players to a salary cap the game could not sustain, whilst other stakeholders continued to be forgotten at the lower non-professional layers of the code.

This was again seen in mid-2021 when the NRL, and with the backing of the NRL clubs pulled out of the Rugby League World Cup to be held in the UK in November of 2021. The event was eventually cancelled and rescheduled for 2022.

The end of 2022 season again saw pay and contractual employment disputes with players, which are still ongoing in mid-2023. That was not helped by the NRL not having set a salary cap or other employment conditions, which gave the players no foundation for future payments or security.

Between late April and early May in 2020 when the NRL, led by V'landys, was trying to get play to resume, players were threatening they would not agree to this start date unless their needs were met around finances, accommodation and safety. This was a poorly-timed public relations stand, with thousands of Australians locked out of work and many found unemployed after Covid, whilst NRL players were continuing to get paid large salaries.

It is hard to ever see clubs and players being able to become statesman-like leaders for the whole of the game. We have seen in the history of the modern professional game, the clubs and players do a lot of great things on and off the field, but putting other stakeholders before themselves in financial resource allocation and influence has not been one of their noted achievements.

Could you ever see clubs and players taking a pay cut to introduce new teams in Perth and Brisbane? Would the players and clubs take cuts to fund other initiatives and projects of the game like country leagues and grassroots?

But can the clubs and players take a back seat and let the commission hold the power and make all the key decisions without input from players and clubs like the AFL? One would think that would cause more discontent, with many large egos at play, who now strongly believe they bring in all the revenue and the game is nothing without clubs and players.

The other side of the coin are the key stakeholders involved in the game at lower levels who have had no say and no voice in key matters outside the professional NRL product, which generates the overwhelming majority of revenue for the game.

The current running of the NRL and ARLC and total game is unorthodox to say the least. You have a chairman, Peter V'landys, who seems to have taken the lead on all matters for the last two to four seasons, such as television deals and other matters with media partners, expansion and all issues surrounding Covid, and seems to have clearly broken the demarcation line between the traditional chairman and CEO role. In addition to this, we have clubs and players (RLPA) dealing directly with V'landys and Abdo, and the commission members at the side not really driving the game or questioning key matters.

What the other commissioners' roles and responsibilities are is still quite grey or unknown to many in the game.

Many in the media today have never asked questions surrounding this. In reality, the ARLC has had a free run and has not had any real scrutiny, as it should have had since its inception. The commission should have been heavily scrutinised and questioned about past decisions impacting the wellbeing of the code.

The game needs strong governance that leads the game forward with a balance of power between key stakeholders that includes genuine independent representation with a blend of football knowledge across all levels of rugby league. It also needs strong operational and professional skill sets, a governance that is not held to ransom by clubs, players (RLPA), media outlets, and NRL HQ, or allows the balance of power to swing too far to one set of stakeholders who have selfish motives and who don't see the entire landscape or between the trees and forest.

Getting all parties in total unity is like herding cats but it is what the game needs if it is to survive and thrive.

VISION

Wherever you are is okay, only your direction is critical!

The promise of the future is an awesome force!

What will it take to put a man on the moon? – The will to do it.

– John Kennedy's question to Werner von Braun

IN PART 2, we spoke about rugby league's vision, which has never really been defined or chased with any real persistent vigour. The NRL may have written strategic plans on the website and talked positively to journalists in the past, but there is a big difference between a wish and a genuine desire. That's all talk, as the old saying goes.

Results are real, everything else is a matter of opinion!

The AFL has backed their strategic vision with concrete plans and actions and achieved some big goals they had for the sport, and it's time for rugby league to let go of petty infighting and conflicts of interest and set some big grand goals for the game at all levels.

Let's outline some clear goals the game and leaders should aggressively set and go after with courage and persistence.

The game's intentions have been muddy for far too long and the code needs to be much clearer on the vision for its future across the whole game that will inspire energy and drive from all involved.

Goals just don't just set the direction. There is real benefit to chasing big lofty goals, in what this will make of you and the organisation to achieve them. That's where the real magic is with big goals: the habits, beliefs, discipline, values, persistence, courage, thinking and customer service that will be required to reach some of those big goals.

Goals could include:

NRL

The NRL is currently the premier rugby league competition in the world and yet there is still plenty of room for improvement

The NRL becomes the number one sport in Australia

Crowds – more fans

Expansion – where will be the next expansion teams?

TV ratings – can we get bigger ratings?

Quality of play – viewer entertainment

Fans' experience – better game-day experience

NRL Draft implementation

Costs

Reaching more supporters

Reaching more interstate fans

Owning the heartland states

Growing international audiences

Grassroots

Juniors – playing numbers

Men's playing numbers

Family experience

Women's growth

Touch football and Oz tag incorporated into the rugby league family

Funding allocation

Management capabilities

Values and ethics

Ensuring enjoyment and fun for all involved

<u>Country Leagues</u>

Restrengthening bush footy

Metrics on clubs and numbers

Stronger middle management

Funding allocation

Code of conduct

Media and marketing plan

International Game

Calendar for international footy

Rebuilding the game and regular top-tier competitions

Having regular international tournaments and tours

Supporting the World Cup

Making the Kangaroos brand globally known and the most popular in Australian sport

Supporting NZ and the Pacific nations

Other

Sponsorship

Government support

Stadiums

Finances

More assets and investments

No one has all the answers, but the code needs to do far more thinking about where it hopes to drive the game. We need to be thinking, questioning and challenging the status quo continually, with a desire to never stop making the game better.

The sport needs some real ambition that is backed with real drive and persistence.

BUILDING A CULTURE

What you do is who you are - Ben Horowitz

Deeds, not words - George Washington

RUGBY LEAGUE NEEDS to change its culture. It is that simple! Over the last 2 decades, we have had players, clubs, senior management, commissioners, media networks, state bodies, consultants and government officials, and many more associated with the game have a take and take attitude from rugby league and not give back in return. Yet in March and April of 2020, after billion-dollar television and corporate sponsorship deals, the game had little money to survive.

Some would say this was only due to Covid, but things have a funny way of coming full circle in life, and you can't blame the virus totally.

The game's key stakeholders have taken and taken and have forgotten the goose that lays the golden egg. And that goose to all is the game itself - rugby league and the fans.

Rugby league needs a complete overhaul of its culture and identity, and this can only be led from the ARLC and senior management at the NRL and then pushed downward and practised at all levels of the code, with the support of media outlets, which often continue to look for negative headlines to trash the game's reputation.

Rugby league management talks a good game, but promises are often empty. We should only judge by deeds, as Washington says.

Your culture = Behaviour + Values + Virtues

Greed and selfish acts have become all too common, and many stakeholders who receive no income from the game and are only involved as fans or involved with grassroots or country games look on with dissent at such stakeholders who continually look after themselves for selfish financial and egotistical reasons.

So, how does rugby league change its culture?

- Rugby league must come first. The game is to be served, not just taken from.

  All decisions must benefit the greater game and all stakeholders, not just an elite aristocracy of people who believe they deserve all the profits and power. The game must serve all levels, from under 6s to playing for the Kangaroos. Long after this generation has come and gone, the game will still be here and it needs to look after the many yet to come.

- The ARLC through the NRL must drive values and deeds that give rather than take and recognise that we are all servants of the game, and profit is not our ultimate goal but serving the greater game and making it the best we can.

- Our values and beliefs should be pushed across all levels of the game and enforced by all involved. We make it clear to all what we stand for and what we don't stand for.

- Strong penalties for those who break the game's code of conduct, that make an example of what the game will not stand for and is a warning to all stakeholders.

- Make integrity and ethics the foundation of the sport.

- Protect the sport's reputation with a vengeance.

- Sub committees introduced from the ARLC that meet regularly to ensure integrity and ethics across the sport.
- Independent audits and reports.
- Clear governance framework for all stakeholders.
- When doing major deals, we must look at all stakeholders not just players, clubs and NRL HQ.
- Updated code of conduct and values developed for the game at all levels.
- Honour the past and what has made the game great.
- Incorporate outside leadership and middle management who come from organisations that put high focus on values, deeds and virtues (integrity).
- Hire people with the right kind of ambition – that is, serving the game and being a great team player.
- ARLC leaders have informal deals with media partners to speak well and truthfully about the code, much like the Melbourne media does with the AFL. Rugby league has been trashed by certain journalists. The game's integrity must be upheld, with an agreement between media and NRL leaders.
- Only sign deals with media partners who uphold integrity and honesty.

The topic of culture within the code has really only been spoken of during player behaviour incidents, but it must include a complete overhaul of the game and all its stakeholders. Misbehaviour, greed and self interest have long been a thorn in the game and must be addressed immediately. Culture with a focus on integrity is the bedrock and foundation of the NRL and sport and must be protected at all costs.

FINANCE

Numbers give meaning, just like words

PETER V'LANDYS HAS stated that the game was in a precarious and dangerous position because of its weak financial position during the initial outbreak of Covid. Both ex-CEO Todd Greenberg and former CFO Tony Crawford paid the price for the game's poor financial position, both leaving the NRL shortly after Covid commenced in early 2020.

As stated, when the game moved to Stage 4 after Covid, the finances of the code were in poor health, with very little cash in the bank and no cash flow available, with the game being paused whilst the virus continued. V'landys made it clear that the game's spending habits were not sustainable and the code would need to make some tough calls to make the game sustainable.

Two recent multi-million dollar television deals had passed through the game but the game spent it all. Expenditure went to clubs, players, HQ, state affiliates, community development programs and other things, and not much was left in the bank.

Ex-commissioner Gary Pemberton once stated the game should have been saving a minimum of $50 million per year and aim for an emergency fund of half a billion.

V'landys has a reputation for being good with numbers, and the removal of two senior executives in 2020 showed his intentions after Covid and the game has now since improved the finances since Covid.

The code announced a surplus of $43m for 2021 and another surplus of $62.9m for the 2022 season, which included operating expenditure cuts of $17.1m for 2022. The code also announced the acquisition of the Gambaro Hotel in Brisbane during 2022 for a reported $25-$30 million.

Despite the larger surplus for 2021 and 2022, these figures may be inflated, with a pause on many services and infrastructure investment during Covid, and the recent profits may not tell the whole story, with operating cuts painting a brighter picture, which may not be as true or easy moving forward, with less potential waste now available.

Whilst nothing can be done now to change the financial mismanagement of the past, the code can still take some great lessons from the past and make powerful new decisions for the future.

- Numbers give meaning - the over-expenditure was called out by a few individuals but there were major warning signs that the game was living beyond its means. We can go back to the last salary cap negotiations dispute between former Chair John Grant and the players and clubs to see the game was in a weak and dangerous financial position in 2015, and the numbers were flashing red that something was not right.
- The game must build assets and cash reserves to fight the next emergency. The AFL, though also impacted by Covid, could last around 18 months longer than rugby league without cash flow. They had built a much larger emergency fund and also the prime asset of the Marvel Stadium provided their game with a real asset that could be utilised to get a bank loan when play was not ongoing. The clubs of the AFL were also, for the most part, in a far stronger position than the NRL clubs. The game must build

an emergency fund and invest in real assets, both physical and non-physical.

- The commission must take far more ownership for the running of the game. Much blame was directed at Greenberg and Crawford, but many commissioners also knew the poor financial position the game had, with limited cash reserves and no assets. Absentee ownership is far too common with many boards, and the ARLC must take an active interest in all matters. The commission has been around since 2012 and the game should never have been in this precarious financial position.

- The game must run much tighter controls around where money is allocated to, such as each club and other stakeholders, including state affiliates, grassroots, country rugby league and any other stakeholders. Numbers give meaning and tell stories and paint pictures just like words!

- The code must reinvest heavily in the sport at the grassroots and domestic levels, both in the heartland and interstate.

- All stakeholders must have voices in the game and know the financial position of each department and the whole game that they are responsible for. There must be true openness and accountability.

- A change in culture, with far more responsibility and accountability with stakeholders who receive funding, with clear expectations around what is expected for receiving the funding. Clear service-level agreements and contracts that are reviewed often between relevant parties when receiving funding.

- Clear weekly, monthly and quarterly meetings with stakeholders to make sure finances are on track.

- As stated in the previous chapter, the game's culture must change from a money-first attitude to the fans and game first on all decisions. Service leads to greatness, but the game has slowly become takers, a culture of: Give me heat, then I will put wood on the fire! Let's change that to: sowing first, then we will reap, or pour the wood inside first.

- Grow the game both domestically and internationally to create larger commercial deals and greater revenues for the code.
- Grow more fans and consumers of content.
- Creator and producer mindset that drives the game, rather than consumerism.
- Future player and club payments pegged to crowds, TV ratings, sponsorships and player behaviour. If the clubs and players want to become part owners of the game, they need to act like owners of the game and have real skin in the game.
- Create more commercial investment outside of television deals.
- Look at building some real assets that are not paper or electronic-based, such as farmland, real estate and commodities or other businesses.
- Look at investment in the UK and Europe for the game, possibly the English Super League or French Rugby League.
- Look at the existing costs. The current players' salaries are highly debatable, if players' pay is to be sustainable long term and the outlay of spending is balanced across the code.

Jim Rohn famously said the poor spend their money first then invest what's left and the rich save and invest their money first and then spend what's left – two different philosophies that lead to two very different outcomes.

The game leaders need to have far tighter controls of the finances at all levels and make sure all stakeholders with some responsibility know their own departments or club numbers, and, as stated, numbers give meaning – they can be a red light with warning signs or a green light showing us the code is in good health.

Investment, responsibility, accountability, productivity and creativity are all keys to the code's sustainability and financial strength into the future.

TELEVISION

DURING THE COVID pandemic when all play was stopped in mid-March of 2020, the NRL and media partners Nine and Foxtel were all in difficult and weak positions. With the competition stopped and no games being played, rugby league was soon in crisis, with potentially no income being provided from media partners. Foxtel may have been in an even worse position than the NRL. With all sports suspended around the world, they had to provide repeat programs and have basically talkback shows and old games as content for subscribers. Foxtel was already in a dangerous position before the epidemic, with the old pay television model being destroyed and many customers transferring to new worldwide streaming platform services such as Netflix, Stan, Disney, Amazon, YouTube and many other streamers who were far cheaper than Foxtel packages. Foxtel laid off a large number of staff in early 2020 and its long-term future is still very grey, but the company has remodeled its business with the cheaper streaming service of Kayo to halt the loss of subscription members.

Subscribers numbers and advertisers from Foxtel were continuing to decline in the face of severe economic pressures and new worldwide competition from streamers. Foxtel developed Kayo as its cheaper alternative, with monthly fees of between $25-$35 per month compared to around $50-$90 on regular Foxtel. It cannot generate the income from streaming subscriptions like the full Foxtel service unless they get a larger subscriber base, but it does retain customers if they transition to the cheaper model, but at lower profit levels unless they gain far more subscribers. Kayo operates very similarly to how Jetstar works for Qantas in chasing the lower end of the market, leaving Qantas with the mid to high-range flights. Kayo will have to gain far more subscribers with the current business model to make up for lost revenue. As of February 2022, Kayo is reported to have 1.03 million subscribers, with the total of the Foxtel group of 4.08 million, which includes a reported 1.782m on residential Foxtel.

In February 2023, Foxtel reported 4.33m paid subscribers with a total of 4.41m subscribers across all platforms.

Nine would have also been very concerned about no rugby league during Covid in 2020. Rugby league gave Nine four of the top five programs nationally in 2019, with the three State of Origins and the NRL grand final match being in the top five rated programs nationally. Rugby league is its main sports product, with cricket in Australia being lost to the rival Seven network and Foxtel after a long history with Nine, and now the network is only showing Australian Open tennis, which runs for just a short period in summer. Ex-Nine boss Hugh Marks utilised and leveraged his media outlets through the Sydney Morning Herald and Nine network programs to attack the NRL after the virus, attacking Todd Greenberg about the game's poor financial position, the option of expanding the league, the costs associated with the media rights and the NRL not consulting with Nine over the restart of play after the virus. Marks was basically looking for a cheaper deal with the rights; he even had senior journalists Michael Chammas from SMH stating that Nine would be happy to walk away from the game. But, as the great state of Missouri says, *Show me, don't tell me.* There was a lot of talk from all parties, but actions and deeds are the only things that really matter.

Amazingly, ARLC Chairman Peter V'landys renegotiated the broadcast rights in this period and gave the Nine network a $55 million discount over 2 years, despite the network trashing the code on its media platforms. Later that year, in 2020, the network again backstabbed the game of rugby league like never before when it used those savings from the NRL's reduced television rights after pleading earlier financial difficulties to secure the broadcasting rights for rugby union's Super Rugby and international calendar. The NRL had given the Nine network a huge discount, only to be betrayed like never before by Nine for its great rival, rugby union.

The influence and power of the Nine network extends well beyond just covering the game on television. The network demanded that the next NRL team come from QLD, as this supports television ratings and sponsors from the game's heartland. Despite other potential candidates for new teams such as Perth, Adelaide and New Zealand, the game announced the Redcliffe Dolphins, to be known as the Dolphins, as the 17th team for the NRL from 2023, with no tender or official application process for the 17th team. The media outlets again got what they wanted, along with support from the ARLC, who are supposed to be in charge and running the code independently.

Fans have been upset for many years with the Nine network and the NRL for always scheduling the Brisbane Broncos every Friday night. The NRL has basically lost control of its calendar and scheduling, as the Nine network decides which teams play on Thursday and Friday night, with the Broncos having a monopoly with prime-time games, as they are the code's highest rating team. This is a very different arrangement to the one the AFL has for deciding which teams get what prime-time allocation during the regular season.

In May 2020, Peter V'landys announced a new TV agreement with Foxtel until the end of the 2027 season, on top of the agreement with Nine until the end of 2022. Both deals were at discounted rates due to the need for security and cash post-Covid. The figures from the Foxtel deal were kept hush, including official reports, with many believing the deal was done for far less money, with the NRL not wanting to publicly announce the figures, for fear of embarrassment from fans and potential AFL deals smashing the NRL's numbers.

In 2021, there was much talk that the NRL would possibly end its partnership with Nine for exclusive free-to-air rights, but this was never really on the cards, as the NRL and Nine would eventually agree to terms in October 2021, announcing a 5-year extension of the free-to-air rights with the Nine network.

The deal was worth $650 million over 5 years, commencing from 2023, which equates to $130 million per year.

The new deal with Nine would include screening the NRL every week, including the finals and grand final, State of Origin, and NRLW, with exclusive rights for the grand final and State of Origin. Nine has also secured the exclusive radio rights as part of the deal for 2GB and 4BC, which the network also owns for the Sydney and Brisbane markets.

In total, the NRL is now earning around $400 million per year from television rights:

- $130m per year – Nine
- $238m per year – Foxtel (unconfirmed)
- $32m per year – Sky NZ

Both the Nine network and the NRL praised the new deal through their media and digital outlets, but is the deal as good for rugby league as has been proclaimed from senior leaders at both organisations?

The AFL was earning around $475 million per year from media outlets after also renegotiating media deals during Covid. The current free-to-air AFL deal with the Seven network expires at the end of 2024 and it is anticipated the AFL will see a good increase on the next broadcasting rights value, which is consistent with many major sports around the world, including the EPL and NFL.

The AFL would renegotiate a deal with both Foxtel and the Seven network in late 2022 that would obliterate the NRL deal.

Despite the new deal, many of the code's fans were disappointed in the announcement of the extension to the media rights with Nine. The NRL has seen massive broadcast deals in the past and yet has never capitalised on them or reached anywhere close to the potential for the sport.

The new deal still does not resolve many of the structural problems that exist within the game and with its broadcasting partner, and no amount of money will resolve those issues.

The Nine network relationship with fans is at an all-time low, and many fans refuse to watch the sport on Nine. The Nine network's high profile employees such as Phil Gould, Ray Hadley, Danny Weidler, Michael Chammas, Andrew Webster and others have trashed the code for many years, with agendas that run against the code, to further the Nine network's own interests and their own personal vendettas.

The code's expansion domestically and a proper international program have been held back by its media partners, including the Nine network, which has no desire, along with the current NRL administration, to expand the game domestically. There is now only a very small scheduling window and virtually no desire to promote international rugby league, with the NRL season now dominating scheduling from February to October and the Nine network likely to object to any scheduling changes to promote the international game during the NRL season.

The current AFL television deal also includes prime-time exposure for non-heartland teams to screen live on free-to-air in prime time for interstate teams such as the Sydney Swans, Gold Coast Suns, Brisbane Lions and other non-eastern state teams such as West Coast, Fremantle, Adelaide and Port Adelaide. The Melbourne Storm, despite their enormous popularity, are still not shown on free-to-air for every game in Victoria, unlike the deals the AFL has struck with the Seven network for interstate teams. These are key differences that have not been discussed in this new deal and will continue hurting the NRL long term in a crowded sporting market.

Whilst $400m per year may look like a huge sum for the game, the new agreement is probably only an average to good deal when you look deeper into the details. The $400m is no increase on pre-Covid television deals and does not factor in surging inflation, contra agreements with Nine that inflate real figures, or the NRL discount of $55 million from 2020. The NRLW is also part of the package, and the NRL disabling and removing investment in its digital arm after complaints from both Foxtel and Nine, who saw the digital arm as a potential threat. The NRL will continue with its strategic plan to own the heartland states of New South Wales and Queensland at all costs and see no chance of growing the game in AFL-dominated markets, with no expansion teams or prime-time coverage on free-to-air main channels interstate.

So, despite the $400m injection into the game each year, which includes $130m per year from the Nine network, there are still fundamental flaws in this deal that will continue to hurt rugby league. The game still has the same writers, journalists and commentators who have trashed rugby league for many years, which has led to many fans disliking and not supporting the Nine network or the sport. The game has removed its digital arm, despite the fact that everything is moving towards streaming and internal production. The scheduling will again be dominated by high-rating teams and will not provide equality for all 17 clubs for prime-time exposure to promote their clubs and the greater game, there will be no Saturday night rugby league on free-to-air during the regular season, there will be no expansion interstate to new markets to draw in new fans as part of the new deal, and the new media deal will not attract new fans interstate, as the coverage will be shown on backdoor channels such as GEM, as seen in recent times. International rugby league will again be put on the sideline, with the network and NRL not allowing for any possibility of a proper mid-season calendar to promote any potential test series or international tours, which will continue to hurt the code, as other sports go the opposite direction in expanding their international calendars while rugby league looks only to a possible October/November window.

The bottom line is the NRL have done a deal with a media outlet who cannot be trusted and who say they are a partner of the game and yet will do what is best for the network only. This goes as far back in time as 1997 during the Super League war when Kerry Packer betrayed the ARL to screen Super League games on the Nine network. The game is becoming enveloped by the AFL, as it persists with a defensive strategy of owning the heartland states and remaining inactive in new markets and dormant in growing the game internationally, which will have long-term ramifications.

The river of time does not stop flowing, nor does it flow in reverse. The game looks like it will get more of its past in the future, despite the lavish and positive statements from Nine and the NRL about a bright new dawn for the greatest game of all.

With long-term television deals now locked in, the game of rugby league will have to soldier on with the current arrangements for a few more years yet.

Moving forward, a number of considerations need to be addressed. One of the key points is understanding what the game really wants and how the media plays a vital role in this. Past decisions have primarily been made on monetary factors alone, with little thought about growth and legacy for the code.

Foxtel has a core and large rugby league base, but the bigger audiences still come from free-to-air, and this has been the major reason other sports such as soccer, rugby union and basketball have returned to free-to-air, even willing to lose money to gain more viewers after being televised behind paywalls with Foxtel.

The British Rugby League learned the harsh consequences of leaving free-to-air television on the BBC for BSkyB subscription television in 1996, with its audience seeing a massive drop in the years, which still hurts the code today, despite the initial cash windfall that has now declined significantly.

Currently, the code has a shared arrangement which covers games from Thursday to Sunday during the regular season. Foxtel shows all games, with Nine showing three games per week.

NRL's weekly schedule:
Thursday 7.30pm – Nine
Friday 6.00pm – Foxtel

Friday 7.30pm – Nine
Saturday 3.00pm – Foxtel
Saturday 5.30pm – Foxtel
Saturday 7.30pm – Foxtel
Sunday 2.00pm – Foxtel
Sunday 4.00pm – Nine
Some Sunday 6.30pm games – Foxtel

Foxtel are screening all games live throughout the season and their ratings are very good; rugby league is the highest rating sport on Foxtel. The games usually range around between 150k viewers at the lower end up to around 350k viewers at the higher level before Kayo started increasing figures. Some games have gone above this with big games, but most average in the 150k-350k bracket, with recently reported Kayo figures included going well above this to near 500k in 2022/2023.

Nine numbers have not grown much over the last few years and seem to be in a stable phase or small decline. Nine televises games on its main channel in NSW and QLD and sometimes in Melbourne when the Storm are playing, and uses its alternate channel GEM to televise into the other states.

With Nine no longer having exclusive rights to free-to-air NRL games other than State of Origin and the Grand Final, both Foxtel and Nine are broadcasting the same NRL games, which has resulted in tensions between the media networks and the NRL in an ongoing ratings war. In recent years, Foxtel has taken a large share of the viewers from Nine, and this will definitely be an issue for the next TV negotiations if this trend continues.

Prior to Kayo, the prime-time Friday night game rugby league figures, including both Foxtel and Nine, usually totalled around 700k-1m total nationally. AFL is usually around 700k-1.3m.

On the return game for the NRL after the virus, the Brisbane vs Parramatta game had a national audience of 1.271 million compared to the AFL's opening game of 1.6 million for the Richmond vs Collingwood game in 2020.

The extra reach into Perth and Adelaide, and bigger numbers in Melbourne, give the AFL an advantage over the NRL in the ratings war. The regional numbers are quite close between the two codes.

AFL goes live into the main channel on Channel Seven in most states, as they are played nationally, and also goes live into Foxtel via its own channel on FOX Sports.

Fundamentally, extending television deals during the middle of a pandemic was a poor decision, and the responsibility for this error lies with Chairman Peter V'landys. The fact that Foxtel's numbers have not been advertised by the NRL tells you the figures are poor or average at best. You can be certain that the AFL were boastful when the next television deals were signed, which they did in late 2022, with the biggest sports media deal ever in Australian sporting history.

The game is now locked in with media deals until 2027, and while Kayo numbers may increase with more subscription numbers, I don't see a lot of new growth for the code, but they could still perform strongly with its existing base.

Longer term, the game needs to get a better balance between profit, growth and keeping fans happy with quality of content.

2027 is still quite a few years away, so the NRL really need to review where it is in the market at present and decide what direction it intends on moving forward before negotiations begin for the next television deals.

The key things are:
- How many NRL teams – 17 or 18?
- Grow the capital city market audience in Melbourne, Adelaide and Perth.
- Strategically place a new franchise in the Metro 5 market such as Perth or Adelaide.
- Grow more in non-heartland areas.
- How to grow the game in heartland regions.

- Grow the game more in NZ and international markets.
- Investigate options with new streaming platforms to grow the sport such as Amazon,
- Paramount, Netflix, and others.
- Build more free-to-air games back into the next deals.
- Should the media rights include more exclusive games for media partners rather than sharing games, which is causing division and tension between media companies?
- Have a Saturday night game on free-to-air across the country. Most Saturday night games are rating around 200k-400k on Foxtel/Kayo for the NRL. The AFL Saturday night games on both free-to-air and Foxtel are normally rated between 600k to 800k.
- Promote the international game, competitions and tours and provide prime-time coverage. Reduce NRL games and replace with more international games.
- More quality and less quantity with schedule. The NRL season can often lose energy and interest mid-year with too many games.
- Understand what fans want from media outlets.
- Consider multiple media outlets to keep more buyers interested in the rights negotiations, which will create more supply and demand.
- Grow the digital department.
- Ensure quality content from media outlets.
- Look at alternative media to Nine and Foxtel. Many fans are stale with regard to long-time media outlets, which at times often make the game more about themselves than the game.

Extending the deals in the middle of a pandemic may have given financial security to the NRL for the short term, but it was not the best for the code financially or to grow the game more. Television money is the code's major cashline, but executives need to see it as not just cash flow but the vehicle to grow and expand the game with. They now have a few years to decide what they want, in an ever-changing media landscape.

MEDIA

RUGBY LEAGUE IS one of Australia's highest-rating programs, and with that comes much attention from the media, both through written and television and radio/podcasts formats. While the game is played on the field, it attracts enormous coverage off the field, for many of the wrong reasons.

The game has the most saturated coverage in the history of the code, with some excellent independent and major sites that provide superb coverage for the modern game, but there is still an ugly side to the media's coverage of the game today from the legacy media.

The game and players are to blame for a lot of problems with the media in more recent times, but the media are also relentless in their attacks on the game and its players and continue to run corporate agendas that deceive the fans and the greater public.

No other Australian sport has the intense media coverage that rugby league has. The Sydney-centric gossip newspapers operate very similarly to the English tabloids, and not even AFL or cricket get the negative press that rugby league receives.

When the game was halted due to the Covid virus in 2020, rugby league's partners attacked the game relentlessly in the media, as well as each other, to decrease the value of the next television deal rights. Rugby league's supposed partners were using their usual tricks to attack the game with a selfish and self serving manner. Nine even purchased the Super Rugby and international media rights from Rugby Australia and placed a bid for the AFL rights in late 2022.

Rugby league leaders should be having meetings directly with our media partners leader such as Mike Sneesby at Nine and Patrick Delaney at Foxtel and News Corp management about the culture and conduct of their businesses in often bombarding rugby league, and how their English tabloids type behaviour is causing serious damage to the code's reputation and losing the respect of many followers of the code.

Peter V'landys and the NRL CEO should be pushing for informal agreements with our media partners about respecting the code and staying away from trash journalism that looks for click bait hits, and presenting the game in an honest and fair manner.

If players, clubs or the NRL behave in an unethical manner, then they should face the consequences, including reports from the various media outlets.

An MOU code of conduct between stakeholders and representatives would also be a good idea to help stop some of the garbage that has become all too common in the digital age. Media deals should possibly also include legal clauses that encourage both parties to work together, and clear guidelines about negative press and attacks on each party.

If the game's partners cannot agree to do this, then the game needs to have some serious thoughts about if they are the right people and companies we want our game to be involved with long term, because sometimes the money is not worth the hassle with some partnerships.

Integrity has to be the foundation for the game both from within and with key stakeholders such as the media networks, and if there is no trust or loyalty between the parties, then the game must destroy those relationships and build new alliances, even if that means short-term pain.

Whilst rugby league is heavily dependent on cash from Nine and Foxtel, both media networks are even more dependent on the NRL and rugby league being shown on these networks. Foxtel and Kayo would see a surge in cancelled subscribers if the NRL walked away, and Nine would lose droves of supporters and sponsors should it not televise the code. The game needs to take a far sterner stance with its supposed media partners and realise it holds great leverage and power over both media parties, despite the poor treatment from both entities since the NRL era started in 1998. Millions of NRL supporters across Australia cannot be easily replaced by another sport for either network when the AFL is also locked into long-term media deals, including with Foxtel. Financially, it would be a disaster for either media partner if the NRL walked away, and no sweet talk could disguise this.

The NRL needs to start talking the language that both Foxtel and Nine understand, rather than the appeasement and devalued rights deals from Peter V'Landys seen in recent years. 300k cancelled Foxtel subscriptions and 250k cancelled Kayo subscriptions is language Foxtel executives understand. No Thursday or Friday night NRL football and ten million people not watching the State of Origin series on Nine is language Nine executives understand!

Rugby league leaders need to get serious about the agendas, betrayal and trash reporting the code has seen for far too long from its media partners. It holds great power and must be clear on what it will and will not stand for and where the line is drawn with its partnerships.

If we don't have total commitment, ethics, trust and loyalty, the code must walk away and forge new alliances and relationships.

COUNTRY RUGBY LEAGUE AND GRASSROOTS

COUNTRY RUGBY LEAGUE and grassroots are critical to the game's future, and, as outlined in Chapter 2, both these fundamental functions of the game need major work to revitalise the heart and soul of the game in regional areas and grassroots to protect the game's future and ensure longevity and strength for the code.

The game faces serious challenges both from within and externally from AFL and other sports and needs to get its own house in order and start running the amateur side of the game with far more professionalism, integrity, quality, higher standards and passion to take the game forward and ensure its future.

The code needs to make urgent changes at the community level if it wishes to change the current direction, and, for this to occur, it needs the right models, people, systems, resources, middle management, leadership and ethics driving the game forward.

In country rugby league across NSW and QLD and in other interstate leagues, the competitions are spread across the states into each area's own region or zone, with their own competitions. The quality of the delivery of the competitions varies greatly across the country areas and metropolitan zones. Some people have told me how strong bush footy is in North QLD, while other regions such as North West NSW or the Riverina have told me of the decline in their respective clubs and competitions from previous times.

So, across the country leagues, we have mixed results of healthy and poor competitions in terms of the delivery, numbers and quality of rugby league in regional zones. This can be measured from a number of metrics, including player numbers, number of teams, referee numbers, filling four grades, systems, governance, committee members, sponsorship, crowds, off-field incidents, finances, marketing, and general overall health of each league.

A common barometer for any successfully run zone or region is always the fruits and results.

For there to be any successful and well-run competition or zone, it needs quality off-field leadership and systems through leadership and committee members at the regional level plus those involved with the clubs. Any time this leadership is not present, we have a sharp and rapid decline in the quality of these competitions, which has been a common occurrence in country and grassroots competitions over the last 20-plus years. As mentioned earlier, everything rises and falls on leadership, and the right people are our most valuable asset, from grassroots to the NRL.

One can also not be too critical of the amateur game, as many involved volunteer their time for the love of their country clubs, local communities and love for rugby league on top of personal and professional commitments outside of the game.

Many of the silent heroes involved in rugby league across Australia have carried the game on their shoulders with limited or no support from the NRL, and without them, we would not have grassroots and country rugby league being played and a long proud historical tradition of bush footy.

The professional head office of the game has been invisible and provided little or no help to the game in the bush, where our great rival, the AFL, has been busy planning and executing an aggressive grassroots and regional expansion of their game, especially in NSW and QLD traditional rugby league heartland markets, on top of their bread and butter traditional core markets in the other five states.

The NRL will shout loudly and defend their involvement, activity and commitment to the amateur game, but everything is a matter of opinion and only results are real! Everything else is just talk.

The game may have strategic plans and management to look after these functions, but the results speak loudest, and for country rugby league, the results have been very poor.

CRL merged with the NSWRL recently, but this organisation merger has resulted in little impact or improvement to the game since the merger took place, in late 2019.

For rugby league to make the necessary changes to country rugby league, a whole new game approach is required that brings far stronger leadership and professionalism to drive the domestic game.

Current Model – Country Rugby League

Rugby league in the bush is basically run by committees across each competition or zone in Australia, with the core competitions being played coming from NSW and QLD. Each region's committee will be made up of an elected group. Nominated members come from each club in the zone, usually filling the roles of any committee something like this:

President
Deputy
Treasurer
Competition organiser
Media
Other committee members

These elected members are usually a representation from different clubs and oversee and manage the local leagues, providing direction and organisation for each league. The committee and clubs take responsibility for all decisions and direction of each zone. The QRL, NSWRL or NRL will generally only step in should there be a serious matter like misconduct, violence or something that may have a negative impact on the integrity or reputation of the sport. The governing bodies may also occasionally support junior clinics or player visits to help the leagues.

As stated, these are volunteer members who do their best in running the leagues, and for the most part, do a great job and are passionate rugby league supporters, with limited support or financial assistance from the NRL. But they are now competing against a billion-dollar AFL machine throwing huge resources and money to dominate the national sporting market and building infrastructure that destroys its competitors.

As Bob Dylan said, *The times they are a-changin',* in his famous song in the 1960s, and rugby league must get its own house in order to ensure the future of the game.

Rugby league is currently running and managing country rugby league with an amateur model, as there has never been any other option other than our great volunteers serving the great game.

The downside of running the game with the current model has created a number of trends and issues that are holding the game back from healthier and better leagues.

Let's look at the issues with running the game with the current amateur model. As mentioned, whilst some competitions may be running quite well if there is a reasonably mature and strong committee, this is not always the case in many regions.

Issues with current model – bottom-up approach

- Lack of committee members to manage and drive league
- Insufficient skills, knowledge and leadership capabilities to manage a league

- Conflicts of interest
- No independence
- Enforcing standards across leagues
- Code of conduct enforcement
- Time, money and resources
- Inconsistent decisions
- Difficult to plan succession
- Executive decision-making power
- No support for finance, PR, marketing, legal, sponsorship
- Refereeing support and voice

These are just a few of the issues identified that many of the zones across Australia face with every season and have done for many years.

Many voices shout loudly about how times have changed and that regional towns have no jobs, which is often false, or there is so much more entertainment or a million other reasons, but rugby league's main focus should be running the code to the best of its capabilities.

The wind will blow on your back sometimes and sometimes it will blow against you, but the set of the sails will determine the direction and destination. The game needs to set a sail that will represent the long-term health and wellbeing of the code well.

New model of management – top-down approach

The game needs to transfer existing clubs, committees, and local competitions to a more polished and professional domestic game model at the lower level. The game needs all stakeholders to work together in complete harmony for this to be achieved. All stakeholders are vitally important, and without all working in a cohesive manner, it cannot move forward.

The old model that currently exists operates from a bottom-up approach, with clubs and committees driving each league/zone, but this also causes challenges, with limited resources and capability challenges to run professional leagues.

The new model should operate from a top-down approach that gives the zones and clubs much needed professionalism, leadership, capabilities and resources to drive the game forward, rather than volunteers having to carry the whole load, but at the same time giving them a strong voice and decision making in supporting the local leagues.

The NRL, NSWRL, QRL or interstate bodies would now appoint newly created positions of operational managers to oversee each league zone or group competition and run the day-to-day operations for each league in a more professional way to coordinate the leagues. These roles would be required to manage the leagues, work with clubs and committees, chair board meetings, organise training and school visits, have executive delegation power when needed to resolve issues, maintain the integrity of the league and also leverage resources from NRL HQ and the state bodies for support with finances, sponsorship, systems, training, social media, news and television reports with local media and marketing. It would be their responsibility to ensure the group or zone was well run and represented the game with the right values and ethics.

The operational managers would be senior roles filled only by candidates with extensive operational and management experiences and who have no conflicts of interest. These would be high-paying roles that would need expertise in leadership, operations, strategic planning, legal, financial management, human resources, communication, working and influencing stakeholders, and marketing, and could come from a background outside of rugby league but have the ability to understand the culture, game and stakeholders quickly.

The game could look at an operational manager to manage a group zone or even look at having two operational managers for larger zones, or have operational managers working together, with admin support and sharing resources for competitions that border on each other. The committee members and clubs would all remain, and committees would still have a strong voice in how each league should be run, and would work closely with the operational manager to manage each league and ensure integrity and that rules and standards are upheld and that the game must come first, to ensure rugby league stays a strong sport.

Once the operational manager is in place and working closely with the clubs and committees in each region, now let's look at some other improvements the operational leader must drive to ensure more integrity and professionalism.

Code of conduct

The whole game would be reset with a new code of conduct for all players, clubs and fans that enforces the image, behaviour and culture the game wants to obtain, and one that respects all involved in the game. The game has a diverse stakeholder base from the young to the old and both genders, and we must all work together to represent the game well.

Too many incidents in recent seasons have occurred in bush footy that have done major damage to the code's reputation within local communities. The game needs to take responsibility and set the standards of the behaviour and image we aspire to reach. Fighting, violence, drunkenness at games, swearing, and clubs stealing players from each other is not the culture or reputation the game needs and must be weeded out.

The code of conduct needs to be implemented and enforced and made clear to all clubs and players that it is each one's responsibility to uphold and adhere to the code. Failure to do so will be dealt with in terms of the offence committed, but the game's number one goal is upholding the reputation and image of the game, well before winning a local premiership or on-field results.

The foundation must be concrete and that can only come from a strong base of values and ethics from the code of conduct that all clubs, players and fans must follow.

Many workplaces such as mining and manufacturing have a zero safety policy to ensure safety and wellbeing in the workplace for all staff and customers. Rugby league needs to apply the same concept with the code of conduct to country rugby league and grassroots to ensure the integrity and future of the code.

An operating manual/guideline would be designed and all clubs and players would have to agree to and adhere to the rules and code of conduct to be able to enter, play and remain in any competition each new season. Clubs and players breaching the code of conduct would be penalised, with deduction of points, suspension, expulsion, players not being allowed to play for other clubs in other regions, fines and removal of funding and support until issues were resolved.

Clubs driving culture change

The operational manager will work closely with each club and committee to ensure that the code of conduct is understood by all clubs and players, and establish a culture where clubs drive the culture change on the ground to improve the behaviour and reputation of the game.

Clubs will train players on the code of conduct and all will be made aware that the operations manager and NSWRL/QLDRL state leagues have the power to deduct points and issue other penalties, should clubs and players not adhere to the new guidelines in the code of conduct.

Operating guidelines agreements should be mandatory for clubs to be a part of a local competition, providing clear guidelines for standards, rules, responsibilities and behaviours that must be upheld to remain a member of any competition.

The clubs must take responsibility and ownership for the running of their clubs and players, as well as managing fans with adequate security and upholding the integrity of the sport.

Metrics

One of the reasons the game has entered Stage 4 and even Stage 5 for many zones in country rugby league is not having a good set of numbers that can read the health, wellbeing and future trends of any organisation. A good set of numbers and metrics can also be the best warning against decline and that the organisation is heading in the wrong direction.

With stronger regional management and a good set of numbers, the game would have been in a far stronger position to see some prior warning signs and take proactive action early, rather than let the game continue down the long road of decline. Metrics will allow far better planning and making better decisions when numbers are flashing red and signalling something is wrong.

What are some of the numbers the game needs to ensure for healthy competition in bush rugby league?

- Player numbers for each grade
- Junior numbers
- Committee members nominated
- Coaching numbers
- Code of conduct enforcement
- Code of conduct breach numbers
- Player behaviour – number of incidents
- Training numbers
- Crowd numbers
- Social media numbers
- Performance of other codes – AFL, rugby union, soccer and basketball
- Whether clubs can fulfill every game
- Referee numbers
- How leagues should be zoned
- Financial numbers of each club
- Canteen requirements of each club
- Marketing requirement each week
- Media requirement each week

- Media and Google numbers
- Bills that need to be paid
- Costs to run clubs
- Sponsorship numbers
- Ground maintenance – fields etc. meeting standards
- Alcohol issues
- Fan behaviour
- Security needs for games
- Accessories – whether clubs have equipment to play each game
- Transport to get to games – buses, cars, etc.
- Government grants
- Junior league support
- Inventory
- Manpower
- Accounts
- Forecasts – numbers, crowds, canteen, toilets etc.
- Variance reports
- Equipment
- Media – newspaper and local TV submissions
- Streaming games
- Insurance requirements

A set of these numbers as an example or designed how zones wish will require work, but the discipline and maintenance of these metrics will enable the game to take charge and drive the game in a far more professional manner that enables the sport to be far more proactive than reactive.

If we do see negative numbers that provide warnings about issues such as low playing numbers, multiple code of conduct breaches for fighting and violence at games, now, through the operational manager and committees, members at clubs can work closely and settle matters much quicker with decisive action, or put plans in place to find solutions to the problems.

Seeing low player numbers or low committee member numbers is a warning for the game that there is a problem that needs to be fixed.

Just being aware of those metrics is a giant step forward for the game. It makes the sport acutely aware of issues and the health of the code, and with greater awareness then comes understanding.

In the biblical Proverbs, Solomon was famous for saying, *Wisdom is the principal thing; therefore get wisdom: and with all thy getting, get understanding.*

A good set of metrics is one of the most important changes that needs to be driven from the operational manager down to the committee and clubs, and should be linked with any funding or support from the NRL or state bodies.

Conflicts of interest

One of the biggest problems I hear from country rugby league folks is that conflicts of interest continue to damage the game's reputation, brand and progress. Many clubs have clubs and committees making decisions for country rugby league where there are clear conflicts of interest when making key sensitive decisions, and sometimes also self interest and the pressures of dealing closely with folks who they have had a long association with. Often the clubs and committees have no other option or resources to defer the decision to.

Conflicts have been seen in player behaviour penalties, disciplining players, ethics of clubs, clubs doing damage to rugby league and other matters. The game must take a new and fresh approach and leave all sensitive decisions involving stakeholders to the operational manager or the state bodies to make any independent decision which has the possibility to damage the game's reputation, image or ethics. The old model has forced many poor decisions to be made, as committees and clubs were left to shoulder responsibility, with no other mechanism or resources to provide support or direction.

The operational manager can now take executive control of sensitive issues and should be totally independent on major decisions, with full responsibility.

Synergistic media plan

Media strategies in bush footy rarely get discussed, but it is one of the most underrated factors in keeping bush footy strong and getting news out to fans. With the decline in regional network resources such as newspapers and many regional news services like Prime News, WIN and NBN now screened from larger cities, it is important the game has a strong media plan to reach country news outlets across Australia and to market and grow their local leagues.

The game and communities need the attention. The players and clubs all love to read, watch and hear about what's going on with their local bush footy competition. It drives clubs and local communities, and one should not underrate the energy and pride it brings to clubs and towns. It is vitally important to the game.

Many clubs have been left to organise this function and generally have someone involved who writes or provides information to local newspapers or regional media networks such as Prime, WIN, or NBN, which generally provide some local games highlights and interviews on the local news, though many clubs do not have anyone working with the media outlets and are now often missing out on key exposure for the clubs and game.

For this to improve, the game can bring far more professionalism to its media strategy for both newspapers and regional news, to much higher standards.

The NRL or state leagues should utilise and fund media staff and freelancers from HQ and the state bodies to support the country rugby league structure, with a much more professional and modern media look for all clubs, and have a flow of stories going out every week and a media plan to cover the footy season.

Let's look at what needs to be done by the media staff:

- Update all clubs' media.
- Update club branding.
- Give all clubs websites and social media. (Some already have this, some don't.)
- Have group and zone websites and social media.
- Have delegated articles going out for each club and region to local newspapers.
- Work with Prime, NBN and WIN to have the best stories for the game and highlights shown weekly on local news.
- Leverage support for clubs from the NRL media department to support the game with media and articles.
- NRL fund freelancers to support clubs with marketing and media plans.
- Have clear guidelines for media requirements for each club that supports and grows the game, upholds the game's image and provides quality content and news to local communities.
- Televise regular season matches, finals and grand finals with media or streaming services on YouTube and social media.

With a sharper and focused media and marketing strategy the game will be talked about, read about and watched more, which is a win-win for the game, clubs and the communities.

Women

One of the better new modern additions to rugby league has been the expansion and inclusion of women's tag rugby league in the men's game day program for country rugby league. It has been a welcome addition to the code. Women have always played an incredibly important role in rugby league through volunteering, working in canteens, as committee members, and being a mum for players and coaches. The mothers involved in the game should never be underestimated. Their contribution and importance to the health of the game, especially in regional areas, is critical.

The AFL has long had a historical relationship in regional areas between the football and netball codes, and the mixing of both codes brings a unique community vibe to their competitions that rugby league has missed out on. This goes far beyond just a footy game. The camaraderie and pride it brings to their respective sports, towns and communities is a great asset to their leagues.

Rugby union has long been known to be a very social game, where many fans, including females, attend games in the bush just for the social side. The atmosphere has a reputation as a place to meet and socialise with people and also get some weekend entertainment whilst watching the rugby.

Country rugby league regions also need these social interactions between genders, and rugby league needs to look to promote more involvement and social interaction with women in rugby league, both on and off the field.

Bringing in ladies' Oz tag was a great step for the women's game, also bringing more women into the clubs and communities of rugby league. But we should not stop there.

Some more ways the game could bring women into rugby league:
- Mandatory female member on each RL committee
- Ladies' day and balls every year for each club
- More social events from clubs that involve women
- Touch football being involved in the code with female teams
- Women's full contact rugby league to follow Oz tag
- Create an environment that women will want to be involved with
- Behavioural guidelines that attract women and families to be involved with the game
- Look to build a relationship with netball clubs like we see in the southern states

These are just a few ideas, but one should not underestimate the importance of females in the game and the social importance for both the code and communities. The code should be definite about involving and attracting more women for the leagues.

U19s

Many kids playing the game will leave the game from around ages 16-19, and possibly younger, for a variety of reasons such as work, school, leaving town, university, other interests, other commitments, travel, being too small, not enjoying the game anymore or many other reasons.

Whatever the reason, rugby league in the bush and the game itself needs to fight as hard as it can to keep young people involved and make the transition to play as easy as possible from juniors to seniors. Many will leave, but many will also go from juniors to seniors and be integral members of football clubs for many years after.

One of the main times junior players leave the code is after finishing u18s and not moving to the senior ranks. Some players at around 17 and 18 are not mentally or physically ready to play seniors and just enjoy playing with their school mates and the social side of the game that comes with playing.

Many players in the bush stop at this stage. Some go and play over in rugby union juniors, where the age groups are usually under 19s, and this allows them to continue playing with their mates and similar age groups. Some will argue having a u19s age group could also take players out of the senior ranks, but the juniors are the lifeline of the game and we need to fight as hard as we can and make the transition for juniors to seniors as easy as possible.

U19s across all leagues should be seriously considered, and research should look into the pros and cons of 18s v 19s or even 20s age competitions. It does not gain much attention, but the age bracket is a big matter for both juniors and senior rugby league, and the proper due diligence should be done to explore what is best for the whole game. My personal view, after witnessing this up close as a former bush player and fan, is the under 19s is a must if it can be delivered across the game.

Anything that keeps more players playing is great for the game, no matter what level.

TOUCH FOOTBALL

TOUCH IS ONE of the nation's most popular sports across all age groups, with both sexes regularly participating across Australia on weeknights and weekends. The game has its origin and rules in rugby league, with the noted difference of no tackles and no kicking. Touch Football Australia is the governing body of the sport, which now has an affiliation link with the NRL.

The NRL see touch football as an integral part for the growth of the code, not just the traditional full contact side of the game we all call rugby league. The NRL understands that the high contact and more physical side of the game is not for everyone and that it is still very important to keep those not interested or able to play full contact involved with the code. Rugby league now has many options outside the full contact model, such as touch, Oz tag and disability rugby league, which is great for a diverse range of stakeholders and has been one of the code's modern success stories.

Up until 2019, touch football had integrated a semi-professional league, with both female and male touch NRL teams, which was well received in raising the awareness and profile of touch football for both male and female players. The competition was halted in 2020 due to Covid and has not recommenced.

The NRL touch football teams played curtain raisers before the main NRL games and it was a great opportunity for touch players to travel, play in front of crowds, experience big stadiums and enjoy the higher profile from leveraging off the NRL competition.

Country rugby league and the whole game should look at integrating touch football, Oz tag and disability RL more into country rugby league and within each club and zone.

The integration of touch, Oz tag and disability rugby league is a win-win for all parties if implemented correctly. It is positive and provides wider exposure and involvement for the code, increases female participation and involvement, supports more youth of both genders playing the game and gets them away from social media and modern digital distractions. It would promote bigger crowds and provide a vehicle that promotes stronger communities, with a fantastic opportunity for healthy sports participation and social interaction.

With many clubs struggling in the bush, touch, Oz tag and disability RL would be great boosters for communities and the whole game, plus enabling the game to leverage off all its key stakeholder base and strengthen the game as a whole.

The NRL has done a good job of bringing the women's Oz tag and touch football into the game. Now is a great time to further this with more integration into country rugby league and the whole game-day experience.

GRASSROOTS

AFTER COVID, THE NRL under V'landys and Andrew Abdo's leadership has been hard at work getting the finances of the game in order. The game has since made major changes to the running of the sport, including massive changes to NRL HQ and potentially other bodies involved with the game.

With some fiscal cuts being conducted in recent times after Covid, where does this leave the grassroots side of the game long term? Whilst the players were guaranteed a large share of their money during and post the virus, other stakeholders were in the grey on what their financial outcomes would be, despite the guarantees of the NRL.

A fundamental difference of significance is how the grassroots should be developed and run. Some believe it should continue out of the NRL HQ through funding of the state bodies, whilst others believe it should be run through each NRL club, which is given a catchment region to care for.

Another question is: What is happening in non-heartland areas to grow participation and code awareness?

The average NRL salary is reported to be $400k today, yet much of the game's income is not reinvested back into key senior and middle management roles for both grassroots and country rugby league. What is a better investment for the code – five development officers on $80k per year to drive the grassroots game in heartland or interstate, 1/2 Country Operation Managers paid $150k/200k per year to lead and manage regional zones, or more money to players and clubs? What gives the best return on investment?

Many involved within grassroots are annoyed that the NRL and the NRL clubs only worry about pathways and taking the best young talent available and not long-term viability for the game for players at all levels of any capability, when only very few players reach the top-level NRL. The focus should be more about enjoyment and reputation than elite player pathways.

Former Australian representative Jamie Lyon is a perfect example. He was a junior star for the Wee Waa Panthers and was signed up with the Parramatta Eels at 16. Now we no longer have a Wee Waa team in Group 4 rugby league in NSW. The code took the Panthers best up-and-coming player and got nothing in return and are now dead as a club. This is a common theme across country rugby league, where NRL clubs take the best talent early and yet give nothing back to the clubs or zones, and the sport now pays heavy consequences for such decisions.

The grassroots side of the game has been facing enormous challenges in recent times from other sports and forms of entertainment. The AFL Auskick program has become the best implemented winter grassroots sports program in Australian sports history, and rugby league also faces new challenges from basketball, with the NBA influencing many of today's youth.

The best outcome, no matter who is in charge or what structure we have, is one that represents the game the very best, which provides great enjoyment to kids and parents, has great delivery and outcomes, is fun for all involved, provides an opportunity for all shapes, sizes and capabilities to play, and leaves kids and teenagers with fond memories of the game and who hopefully will last a lifetime as fans of the sport.

Statistics released by the NRL say the game is growing, but it is highly debatable on how this is actually being measured, with nearly all professional sports in Australia glossing their figures to make them look better for sponsorship and government funding. Figures can now include anything from a school visit, an online program or training camp. which are not the same as signed registered junior players who play each weekend.

Numbers at the grassroots level are also glossed up, with women's and other forms of football such as touch football often included in the contact figures. The women's game is very new and is starting from a base point, and, as expected, their numbers are in a phase of rapid growth compared to the boys' groups, whose figures are possibly in decline. This makes the total figures look better than they really are.

Like country rugby league, we have seen a decline in grassroots over the last 2 decades in many regions, and much hard work and maintenance is required to turn this around and make the grassroots vibrant and strong again.

Many of the core issues with the grassroots game are the same issues that are hurting country rugby league and can certainly be applied to improve grassroots.

Some key grassroots issues are:
- Leadership
- Culture
- Behavioural issues
- Code of conduct
- Resources
- Funding – costs to play/insurance
- Weight age groups
- Management
- Ethics
- The loss of white and smaller players due to a variety of factors
- Polynesian kids dominating and white players' flight

- A model focused on elite pathways rather than enjoyment and fun

The NRL has long believed that it can possibly fund its way out to improve both grassroots and country rugby league. This philosophy is totally false and no amount of money will fix the structural issues within the game at the grassroots levels. It will take hard work with heart and soul to reinvigorate the grassroots game.

The NRL needs to stop focusing on the results and effects and start paying more attention to what they are doing and how they are doing things.

Bill Walsh, the famous San Francisco 49ers' head coach said the score will take care of itself, and that's the attitude rugby league needs to take with reinvigorating the code at the grassroots level.

Let's focus on what we are doing, how we are doing it, what we can give and how we can make the game an enjoyable experience for all to be involved in.

Here are some brief key points to improve grassroots on top of the points outlined to improve country rugby league, which can also apply to grassroots.

Leadership

Leadership has been a common theme throughout this book, but again, it is the foundation to a strong sporting organisation. Without it at the core, the game will continue to decline at the lower levels of the sport.

Strong leadership sets the vision and standards for grassroots, upholds the integrity of the game and is on top of issues when they become present.

Leadership that drives the sport forward and that has ownership of regions, will ensure strong and vibrant competitions with good numbers.

Leadership must uphold the reputation of the game for all involved and make the game an enjoyable experience.

Culture

Parents fighting, players fighting, brawls, swearing, abuse, and referee attacks have become all too common with the underage game and this needs to be stopped immediately.

The grassroots game has a poor culture and needs a drastic makeover. One of the reasons for this has been the lack of leadership from the NRL and state bodies in driving and enforcing standards at the lower levels.

Many parents do not want their kids involved with the sport, and for good reason, with some of the atrocious behaviour we have seen in recent times.

Culture is nothing more than what we do and what we stand for!

Like Country Rugby League, the NRL needs a whole new approach to enforcing the code of conduct and behaviour. Just like a worksafe site with a zero safety policy, the game needs to enforce zero behaviour policies for players and parents to ensure the image of the sport is upheld. This is grassroots with young kids playing and should be all about fun and enjoyment and not the ugly things we see too often on the sideline.

Code of conduct

What behaviour and actions the game no longer accepts must be enforced through the code of conduct, which will be the Bible for enforcing the rule of law and behaviour across the game. Players and parents can only be allowed to play after being educated and becoming aware of the code of conduct and their responsibilities to uphold the code.

Without the rule of law, we have the Wild West, where we have seen many ugly incidents in recent times across grassroots.

The code of conduct must be designed to stamp out bad behaviour and enforce the image and reputation of the game, no matter how good a player may or may not be, and this applies to families and spectators as well.

Genghis Khan and Toussaint Louverture were both known for utilising shocking and explicit rules to enforce the culture and behavior they wanted. The Japanese Bushido Code is one of the world's most famous set of principles and practices to enforce a culture.

Cultures tend to reflect the values of leaders and are often an extension of the leader's personality in any organisation.

Resources

In recent times, players and clubs have taken a large share of the game's total revenue. Some believe this to be fine, as the clubs and players bring in the most revenue; some argue the other side: that the clubs and players are taking too much money, and not enough is being provided to the grassroots.

More money and resourcing is needed for grassroots, but how that is spent is key. I spoke about how in the country rugby league we have a bottom-down approach, and the same is true for the grassroots. Committees, parents and volunteers are doing their best to run the game in each zone and region across the country but facing stiff competition, often with more firepower, professionalism and resources.

The game needs resources in key leadership roles to drive grassroots zones and regions. These roles, just like the operational manager position for country zones, will be responsible for leadership, strategy, code of conduct, upholding image and reputation, ensuring a positive playing experience and other managerial duties.

Funding – costs to play/insurance

The financial cost to play the game and insurance costs to both clubs and players is one of the biggest issues on the ground in grassroots. The prices can range from $60 at the base age to around $350 for senior players. This is a large cost for both clubs and players, and the NRL needs to do more to offset some of these costs.

Many involved with the game in grassroots are pleading with the NRL to take some of the burden off clubs and parents for these costs.

Enormous money in recent times has gone to clubs and players, and some of this needs to be reallocated to the lower levels of the game to ensure the game's future.

Weight age groups

In recent years, the game has been dominated by Polynesian kids in the grassroots format, with these Pacific Island kids being much bigger and stronger than children of the same age, which has caused many kids to stop playing or not want to play.

This unfair advantage is hurting all parties, and no one is to blame. But boundaries need to be in place to ensure the code can be played by kids of any background or size. Weight age groups have been implemented in NZ and this should also be the case in Australia. This ensures the health and wellbeing for all players and creates a better environment for kids to want to play the game.

NZ junior rugby union already has done much of the due diligence, and rugby league should jump on the back of what they have done, to implement age and weight classes for grassroots football. Senior management should oversee any changes within the group to ensure fairness and enjoyment playing the game. The grassroots format focus should be about making the game as enjoyable, safe and friendly as possible for all players, regardless of their age, shape, size or capability.

Rugby league has a diverse background of people who play the sport, but if we don't implement weight age groups, we will lose this diversity, which also is a representation of society, and have only Polynesian kids playing the game. The game is seeing a surge of white flight from playing the game and this is now also seen in the NRL, with 46% of players coming from Pasifika in 2018, up from just 9% in 1998 and looking to be only going higher each year. The Pasifika represent only about 1.5% of Australia's total population and yet we are now moving towards more than half of the NRL players being from Pasifika ancestry. White flight could have disastrous long-term consequences for grassroots' future, national interest and commercial deals, and steps must be taken urgently to ensure the code is represented by all of society.

Without weight age groups, we will lose the next little Caucasian and Aboriginal players, the future Allan Langers, Geoff Tooveys, Preston Campbells, Jonathan Thurstons, Billy Slaters and many more.

Current NRL star Nathan Cleary, who spent some of his junior years in NZ, stated recently that if there were no weight and age groups in NZ, he would have quit the sport.

Weight and age categories are essential and needed urgently for all of grassroots football and to ensure we have a diverse set of demographics playing the sport, not just Polynesians but one that reflects society.

MIDDLE MANAGEMENT

WHILE MOST ATTENTION from the media for off-field matters goes directly to Peter V'landys, the NRL CEO Andrew Abdo, ARLC Commissioners or senior management within the game, often overlooked are roles that have some of the most importance and significance – the middle management roles across the game.

These roles are varied and can be involved in country rugby league or grassroots. A key financial role, a key marketing position or a senior professional role in HQ or the state bodies are just some examples of middle management roles within the game.

One of the major reasons AFL has become the number one sporting code in Australia is due to the capabilities and resourcing of their middle management roles.

Middle management has driven Auskick nationwide implementation and participation across Australia. Their sponsorship and government funding is the largest in the country. Regional country leagues are of better quality and standard than other sports. These are just a few examples of the importance of strong middle management.

For any organisation to be successful, there needs to be a blending on the ground between middle managers and the senior management. The middle managers have the knowledge, awareness and details on the ground; the senior management have the power to execute decisions.

Middle managers often know problems of downward or upward trends long before any other employees in an organisation. A farmer knows the condition of the land and livestock long before any politician in Canberra starts discussing it, a salesman knows the trends of sales and profits on the ground long before senior management discuss potential profits or losses, police know the behaviour of kids in towns/cities long before media start raising the issue about behaviour and crime in specific zones.

Knowledge and power need to work together, not against each other for optimal results. Far too often in organisations, the senior leadership will not listen to the middle managers when they are raising concerns about matters inside the business. But high quality leaders should listen and value the knowledge and awareness of the middle managers on the ground to make sound decisions. The pain it can save is immeasurable to any organisation, and many times, leaders have had to learn some bitter lessons.

If rugby league had had stronger middle management over the last 2 decades, it could have identified many of the downward trends within the game and made amendments to rectify the numerous problems, such as country rugby league, grassroots, codes of conduct, media, finances, culture, declining player numbers, and governance, which were all lacking strong middle management, who, if they had the knowledge and awareness to raise these issues with senior management long before they became larger issues, may have stopped or limited these problems from becoming far bigger issues.

More leadership equals more horsepower, and rugby league needs to build the whole game with higher quality middle management, who bring the right experience, knowledge, character, confidence and capabilities that will drive the game forward and be the sounding board for senior management to identify upward and downward trends within the game that may or may not be future concerns.

Middle management on the ground with strong knowledge and awareness of the game, working together with senior management who have executive power, is real synergy, which the game needs to see much more of.

NRL PRODUCT

RUGBY LEAGUE IS in the entertainment business, not the sporting business, as many believe, but somewhere over the last 10-20 years, the game has lost its compass and awareness about what made rugby league great in the first place and what resonated with fans from all walks of life.

The current game is anchored down by bureaucratic processes from HQ, the search for perfection that does not exist, with technology, silly new rules introduced, coaches' overextension and influence for selfish gain, poor game models that do not improve the game, continual video referee interference and a lack of courage and acute awareness from senior management to show some backbone and do what is right for the game and fans against biased internal stakeholders and aggressive media.

The players today are bigger, stronger, fitter and faster than ever before in the history of the game, but this does not equate to a better product, football game or entertainment and game experience for fans.

Bigger, stronger, fitter and faster athletes and modern rules have made the current product dull and boring to many. Nearly every team runs the same second man plays in attack and bombs for wingers on the last tackle, and every team aims to dominate the ruck and slow play the ball with wrestling and rolling players on back or in other positions to slow the ruck speed down – not the sort of thing you want to be paying good money to attend.

The players are bigger, stronger and more athletic than ever before, and the mixture of shapes and body sizes from players from past eras is now also becoming a thing of the past. The modern era has eroded many of the smaller players and even the really big giants of the game, with players from second rowers to centres to wingers nearly all of a similar shape and size today.

The game's little men have played a massive role in the game's history and popularity. Players like Allan Langer, Preston Campbell, Trevor Gillmeister, Geoff Toovey, Johnny Raper, and Paul Vautin were not some of the biggest players, but their legacy and influence in how they played the game will live on in the minds of many.

The interchange rules and non-stop video referee intervention has lessened the fatigue and endurance factor in the game for those who made their name by being endurance players and who may have lacked size and power but made up for it with excellent cardio, heart and mental toughness. The modern game disadvantages these players and yet rewards bigger and more athletic players who can recover more with interchange and non-stop video intervention.

Players such as Brad Clyde, Gary Larson, Bob Lindner, and Luke Ricketson were synonymous with being fit endurance players with massive hearts. These players have been slowly replaced for power and more multi-skilled athletic players in the modern game.

Even the game's giants are slowly being removed for more athletic modern day players. Men like Paul Sironen, Steve Roach, Mark Caroll, and Martin Bella would all find it hard to play in the modern game.

The code's implementation and continued use of the video ref has been a disaster. Its non-stop involvement in the game now includes its very own million-dollar bunker where officials review everything, and has become one the fans' biggest gripes. So much focus has been taken away from on-field game discussion to off-field discrepancies with the video ref, as the match officials now default power and decision making to technology and the bunker.

Its involvement has far overextended its initial role. The non-stop interaction of the video ref stops the motion and flow of the game and makes for far weaker viewing and sometimes makes a game unwatchable. It has now impacted the endurance side of the game and the ability to force players to make decisions when there is high stress, fatigue and pressure. Origin seems to be one of the few games where stress can still play a part of a game, with Origin 3 of the 2022 series being the perfect example of high stress levels in a game.

Senior management at NRL HQ have a philosophy that perfection will make the game better, modeled on the NFL in America. The NRL leaders think they can utilise the video ref and technology in similar manner to how the NFL utilises its technology to make rugby league better.

This is completely false. The NFL is a game built on more short bursts of power and stop/start play, where players whose body shapes are designed for power and strength compared to endurance. An average NFL game will take 3-4 hours to be played. Rugby league non-stop motion and simplicity is what has made the game different to rugby union and other sports and what has made it loved by the fans.

When played with the pure essence of the sport's DNA, its characteristics include fatigue, endurance, collisions, courage, tenacity, brains, risk, and ball movement qualities that have empowered the game since its inception, but over the last decade have been removed in the search for perfection, power, speed and repetitiveness.

In May of 2020, Peter V'landys made the announcement that the game would revert to one referee following the fiscal measures after Covid. Whether the decision was based on financial reasons or for improving the product is not known, but it is the right decision, and many more need to be made if the game is to resemble how the game should be played and watched.

V'landys also introduced the six-again rule when the NRL resumed on the 28th May 2020 to try and eliminate wrestling in the game and speed up play. This rule has now become a lottery and complete disaster. I can't recall a rule in the code that has had such an impact on the outcome or momentum of games.

The rule was never tested in any lower leagues or trial games. It is beyond belief that a new rule would be implemented in a professional league that has such an influence on games without any prior trial or testing.

The rule was designed to stop wrestling, but now fans and players have no idea what the referees are actually blowing six-again penalties for, and thus has made the spectacle even worse viewing and the game too fast. The refs also have no accountability with the new rule, which has frustrated many stakeholders.

Never has a rule changed the momentum of games so much, with teams looking dead in the water, then being brought back to life with favorable six-again calls and a giant swing of possession. It's a complete lottery and many fans hate it, including myself.

During Covid whilst the game was suspended, Foxtel were showing some of the older games, as no games were being played. Commentators and many fans made comments about how much better the game was to watch in the '90s, with more ball movement, no wrestling, quicker play of the ball, more unorthodox attack, more short kicking, more little guys, more endurance players, more fatigue, more heart required, less interruption and more one-on-one challenges between opposing players.

In a nutshell, the game was far more entertaining and fun to watch. Today the players may be bigger and stronger, but the content today, mixed with modern rules and technology, is of far poorer quality and entertainment. Many have known this for a long time, but people in key leadership positions involved with the game have not, and continue to dig a deeper hole for the code.

AFL has made big strides on rugby league in attracting more viewers, as their code is not marred by controversy with referee and video ref decisions like rugby league is, which has plagued the code since the NRL era began.

Peter V'landys stated, when appearing on 100% Footy, that the one stakeholder the game had forgotten about in discussing the rules were the fans. He was 100% right. The fans are the most important stakeholder in the game and what they want is an extremely important factor in the rules and product of the game. Sadly, V'landys has paid very little attention to his own advice.

The early '90s product may have been the best content and quality the game has ever delivered for pure joy and entertainment. The superstar teams of that era, including the Brisbane Broncos and Canberra Raiders, were the glamour teams of that period, with their offensive-minded attacks, with huge long passing from Ricky Stuart, Laurie Daley's direct running game, Mullins' electric runs from the back and big Mal's power game out wide, alongside flash wingers in Nagas and Nadruku.

Brisbane had Alfie Langer with his unorthodox bag of tricks such as the chip and chase, dummy and running game that had every defence on high alert; and the Walters and Renouf combination with Walters' great ball playing in sync with Renouf's electric speed, fend, swerve and balance. The Penrith Panthers 91 premiership team had Greg Alexander's unorthodox brillant attacking play, Freddy Fittler's huge step and Mark Geyer's off-loading game, which was appealing to viewers.

Canterbury had Ewan McGrady carving up defences with natural brilliance, and Terry Lamb, the great leader and ball supporter, always following the ball.

Probably the most attractive footy seen since that era was the Wests Tigers premiership team from 2005, who based their game on skills and ball movement to great effect against bigger teams.

Those are just a few teams and examples, but the philosophy and attitude across the entire league that included less structure, smaller players, more adlib attacking play, no video ref, and higher fatigue created the right environment for the game to be a very attractive product to existing and new fans, and one the game must get back at all stakes to ensure the long-term success of the code. The early to mid-'90s is still the fastest growth phase in the sport's history and there are reasons why it attracted so many new fans.

The game's product needs new rules. Let's look at some key changes that need to be made:

- One ref – The move back to one referee from two after Covid is the right decision. Two referees have complicated things more, with disagreements between refs, which results in inconsistent rulings and decision making, and extra costs to the game, with more officials. Rugby league's simplicity is one of its strengths. Where things have become more technical and confusing, the result has been poorer quality rugby league and more attention on officials and technology. The one referee also empowered the referee officiating the game with accountability, confidence and responsibility.

- Remove the video ref and bunker – The video ref role has expanded far beyond its initial role and this has been to the game's detriment. Perfection in rugby league does not exist and the game should never try and think that because the NFL utilises video technology to officiate, that it would work well in rugby league. Rugby league is meant to be played with end-to-end action with limited stoppages. That is what has made it great and separates it from rugby union and the NFL. Its flow and imperfection adds to the drama and entertainment. Non-stop interruption from technology is excruciatingly painful to a game and stops momentum and never lets a game flow and rise to its peak. The video ref must be removed for end-to-end action to return that puts more pressure on players, brings more stress and decision making and tests the players' endurance and mental strength far more.

- Wrestling – Probably the fans' biggest groan is in relation to the infusion of wrestling into rugby league. Many fans argue it's not in the spirit of the game and is not what rugby league is about. Craig Bellamy and the Melbourne Storm were the founders of this practice, with every club in the game now following the Storm's lead and utilising wrestling and martial arts practices such as jujitsu and sambo tactics to dominate the ruck. The Storm are well coached, have great discipline and have a great club culture, and many great players have donned the club's shirts, but their ability to wrestle has been one of the leading factors in much of their success. They would still be a good team, but wrestling has been the major reason for their huge success during the Bellamy era. Every club now has wrestling and martial arts coaches to control the wrestle and the speed of the ruck. Rugby league should have stamped this out years ago and has to do it now to regain the confidence of the game and fans. Many fans argued in early 2019 about the refs blowing penalties to stop wrestling in the ruck. Some liked this to stop wrestling, but some said 20 penalties a game is terrible for the viewer. The NRL must be ruthless towards wrestling and do whatever it takes to get rid of this in our game. The NRL leadership and officials need to set the direction and not worry about the grievances of coaches and clubs. Wrestling is a terrible blot on our game: it takes the spectacle away, slows the ruck, allows defence to dominate, creates more structured and repetitive plays and is not in the spirit of the game. No half-hearted measures will work here; only a total revolution of how our game should be played and officiated will succeed. The game should ban all clubs from any wrestling and martial arts coaches. No video ref will also bring more fatigue back to the game, which limits wrestling, plus reduced interchange to bring more fatigue back, and officials should be ruthless in removing wrestling and clearing the ruck. Blowing penalties is not sufficient; the penalty should include sin binning and suspension. The game needs to have a totally new attitude and philosophy to stamp wrestling out at all costs and clear the ruck up once and for all.

- Interchange – Reduced interchange to four interchanges per game should help reduce wrestling, bring more fatigue back into the game and more opportunities for endurance and smaller players, and allow more diverse body shapes. The reduction in interchanges will bring more expansive attack and ball movement and create less repetitive rugby league. Tiredness, both physically and mentally, creates more space and stress in games, which creates more exciting football. Fewer interchanges is better for fewer injuries and concussions, as fresher and stronger players equals more high-intensity body clashes and collisions and far more chance of injuries and concussions occurring.

- Captain's Challenge – Completely remove it. It creates more stop-start play and kills momentum and rhythm. Again, the pursuit of perfection kills what has made the game great. Captains, at times, will use this play to deliberately bend rules and stop momentum. The game needs motion to flow more, but more interruptions means games losing rhythm, which affects the quality of the game. Simply get rid of it.
- Remove golden point. The game is not played in the right spirit of the sport with golden point extra time. With the focus on field goals, teams can lose games without even touching the ball. A draw is a fair result during the regular season. Extra time, with a set amount of time not based on the first point scorer, should be applied during finals.
- Remove seven-tackle sets and have six-tackle sets and nothing else. It is a terrible rule that must be scrapped immediately.
- 50m penalties like the AFL has for stern infringements could be a welcome addition.
- Create a rules committee that has no conflicts of interest and includes a diverse range of voices, with its focus on making the game more exciting and challenging, and questioning the status quo, and hire wrestling experts to support the committee to identify wrestling techniques which need to be removed from the game.
- Bring in more rules that require thinking by the players and can result in some momentum changes to a game, which creates unexpectancy and excitement. The 40/20 rule has been one of the best rules introduced in recent memory and has the ability to change the momentum many times in a game. The game should look at a few more of these types of rule changes to create excitement and more thinking.

One of the criticisms of many is the predictability of teams' offence where the fifth tackle bomb for the flying winger and continuous second man plays in attack with the shape of player movement that every team continually runs. Possible rules could include:

1. If a bomb is kicked and caught by the opposing team in the in-goal, instead of going back to the 20m for a tap, the game could consider the ball going back to the 40m or 50m line. This would make offensive teams think twice about kicking a bomb to the corner and would require players to think more about the positives and consequences of any strategic attack in offence.

2. Limit the amount of decoy runners and second man runners. This would be hard to implement, but the saturation of second man decoy runners plays is utilised by every team and should be reined in by the NRL. Possible options include limiting to one second man or decoy runner per play.

3. Tries inside attacking teams' own half could be given an extra one or two points for any try. This would encourage more long-range attack, which would bring more unpredictability to the game

4. If the endurance of the game and fatigue is brought back and if players are more tired, the shoulder charge could be considered. It brought a lot of joy to fans but many also disliked it, and many medical reps would not advocate for its reintroduction.

Making the game more enjoyable for fans is a must to bring value and entertainment to our most valuable stakeholders, the fans. Playing to the game's strengths is the best way to implement this, through more fatigue, less wrestling, no video ref interruption – a game that stays in motion and has stress and pressure, which causes more unpredictability and brings more ball movement, reduces the modern athletic players and puts more creative decision making onto players.

**Wherever your awareness
and focus go is where your energy goes!**

The current game model is designed to focus on errors, captain's calls, and video refs, and takes the spectacle away from the game. This is the biggest fundamental change needed! Where the focus and awareness needs to go is on the game itself, that is in motion, not on technology, referees or wrestling.

NRL SCHEDULE

PLANNING A SCHEDULE that provides all levels of the game with balance and opportunities is a hard juggling act and one the game has never quite got right in the NRL era. In pursuit of big television deals and not having widespread stakeholder governance representatives, the game's regular season now extends to around 24-26 rounds per year plus a finals system. The NRL season starts in early March and the grand final is held on the first weekend of October, with clubs also having early season trial games, which can start in late January and run through to early March.

Having the NRL season run from March to October and late January, if you include trials, does not allow the game much room to expand the international games calendar, which has been forgotten and under-utilised, to the game's detriment.

The code's modern tradition is occasionally playing a few post-season internationals and some short tours to Great Britain, but this has become rare in modern times.

It is often debated when State of Origin should be played, with recent series playing Games 1 and 3 on the traditional Wednesday night, with Game 2 of the 2022 series in Perth being played on Sunday night. Many clubs and players complain about the length of the season and its demands, both mentally and physically. Many argue that having Origin during the regular season takes much fanfare away from the NRL season, with rep players unavailable and all attention from fans and media on the State of Origin series.

In 2020, due to Covid, the State of Origin series was moved to November after the NRL season concluded. Many called for this to continue into the future, as it does not interrupt the NRL competition, but with the lower ratings compared to Origin played mid-season, the cricket season and other events, it would not seem logical to continue playing the Origin series post-season in November.

The game has three main products it can sell:

- NRL
- State of Origin - three game series annually (NSW vs QLD)
- International game involving Kangaroos

Most attention at present is going to the NRL competition and the annual State of Origin series, as they create nearly all of the income for the game, but a balanced schedule that focuses on quality rather than quantity and grows all three levels of the game is the best schedule to take the game forward and reward all stakeholders and fans.

Major American sporting organisations such as the NFL and MLB predominantly focus on their core national league brand product, but rugby league is blessed to have three levels of the game it can sell and promote, and this is one area where the game has great leverage over AFL. AFL only has its national core league, the AFL, but does not have the benefit of an international game, and its State of Origin series has ceased in recent times and only brought back in 2020 as a fire relief fundraiser.

Rugby union has a thriving international scene but does not have a State of Origin series like rugby league or a thriving Super Rugby championship, which is currently going through a large restructure.

Soccer in Australia has a struggling A League national competition that is declining in popularity. After a very promising start to the A League, it has no state representative series but is by far the most popular international sport in the world, with the Soccer World Cup being the biggest sporting event in the world. Anytime the Socceroos are playing big games to gain entry or compete in the World Cup, this draws huge interest from fans and media.

Rugby league is very lucky to have three professional levels, with clubs, state and international representation, which provides the game with great potential to leverage the game to a wider audience and provide quality content.

The international game has the most untapped potential for the game to drive growth, revenue, media, and sponsorship, attract new fans and bring more awareness to rugby league. International sport has the ability to lure casual or non-fans that club content cannot provide, with the patriotism of their country playing attracting new fans. The Wallabies and Socceroos have shown what the power of national branding brings in terms of interest and attention. Whenever these teams play, the game gains far more media interest and exposure compared to any A League or Super Rugby game.

Never was this more evident than the Matildas match against France in the 2023 FIFA Women's World Cup, which had TV ratings of 4.013m nationally, outrating the 2023 State of Origin games and NRL and AFL games.

As identified, rugby league has three key functions in the professional game that can be utilised to grow the game's audience, create revenue and sponsorship, and satisfy all fans, with a balance of club, state and international rugby league.

Possible Schedule

NRL Premiership – For a balanced mix of all three leagues, quality, quantity and the benefits of player health and wellbeing, the NRL season must be reduced to allow the growth of the international game.

NRL -18 to 22 NRL club rounds plus a final series would be our recommendation.

State of Origin - Don't change a winning thing. You take a great risk when you chop and change one of your game's biggest events that has made it unique and special in the public's eyes and is awaited with great anticipation each year. State of Origin is a special event and rivalry that most sports would die for, so don't change anything. It brings so much of the good to the game, passion, the best against the best, history and tradition, stories, a huge audience and massive income.

- The game must remain being played on its traditional Wednesday night. The midweek event is one of the main reasons it has achieved such success. It has a special feeling playing midweek and the ratings have always backed this up. The move to Sunday takes this away, with 2020 and 2022 ratings showing the game rates far better on Wednesday than Sunday. Simple: Keep it played on Wednesday.

- The series must start between late May and early July and run for 6-9 weeks to keep momentum. Clubs will cry about losing rep players, but tough luck - suck it up. The early season discussion around who will and won't be selected adds great anticipation to the series and is one of the reasons for its success.

- The expansion of Origin to include neutral cities outside of Sydney and Brisbane has been a wonderful success, with Origin games now being played in Melbourne in 2018 with 87,000 in attendance, Perth in 2019 and 2022 with record crowds of 58,000 and 60,000, and Adelaide in 2020 and 2023, and the game should continue to look interstate and possibly overseas to continue growing the series and rugby league. Origin interest now goes well beyond the two states competing and has become a huge sporting event on the national calendar.

- Player eligibility has been the subject of much discussion in recent times, and this is one the game must protect with a vengeance. Origin should only be open to players who are born in either state or moved at a very young age. We can't have players playing Origin and then playing for other nations such as Tonga, Samoa or Fiji. This would make a complete mockery of the rules and hurt the game significantly. It would tarnish the jewel in the crown and do serious damage.

International Game – The IRL (International Rugby League) is the head governing body that oversees and leads the international game, but for the international game to expand, it needs to be led by the NRL with English Super League backing so a regular and planned calendar is not clashing with the Australia and English leagues, and so both competitions endorse, support and promote the international game. The NRL and clubs have put the club competition before the international game for far too long, but this needs to change immediately, and the NRL with the IRL should show by deeds with regular and meaningful games and a long-term schedule how important the international game is.

The international game needs:
- Regular competitions or series every year.
- Meaningful games woven into series, tours or competitions.
- To help the build-up to the World Cup, which is played every 4 years.

Regular games for the Kangaroos and meaningful competitions and series need to be incorporated into the rugby league schedule, and, with reducing the NRL competition, the game can have more space to expand and play the international game.

The Kangaroos should be looking at playing four to eight games per year against multiple opposition, and these could be mid-year series or end-of-season tours series or tri or quad series, like competitions played between three to five nations.

The NRL with the IRL should also be working on the Pacific nations joining the Kangaroos and Kiwis in playing regular and meaningful series that move away from one-off games always in Australia. Many of the players representing these nations play in the NRL and states leagues in NSW and QLD. Much improvement from the Pacific nations now sees them ready to move to the next level, and, like the Kangaroos, they need to play more in meaningful leagues that grow their brand and the international game as a whole.

INTERNATIONAL

RUGBY LEAGUE HAS the NRL competition and State of Origin series firmly entrenched in the game schedule. And now the NRL, with the support of key domestic and international stakeholders within the game, must place high importance on revitalising international rugby league and building the profile and prestige it deserves.

The Rugby League World Cup was held across England in October and November of 2022, after previously hosting the Rugby League World Cup in 2013, which is regarded as one of the best World Cups ever. The same people involved in the 2013 cup were again involved in organising and managing the 2022 Rugby League World Cup.

The World Cup brings extensive worldwide attention to the game and is one of the biggest opportunities the game will ever have to market and promote itself to a global audience. It is a must to use this platform to start revitalising the international game.

The NRL has been indifferent about promoting and marketing the international game for a long time now, with all its focus on the NRL and State of Origin, the code's main revenue drivers.

The NRL has never worked with other stakeholders in planning an aggressive calendar for international rugby league. Usually internationals are only scheduled when there is a free space in the calendar or it does not clash with other key events in its own schedule.

Nonetheless, the game needs to show by its actions (and not continually draft plans) that it intends to promote, play regular matches and revitalise the international game. The 2022 World Cup in England was the perfect time to relaunch the international game.

The game's key stakeholders around the world, such as the NRL, Super League, French RL, NZRL, Pacific RL, Europe and Pacific nations and the IRL should all work together to have an extensive program to continue the momentum after the 2022 Rugby League World Cup. This can only occur with full support from all stakeholders, especially the NRL and UK Super League.

The game needs to develop unity and cohesion to allow for a vibrant international game. The schedule currently is inconsistent, with only the odd flickers of light, and it never flows to allow the game any real momentum or build up rivalries between the nations to raise a bigger profile.

The leading key stakeholders – the IRL, NRL and Super League – have never been on the same page about the future and direction of the international game, with the NRL being the main offender, despite some efforts in the Pacific in recent years. The game will never reach its potential as long as all parties are going in different directions, with no communication, no shared vision, common goal or schedule for the international game to aim for.

The International Rugby League has copped much criticism for its incompetent performance over the last decade plus with the international game. Much of this criticism is from the UK fans and media and aimed at former CEO Nigel Wood from England about the international game's decline in the media and lack of awareness of the code. Wood was seen by many UK fans to be on a massive salary and to have sat on his stool and let the international game decline, delivering on nothing.

The management capabilities and performance of the Rugby League World Cup leaders in England in 2013 and 2022 are miles ahead of anything Wood or the IRL have shown the game in the last decade. These are some of the people the game needs involved with the code: intelligent, enthusiastic, driven, with strong skills in management, social media, marketing, promotions, and operations, who have brought much more professionalism off the field.

So what are the steps the game needs to take to rebuild the international game?

1. Governance

As stated earlier, there are numerous stakeholders involved across the world with the international game but unfortunately are all often going in different directions, with no unified governance, and this has led to an inconsistent international program that can never gain momentum and reach its full potential.

It will be impossible for the game to succeed if some international members are never fully supportive of the international game, and this has been an anchor to the ship of progress for some time now. The English RL were very disappointed in Australia cancelling the 2020 Ashes test series and the 2021 Rugby League World Cup, but this tells you more about the indifferent attitude from NRL leaders. The recent cancellations have not been the first time Australia has been indifferent about the international game.

The game's representative leaders must get together with each other and agree to firm guidelines around the future of international rugby league. One would think this would be led by the IRL, but it needs total support from the big players in the NRL and English Super League to allow the IRL to have far more leverage and capacity to grow the game and plan a regular schedule with the other bodies.

How can the IRL become a governing body that can grow international rugby league?

These guidelines should include:

- Clear rules and guidelines for international rugby league
- Clear buy-in from NRL and Super League on the IRL to grow the international game
- Contractual agreements
- Agreed schedule that promotes the international game
- Regular competitions and tours
- Development around the globe
- Sound finances with agreed budgets
- Priority and focus of international game growth
- Leadership
- Media deals locked in and negotiated outside of club rugby league
- Planning and running the international game from the IRL
- No conflicts of interest, or minimised to eliminate biased decisions
- Who is on the IRL Board? Selected members from each country with strong experience and qualifications
- Total commitment to growing international rugby league across the globe from all parties
- Government investment and sponsorship contractual agreements
- Working towards better media, commercial interests and revenue for the game
- Reinvestment plan to grow the sport

The governance function of the International Rugby League has to be solid if the international game is to have long-term success. The game had some tremendous people working and managing the Rugby League World Cup in 2022, but it needs to have a clear strategy and plan for the momentum to continue after the World Cup in November 2022.

This can only occur if the clubs, NRL, Super League and IRL are in complete harmony about growing the international game and allowing a regular program of quality content, even with the reduction of the NRL and Super League games.

If the stakeholders can get the right leaders and people involved, with unity and alignment, the game can move mountains. But, as we know, rugby league has a long history of the complete opposite occurring.

2. Regular Matches, Series and Competitions

After governance and unity between stakeholders, the single most important thing to revitalise the international game is for a proper international program with far more consistent and meaningful games to be played, which includes regular test matches, series and competitions between the top nations and other developing nations.

Australia does not play anywhere near enough international rugby league and neither do other nations around the world, and this must change. The only way it can change is if governing bodies reduce the NRL and Super League regular seasons to allow for more meaningful games to be played.

The 1992 Great Britain Lions Ashes Tour to Australia mid-season which included both club games and a three-game series against the Kangaroos was far more anticipated by the fans than the State of Origin series which was played just prior and is a great reminder of what has been lost to the game.

The Kangaroos were once one of Australia's leading brands for the national team, and have been surpassed by the Wallabies and Socceroos for national team profiles due to the quality of competition and their inactivity. In the UK, the game has a much smaller profile compared to Australia, and plays second rate in the media to soccer, cricket and rugby union. The national team is one of the most important instruments the game can utilise to raise the code's profile. The All Blacks are the biggest thing in NZ and the game needs to utilise the Kiwis' national team to grow the game far more there also. Regular and meaningful games by the leading nations can only be a healthy thing for the code.

The Pacific nations and other European home nations play vitally important roles in growing the game outside the big three, and they need regular competition to continue their promising development. Tonga, Fiji and PNG have made great strides, with good wins from all three nations in the 2019 internationals, but much more work is to be done. If rugby league can get close to 10 teams of high quality (with local born and bred players), who all have the ability to defeat their opposition, you would have an incredibly vibrant international game and one the code should aim for, and that is quite possible. The game has made small steps towards this but must continue to finish the job and let the fruit be seen for all. Only hard work and regular competition can make this happen.

So, what options should be considered for a schedule?

There is a core group of nations which need regular and meaningful matches in both the southern hemisphere and the northern hemisphere:

Australia
New Zealand
England and Great Britain
Tonga
Samoa
Fiji
Papua New Guinea
Wales
Ireland
Scotland
France
Cook Islands

There are many other developing nations which also need support and opportunities to continue their growth.

The schedule needs a short and long-term plan. There are many options to be considered for a meaningful schedule:

- Regular matches for top-tier nations
- Australia, NZ and England to lead the way
- Continual World Cup every 4 years with different hosts
- Southern hemisphere four, five or six nations, with teams such as Australia, NZ, Tonga, PNG, Fiji, Samoa, with focus on quality
- Australia vs NZ – three-game series
- NZ vs Tonga/Fiji/Samoa/PNG
- France/Wales tour NZ and Pacific
- Australia vs PNG
- Regular Eng vs Wales, France, Ireland, Scotland internationals
- Great Britain tours to play southern hemisphere nations
- Ashes series both in Australia and UK
- Aus/NZ/Tonga/Fiji/PNG/Samoa tours to UK and France
- France vs England, Wales, Scotland, Ireland

Those are just a few options the game has to reinvigorate interest in international rugby league.

Let's look at a Kangaroos potential schedule that could grow the game over the next few years:

(2022 – World Cup in England)

2023 – Mid-year test series against NZ – two/three games and Ashes tour to UK at end of 2023, playing Ashes, Super League clubs and European countries such as Wales and France

2024 – Southern nations four/five/six series between the best teams in the southern hemisphere with final for top two teams. UK and France could play games in the north.

2025 – GB tour to southern hemisphere playing Ashes against Australia and against NZ and Pacific nations mid-year, like the 1992 tour

2025 – Mid-year tests against southern hemisphere nations before World Cup – PNG, Tonga, Samoa, Fiji, NZ

2025 – World Cup – host TBC

2026 – Mid-year test series against NZ, end of season matches against Pacific nations, NZ tours UK and France

2027 – Australian Ashes tour to UK and France, mid-year games against NZ or Pacific nations

Wouldn't that be exciting to look forward to and see that for a schedule: regular and meaningful games for the Kangaroos both at home and abroad?! That would have many fans in a frenzy, with the prospect of high-quality international football. Other nations could work with the IRL to plan and deliver similar programs for their countries.

From having an inconsistent or non-existent international program, all of a sudden, the game has consistent and regular quality international rugby league all around the world that could be sold via multiple media outlets.

In August 2023, the IRL announced an itinerary until 2030 which included an Ashes series downunder in 2025 for both men and women, Kangaroo and Kiwi tours, northern and southern hemisphere tournaments, the Men's World Cup being pushed back to 2026, with a standalone Women's World Cup to be held in 2028, and Australia and New Zealand to tour England in 2027 and 2028. The sport has a long history of drafting international itineraries and plans and then failing to execute the plan.

Conclusion

The fans have been begging the game for more international rugby league for a long time now, and rightly so. It is the code's greatest growth opportunity to expand the game globally and raise awareness of rugby league.

It's time for the game's leaders to listen and see the importance of international rugby league with real action. Not only will it revitalise international rugby league and bring much exposure and many new fans to the code, it will also have a ripple effect for the NRL and Super League and grow their brands and competitions.

WORLD CLUB CHALLENGE

WITH A LIMITED schedule of availability between the NRL competition, State of Origin and the international game, there is now little space for the World Club Challenge to be expanded. Nonetheless, the concept is still of vital importance to the game for both the southern and northern hemispheres, as it has much potential to become a high-profile game of significance that raises much publicity and media awareness for the code.

As stated, the one-off game is currently played in February of each new season and this is usually hosted in the UK. But Australia has hosted the concept, with Melbourne being the last NRL team to host the game in 2018 against Leeds, until the return of the competition in 2023 with Penrith Panthers hosting St Helens.

The question is: What is the point of the game being played and what is its purpose when so many have opposing views?

The simple answer is to find out which is the best rugby league club team in the world and for the winners of the NRL and Super League to face off and find out which is the best team. This is all the game needs to sell the

WCC concept: the best against the best from both leagues to find out who is the best team in the game.

Quality always sells, and when these teams don't play each other during the regular season, it raises the mystique and intrigue about the game even more. This has been proven in the UEFA League, which has overtaken the FA Cup and Premier League to become the biggest trophy in world soccer for a club competition.

Presently, the game is being treated more like a trial, played in the following season and calendar year after each winner's grand final victory in each hemisphere. The game still gains reasonably good traction with the media, TV viewers and match attendees, but there is no doubt that the game can definitely make it a much bigger game and event on the code calendar.

One of the last really big WCC events that involved great anticipation was back in 1994 when the Brisbane Broncos hosted the Wigan Warriors. They were the two glamour teams of the '90s, filled with superstars, and many trophies for each club. The game was a brilliant spectacle and event that was won by Wigan in front of over 54,000 fans in Brisbane.

The World Club Challenge has the ability to rise to this level again and become an even greater event, but the game's leaders need to market and promote it with the attention the game deserves.

How can the World Club Challenge gain the respect and attention it deserves? One of the first actions is for the leaders from both leagues to stop treating it like a trial game for the NRL and Super League clubs. Actions speak louder than words, and the WCC demands respect and is one game the fans are very interested in.

One of the biggest decisions with the game is when it should be played. To give the game the attention it deserves, it must be played 10-21 days after the GFs of each respective league have been completed, and locked into the calendar before the season even starts.

This allows the same teams from the winning grand final teams to play, whereas, with the current model, the teams can be completely different when played the following year, that is, four to five months after the grand final, with potentially new squads, retirements and other changes. Let's have the best against the best, with the teams fielding the same teams as played to win each league title.

Playing the game roughly 2 weeks after the respective grand finals of both leagues allows the maximum leverage in promoting the game with the momentum still flowing after the GF, and provides the opportunity to turn attention to the WCC. Playing it in February the following year roughly 4 months after each respective grand final still creates a momentum, but nothing as fresh as straight after the GF.

The game should be alternately hosted between the NRL and Super League each year to give each club and fans the opportunity to attend the game, and to provide greater awareness and media attention of the fixture, with both hemispheres hosting the game.

Making it an event rather than just a game and an honour to be a part of means building it up and having quality off-field entertainment on the day of the match, with both leagues putting money into the promotion for entertainment.

Strong marketing and build-up from the media to give the game the attention it deserves, the best against the best and some great rivalries from players, clubs and coaches, will guarantee the game attracts attention.

Looking at playing the match on a mid-weeknight to give the game an even more unique feel to it would be an option that I think would succeed! The Broncos v Wigan game was played on a weeknight, and playing State of Origin on a Wednesday night has been a massive success, adding to the Origin legend and creating a great build-up for fans that is the best in the game.

A midweek event would rate very highly on television if played in Australia. The UK may work better with an afternoon kickoff that screens in Australia later at night, similar to Ashes cricket, but may have to be played on the weekend for a Saturday or Sunday night prime-time audience in Australia.

If the Super League clubs can start having the success that the Wigan Warriors had in the '90s and St Helens had in the early 2000s and in recent years, the concept can only become bigger and better. The UK teams which have been dominated by the NRL clubs in recent times until St Helens shocked Penith in 2023, must take responsibility and stop making excuses and become better. Super League must raise the standards and profile of its league and stop believing they are inferior to the NRL.

Could we see an expansion of the World Club Challenge? Based on the limited time in the rugby league schedule and if the international game was expanded, there would be no time to really expand the World Club Challenge concept, though that does not and should not stop the game from considering expanding and building bridges between both leagues.

Some options could be:
- Games in Jan/Feb between NRL/Super League clubs
- A mini tournament
- Tours from clubs playing against other clubs in their opposing league. Wigan and Hull toured Australia in recent years and some Australian teams have also gone to the UK.
- Clubs playing against national touring teams such as Kangaroos, NZ, England, Wales, Tonga, France, PNG, etc.
- Winner from the WCC challenge gets rights to play touring English or Australian teams on Ashes tours

The World Club Challenge is a great concept and event that is seriously underrated by the game's leaders but loved by the fans, and a great instrument and event to raise awareness with the media and non-followers of the game. It deserves far more attention and recognition, and playing it after both leagues' grand finals on prime time, giving it plenty of promotion, will ensure the concept becomes bigger and better. The game needs to believe more in the game, and the World Club Challenge is the perfect example of this. This can be one of rugby league's premier events on the rugby league calendar.

EXPANSION

EXPANSION SEEMED TO be the last thing on the game's leaders minds after Covid had shut down the economy and left the game in a dire financial position. But nature abhors a vacuum and if you don't keep moving forward, someone or something else will quickly take your place.

You're either growing or dying is one of the universal laws of life and the world! Nothing stands still, and this applies to nature, such as a tree and grass transitioning through the seasons of life, as it does with an individual or organisation. The game must keep growing and believing it can take the game to new audiences or face the reality of becoming less and less and thus going backwards.

Rugby league, when played in the true spirit, is a tremendous product, but the game's leaders, for whatever reasons, have never had the faith, courage and commitment to decide that we as a code shall grow and expand. Instead, we have chosen to remain in safety and not sail in the deeper waters. Intelligent activity and boldness has a funny way of finding success. There can't be success without great risk.

The AFL has successfully expanded their game nationally and now has a strong footprint across the country. It is now implementing its northern strategy of moving hard into heartland rugby league areas through the Auskick junior program, development officers and the development of new regional AFL leagues to compete with rugby league and other sports.

Before Covid, V'landys publicly stated that the NRL wanted to expand the competition to 17 teams and bring in a second Brisbane NRL team, and this was confirmed in October 2021 with Redcliffe Dolphins (or Dolphins, as they were to be known) to enter the NRL league in 2023. This decision had the full support of both media partners, Foxtel and the Nine network, which both benefit from a second Brisbane team, with Queensland driving sponsorship, advertising, ratings and subscriptions which will benefit both parties.

Brisbane is a strong rugby league city, and the Broncos have had a monopoly on the city and market since the South QLD Crushers were removed from the league in 1997. The Broncos are the game's biggest brand, with the highest crowds, best stadium, highest ratings, large government support and the biggest sponsorship of the league. With a population of 2.5 million plus the surrounding region, the city clearly has enough room for another NRL franchise, which would also add a Brisbane derby match to the NRL schedule and enable the media partners to screen a game in Brisbane prime time every week.

The Redcliffe Dolphins have a long and proud history in Queensland Rugby League and have been one of the strongest clubs in the QRL since its inception. The club has a new boutique stadium in Redcliffe that has a capacity of 11,500, and Wayne Bennett has agreed to be the team's inaugural coach for 2023.

Despite expanding the league to 17 teams, V'landys and the NRL have shown no appetite in expanding into new markets, either in Australia or New Zealand.

V'landys was quite blunt on expansion, stating that he wanted to own the heartland areas of rugby league and not invest in new areas like Perth or Adelaide, which are dominated by AFL, and New Zealand by rugby union.

V'landys stated on 100% Footy he would not expand into AFL territory!

V'landys' statement was very disappointing but not unexpected from the chairman or the NRL, who seem content with the NSW and QLD markets.

This outlook from V'landys shows the lack of courage and boldness from the leadership in the game and provides little hope to expand our great game for existing stakeholders in these regions such as Perth, Adelaide, and NZ. It was the complete opposite statement to what previous ARLC Chairman Peter Beattie had said only recently, when, as chairman, he declared the game must expand or fall backwards.

The refusal to look at expansion outside of rugby league heartland is a strange and interesting decision and makes you question what the code's goals and short and long-term plans really are. The move to 17 teams makes no financial sense when you can't sell an extra game as part of media rights to pay for the additional costs of a new team.

For years, the game has made empty promises to Perth about the region's future and potential NRL team in the west. Over the last few years, numerous clubs such as Manly, South Sydney and Canterbury have taken their home games to be played in Perth in front of solid crowds. The 2017 test between Australia and NZ was played at NIB stadium in front of a capacity crowd, and Game 2 of the 2019 and 2022 State of Origin series was played at Optus Stadiums, with sell-out crowds to both games. Perth also hosted a double header in 2018 at Optus Stadium to open the season, and the 9s were hosted there in 2020, with strong attendances.

Adelaide also got a taste of rugby league, hosting the second game of the 2020 State of Origin series at Adelaide Oval, and hosted another Origin game in 2023.

Despite taking one-off event games on the road, V'landys says there will be no new teams outside of rugby league heartland. This was stated before Covid and confirmed again in June of 2020 in a television interview. What is most interesting is that no proper analysis or due diligence process has ever been completed about the viability of new expansion teams and the pros and cons of each new team, with the commission still being heavily influenced by existing stakeholders, often only looking out for selfish gains and not the game's long-term best interests.

It seemed the backing and support of Foxtel and Nine was the key influence in the NRL agreeing to expand to a second Brisbane team for the 17th NRL license. Governance and leadership had to again be questioned, with the ARLC supposed to be driving the strategic direction of the game. But media partners were telling the NRL where they wanted the next expanded team, and V'landys was quickly in support of this.

So does the game expand and how should it look into this?

Many are not supportive of the game expanding beyond 16 or 17 teams and believe the status quo should remain. The reasons are valid and include: too many teams, it will dilute the quality, not enough talent for more than 16 or 17 teams, financially the game can't afford it, the game does not have the structures in place or AFL is too strong in those areas.

Let's look into this a little further and how the game should be deciding these key strategic decisions.

Step 1 - What's the Vision?

What is the strategic plan of the game? What does the game want the NRL to look like? What are its short and long-term plans? We talked earlier about vision as a key component the game needs within its leadership function. What is the game's vision? For far too long, the game's vision has been grey and very unclear, whilst the AFL leaders and commission has had definite targets, including a national presence, which they have achieved over the last 30 years with new teams in Sydney, the Gold Coast, Perth and Adelaide, and are now in the final process of a Tasmanian team joining the league in 2028.

Step 2 - Due Diligence

Far too often in rugby league, opinions are thrown around by the media, fans and other stakeholders, with no real empirical evidence to support their beliefs. Other times, key individuals have vested interest and only push a decision that supports their own personal agenda, at the expense of other possible good ideas, which may be the case with the second Brisbane franchise (Dolphins) from certain media outlets, which will gain direct benefits from the decision.

Before any decision is made, a thorough due diligence process must occur from the head office on the pros and cons of expansion, and if expansion does occur, where the best places are for the game to grow and succeed.

Some basic answers the game needs to know:

What would it cost to run a new club?

What would be the impact on the other 16 or 17 teams?

For how long should a license be given?

Do we have enough player talent?

Can we get the right people leading the new club?

Should we have a tender process or directly appoint new teams?

Should it be run by the NRL or a private entity?

Do we have stadiums of high quality to be played in?

What would be the costs of travel for any new team?

What are risks with private equity vs NRL ownership?

Will the government provide funding to support a new team to bring tourism to each state or country?

What can sponsors pay for the new club?

Will it help or hurt the next TV deal?

What are the opposition sports doing in these regions?

If we don't expand, what are the potential consequences?

Does this allow AFL and other sports a leg up on our code if we do or don't expand?

Do we have any grassroots and domestic structures in place?

Do we have development officers and internal structures in place?

What crowds will new teams attract?

What are the break-even minimum crowd numbers?

Can it bring in more revenue to the game?

Can we sell new television time slots with new teams?

How well do we know the industry and market of proposed new teams: market, jobs, economy, government policy, development, industry, unemployment, expats, etc?

Can we sell an extra game to the media outlets?

These are just some examples of key questions the game needs to ask to gather better information, understanding and awareness in any due diligence process, plus looking internally at the financial position and vision and strategic plans the NRL has. A strong due diligence process provides you with the facts, which allows the decision-making process to be of a much higher quality. The Bible says, *Know the truth and it will set you free,* and the gathering of real facts will set the game free with regards to whether to expand or not.

Step 3 - Feedback

Once the game has gone through a proper due diligence process and gotten the actual facts about the pros and cons of expansion from within and externally, the decision will be simple.

Does the game expand or not?

The answers are simple:

Yes.

No.

Maybe – within a certain time frame or requiring more investment and work from potential new teams.

If it is a yes to expand, the game then should start looking if it will be a direct appointment for entry into the NRL or go through a tender process to select the next new team.

If it is a no or maybe decision, the game needs to be clear and concise with fans, media and potential new expansion teams. This has been one of the game's failures in the last 20 years, especially for past interested Brisbane franchises and Perth consortiums, which have been promised and promised for years, and yet the NRL has drifted aimlessly for many years and given these teams and investors no clear direction or understanding about where they stand and what they need to do and what criteria they need to meet to enter the NRL.

Fans are in the same boat and often ask about expansion when given the opportunity to speak to NRL leaders through social media, but the NRL has had no clear vision for the game around expansions and hasn't completed a due diligence report, which would provide insight on what the game should do long term.

If the NRL knew what it would cost to run a new team and had a clear selection criteria that potential new teams must meet to be granted entry, this would give new franchises a much better opportunity to prepare and succeed in laying the groundwork for stronger business models and allow for much higher quality of applicants.

Step 4 – If Yes, Proceed to Tender Process

If the game has done its due diligence process correctly, it should have a good idea where they want a new team and what is best for the game and its long-term success that links with its strategic plans and vision for the code.

The game's due diligence process should cover key components such as:

Operating costs
Funding
Stadium
Crowds
Government support
Private or NRL owned
National presence of game
Sponsorship
Internal management capacity
Media coverage and deals
TV ratings
Strategic importance to other sports
Grassroots and domestic structures
Franchise fee to enter competition

The key contenders for any possible new franchise for the NRL would include:

Brisbane Bombers (QLD)
Brisbane (Easts) Tigers (QLD)
Ipswich/Logan (QLD)
Perth (WA)
Adelaide (SA)
Central Coast (NSW)
Sunshine Coast (QLD)
Wellington (NZ)
Christchurch (NZ)
Second Melbourne Franchise (VIC)
Papua New Guinea (PNG)
Central Qld (QLD)
Cairns (QLD)

All potential new teams have strong claims as the next team to be permitted entry to the NRL competition, but realistically, since the Dolphins were announced as the 17th team, the NRL will have to look into new markets if the sport is to grow and push back against the AFL, though many supporters in Queensland will believe the state demands another team.

The leading contenders in new growth markets are:

Perth (WA)

Adelaide (SA)

Wellington (NZ)

Christchurch (NZ)

Second Melbourne franchise (VIC)

Papua New Guinea (PNG)

As discussed, with 17 teams, you cannot sell another game to media outlets to create additional income, and you lose the opportunity to expand into new markets, which can grow the NRL and push back against the AFL in this sporting battle.

So should the NRL decide to expand to 18 teams?

Yes, the game needs to show some boldness and real ambition! If the code does not expand, the AFL will only extend its gap as the country's number one sport, with a larger scale and magnitude of audience and fan base.

Many will argue the game cannot support another team both financially or player talent wise, and it will dilute the current league. But, as stated before, you're either growing or dying, and the game which once had the boldness to expand the game with four new teams in 1995, needs the same bold spirit and leadership today.

With the Dolphins confirmed as the NRL's 17th team, the game needs to take some chances on the 18th team, and the one that stands out is a new team from Western Australia based in Perth.

Adelaide and potential new teams from Christchurch or Wellington in New Zealand could be expansion options, but Perth is clearly a stronger candidate to enter the NRL on all levels at present, including structures, grassroots base, stadium, sponsorship, past results with NRL, State of Origin and a test game played in Perth in front of excellent crowds, finances, private investment, and the overall benefit to the game and NRL a WA side would bring to the code with a stronger national presence.

One of the big leg-ups the AFL has over the NRL for ratings, which lead to bigger TV deals, corporate sponsorship and media exposure, is the five-city metro TV figures, based on Australia's five biggest cities: Sydney, Melbourne, Adelaide, Perth and Brisbane.

The AFL has a much stronger presence in these five cities and gains leverage to win the five-city metro ratings (regional not included) comfortably over the NRL. The NRL, whilst strong in Brisbane and Sydney, has a limited presence in Adelaide and Perth, and only gains traction in Melbourne when the Storm play, often put on back channels on free-to-air.

Whilst rugby league has a strong regional following, which accounts for about a third of all television viewing, the five big cities gain attention with media outlets, are always on the rating sites, and bring attention to their brand for sponsorship, media and advertising.

Perth, which was once in the old ARL as the Western Reds, joining the league in 1995, was one of the clubs culled during the Super League civil war. The club performed quite well during this period, but the whole game suffered greatly during Super League and was never the environment for any team or the code to succeed.

The benefits of bringing a new Perth team are many: not only does it expand the game across the country but also in one of the major capital cities for the important five-city ratings, which gives the code many benefits.

New Perth team benefits:
- Expansion in non-traditional rugby league heartland
- Gives code national presence
- Raises awareness of NRL and rugby league in WA
- More exposure to national media, not just QLD and NSW
- Does not let AFL control everything

- Government support
- Western Force Rugby Union was not playing in top-tier Super Rugby, though is back now in Super Rugby
- Two million plus population in Perth alone
- Big resource sector, which has driven the national economy in the last 2 decades
- Sponsorship potential
- Many expats work and live in the west who follow the code
- Great stadiums
- Sound infrastructure of rugby league through WARL
- Solid grassroots across all of the state from Bunbury to Broome
- Gives WA a local team to support
- Timezone difference, which means a game can be shown in prime time on east coast – great time slot for 6.30pm Sunday night on east coast
- Allows code to sell extra game as part of media deals, possibly to other media companies to increase demand

Perth would bring many benefits to not only rugby league in Perth and Western Australia, but also give the code a huge boost with a national presence for more media exposure and to push back against other sports. They also bring many benefits to the game both for the NRL and long-term strategically to further the code.

The wildcard option for any expansion is a team from Papua New Guinea. Rugby league is a religion in PNG and the country has made great strides in recent times with entry into the Queensland Cup and building a first-class stadium in Port Moresby. Despite the improvements, many still have concerns around the security and safety for players and staff travelling to PNG, which has become an issue in recent years, needing federal government support.

The reason why PNG could be a smokie as the next team to enter the NRL is all related to politics and national security. China is becoming a huge threat in the Pacific region and they have built many new relationships with Pacific countries through the belt and road initiative. Many politicians in Canberra fear the expansion of China in the region and in PNG, which is so close to Australia. Prime Minister Anthony Albanese made a visit to PNG in early 2023 to build an alliance with our northern neighbour, with Albanese using the opportunity to use rugby league and his support for a PNG team in the NRL. Albanese called for both countries to deepen ties across security, economics, trade and sport.

Realistically, PNG is a long way behind in the expansion pecking order, with teams from Perth, QLD, NZ and Adelaide looking stronger both economically and on other metrics, including security, infrastructure, and commercially, but this could all change with the threat of China rising.

Albanese and his government know he needs a strong alliance with PNG to fight off the possible China threat, and he may have to charm our northern neighbours. The best present of all would be a PNG team in the NRL.

As crazy as it sounds, the federal government may force the NRL to expand to PNG, if that means boosting national security. The NRL may have no other option if pushed hard from government when they are receiving tax-free exemptions and large state and federal funding for events and stadiums. Albanese may force the NRL's hand!!

The NRL could now possibly expand the competition to 18 teams, with a new team at no extra cost, as the federal government is likely to cover any costs associated with a PNG team in the NRL, which would likely include travel, infrastructure and other costs associated with expansion in PNG.

The Albanese government would be happy to pay for a PNG team in the NRL if that ensures a stronger alliance between both countries. Only a few years ago, the thought of a PNG team in the NRL was just a wild dream, but with rising geopolitical issues in the Pacific, they now may be the front runner as the next expansion team in the NRL.

Who would have thought PNG may get an NRL team because of rising China geopolitical threats in the Pacific? That is one of the few carrots the Albanese government has at its disposal to charm and persuade our northern neighbours. It certainly is a crazy world!

Conclusion

If the code does its due diligence in the expansion process and it is sustainable both economically and player wise, as well as meeting the game's strategic objectives, new teams from Brisbane and potentially Perth would be wonderful additions to the code. The second Brisbane team (Dolphins) strengthens our presence in heartland QLD and provides Brisbane with a derby game with the Broncos and lays more foundations for rugby league to continue to own and be the number one sport in Brisbane and QLD. Perth gives the game a national feel once again to match AFL. It provides more media and sponsorship opportunities and an extra TV slot the game can sell in prime time on the east coast. The game needs to believe in itself more, and expansion shows real boldness that our code deserves and that it wants to get bigger.

PNG is the wildcard in all of this, with their hopes lying with China's movements in the Pacific and what sort of response we could see from the Albanese government, which may need to flatter our northern neighbours to keep the alliance.

Other regions which are not ready for a NRL team are still vitally important to the future of the code. Cities and regions such as Adelaide, Wellington, Christchurch and the Sunshine Coast are vital partners for the code and the long-term health of the sport. The code should still support these regions by strengthening local leagues, increasing playing numbers, building the grassroots base, building infrastructure and playing top-tier rugby league to organically grow the sport in these regions. In the future, after heavy and committed investment, regions may be ready for the NRL.

SUMMARY

There is a tide in the affairs of men.

Which, taken at the flood, leads on to fortune;

Omitted, all the voyage of their life

Is bound in shallows and in miseries.

– Shakespeare

2020 WAS ONE of the most turbulent years in the code's history. The regular season was stopped and then restarted, the game was facing potential financial perils with no income during Covid, new television deals with media partners were rashly negotiated during the pandemic, Todd Greenberg was removed as CEO, Andrew Abdo was appointed as interim and then permanent CEO, and Peter V'landys had taken over the running of the game and seems to now have executive power for the board and the day-to-day decision making of the NRL.

Many fans and media representatives saw Peter V'landys as the saviour of the game, but very few studied his background or knew the man. This thinking was dangerous, as no one person ever has all the answers or solutions, and often any organisation that puts all its hope and faith in one man is destined for big trouble.

I initially started writing this book at the beginning of 2020, with concerns about the direction and future of the code and looking deeper between the trees and forest to see what were the real core issues holding the game back and how they would have to be confronted if the code was to keep evolving and remain a dominant player in the Australian sporting market. I then had to amend the book when Covid appeared.

Fast forward to the end of 2022, and the things I started writing about are as relevant as ever in the battle of the codes and the infighting that continues to hold rugby league back.

The 2022 NRL Grand Final was watched by 2.76m nationally, one of the worst-rated grand finals in the NRL era, with the five-city metro numbers the worst in the NRL history since 1998.

The AFL in late 2022 would sign off on its media deal with Seven, Kayo, Telstra and FOX Sports and make a complete fool of Peter V'landys and the NRL, despite plenty of talk and self praise from the chairman over the last 2 years. The new AFL deal would be the biggest sporting deal in Australian sports history, worth $4.5 billion over 7 years, with the NRL's media partner, the Nine network, embarrassing the sport further with a failed bid for the AFL rights that dwarfed the NRL extension in late 2021 with Nine.

The new AFL deal will equate to around $200- $250 million more per season than the NRL, with the AFL earning $277 million more than the NRL in 2022. That extra money will allow the AFL to further its goal of growing the game in heartland NRL markets with more development officers and investment. Since 2012, the AFL has earned over $2.5 billion more than the NRL, as the gap continues to widen between the codes.

The V'landys and ARLC era has not made the game any better, despite the many promises and the blatant propaganda from Nine and Foxtel/News Limited.

Many fans are now really seeing what sort of leader Peter V'landys is and what he stands for! Two years is a long time in rugby league, and V'landys has been terrible for the game, despite the media's lavish praise for him.

The NRL has a competitor in the AFL, who are hell bent on further dominating the Australian sports market and now want to annihilate Peter V'landys and the NRL. Rugby league also faces challenges from other codes which look to rebound, such as rugby union, soccer and basketball, in an ever-changing professional sport market.

The AFL is an organisation to be respected, but the biggest challenge and threat to rugby league is rugby league, and this has always been the case! If the game could ever have unity with all stakeholders across the game, it would move mountains and reach the moon. But that is like herding cats and has been an impossible task for many years and looks more unlikely than ever, with new media deals extended and the current governance model. This was seen again with the industrial dispute in the middle of 2023 between the RLPA and the NRL.

The code has a serious fight on its hands to keep country rugby league strong and attract young people to play the sport. The code under V'landys has become an even worse spectacle, with new rules introduced, making the viewing product even worse, alongside technology interference and wrestling that is making the game unwatchable at times.

The governing body has been lost to a new elite aristocracy, with outsiders now controlling the sport and lovers of the game removed from power. The commission has made the game more political than ever before, and those at the lower and community levels have no voice in the running of the game.

NRL clubs and players again got a bigger slice of the pie, with an upgraded salary cap at the end of 2022, whilst the lower levels of the game continue to be forgotten.

International rugby league, despite the recent World Cup at the end of 2022, is still dormant and does not have the full support of the NRL to be revitalised and create a new renaissance for test match footy.

Maybe the most dangerous matter for the sport is the denial by its leaders of the potential risks and liabilities within the game. For 2 decades, we have seen an ever-revolving door of leaders continually turn a blind eye to the many issues within the game and only focus on the positives. The outside still looks strong, with large media deals, a sport that dominates two states and a strong fan base, but the outside does not always show a true reflection of the sport, and only by going deep on the inside and getting close do you see the whole story and the health of the patient.

Paradoxically, for the code to move forward, it would have to enter a mindset of destruction, destroying the negative beliefs, thoughts, addictions, emotions, fears, behaviours, relationships and old paths that have stopped the game from reaching its potential. Only by destroying what holds the game in slavery can the game move forward to a new creative phase and find mastery, truth, purpose, renewal, transformation and growth.

Rugby league will always survive, such is its tenacity and resolve, as seen for more than 100 years, but the real question is: in what capacity and strength?

This book has hopefully raised some awareness about the challengers that the code faces to secure its future.

DUTY AND HONOUR

RUGBY LEAGUE HAS been a game that has always given and given to many over the years, and yet so many in key decision-making positions continue to take and take from the game. Rugby league gives joy and entertainment to fans each week, it gives employees something to chat about on Monday morning or Friday afternoon with work colleagues, it provides endless memories for many involved with the code, provides entertainment for retirees who enjoy relaxing on the weekend and watching the footy, it gives the pubs and clubs entertainment, it unites country communities with local bush footy, it gives the kids excitement when watching and playing the game, it provides unbelievable opportunities for players, media and professionals who are working within the NRL to live the life of their dreams, and it unites Australian states during the State of Origin period with raw emotion that no other sport can match. Rugby league can pick you up no matter how difficult life can be, and give you meaning and something to look forward to.

The game has always given and never asked for anything in return, no matter how badly some egotistical and greedy stakeholders have treated it.

Duty and honour are what we want, need and expect from our leaders involved with the game: the duty to do what is best for rugby league and put the game first for once, the game that has given to so many, the duty to make sure the game is strong for many generations to come, the duty to grow the game both in Australia and internationally, the duty to put the game before money and greedy stakeholders, no matter the cost, and ensure its future and wellbeing for many years to come.

www.ingramcontent.com/pod-product-compliance
Lightning Source LLC
Chambersburg PA
CBHW020315010526
44107CB00054B/1846